FIRST CHAPLAIN OF THE CONFEDERACY

Father Darius Hubert (ca. 1885), wearing his Army of Northern Virginia service badge and Savannah "Good Samaritan" medal. From Albert H. Biever, S.J., *The Jesuits in New Orleans and the Mississippi Valley, Jubilee Memorial* (1924).

Contents

Illustrations

Preface and Acknowledgments

In the time it has taken to write this book, the landscape of Civil War memory has come under prolonged and intense scrutiny, one result of which has affected the physical landscape of many Southern cities and towns, where Confederate monuments and symbols have largely vanished from public view.[1] No effigies of Father Darius Hubert, the subject of this volume, were ever commissioned, though he was prominent in blessing the monuments and honoring the memories of others who died in Confederate service. He was, however, the subject of several notable portraits, two of which are known to have survived, though neither has been displayed for decades. Both represent him in his declining years, as do several extant photographs taken in New Orleans in the 1880s. It is difficult, therefore, to visualize him as the "young dandy" whom a fellow Jesuit, Father Hippolyte Gache, was shocked to encounter on a road near

1. Among important recent scholarly volumes, see especially Barbara A. Gannon, *Americans Remember Their Civil War* (Santa Barbara, CA: Praeger, 2017), an exhaustive survey of scholarship examining competing "official" and "vernacular" memories of the war, from the immediate aftermath of Appomattox to the 2015 Charleston church murders, and Caroline Janney's *Remembering the Civil War: Reunion and the Limits of Reconciliation* (Chapel Hill: University of North Carolina Press, 2016); also David Blight, *Race and Reunion: The Civil War in American Memory* (Cambridge, MA: Harvard University Press, 2001), and an older but still valuable examination of the first generation of postwar memory in the South, Gaines M. Foster, *Ghosts of the Confederacy: Defeat, the Lost Cause, and the Emergence of the New South, 1865–1913* (New York: Oxford University Press, 1987).

Norfolk in the early months of the Civil War, looking not very Jesuitical at all, but bearded and resplendent in an officer's coat with bright pelican buttons, pressed trousers, and comely boots. Yet that image, if we had one,[2] would mislead us in envisioning the man honored and loved by so many, from his young, orphaned student Celeste Repp in Baton Rouge, who wrote about him affectionately in her 1859 school journal, to the soldiers whose misery and exhilaration he shared in Robert E. Lee's army.[3] For the former, he was a kindly, cassocked spiritual father. For the latter he was a battle-worn comrade, often as ragged as they, and sometimes shoeless; he gave away his gleaming apparel early on and wore what hand-me-down garments he could muster in the towns and byways of various campaigns.

Descriptions are almost as hard to come by as images. In a newspaper retrospective written nearly a decade after Hubert's death, the writer faltered: "Nothing is more difficult than to indicate in precise terms the picture of his life. His character and qualities were well known to his comrades, but we are powerless to leave behind any adequate idea of his personality. Indeed, it would be impossible to imagine a more perfectly rounded character than Father Hubert, and to know him truly, it was necessary to have served with him."[4] His service records contain an unusually laudatory yet similarly cryptic commendation by one of his commanders:

2. *Frenchman, Chaplain, Rebel: The Civil War Letters of Pere Louis-Hippolyte Gache, S.J., Tenth Louisiana Infantry*, ed. Cornelius M. Buckley, S.J. (Tuscaloosa: University of Alabama Press, 1981; 2007), p. 60. A colored plate illustrating the attire of Catholic chaplains in Confederate service, created by Peter F. Copeland for the Company of Military Historians in 2003, purports to depict Darius Hubert and his Jesuit colleague Fr. Joseph Prachensky, alongside Baptist chaplain J. William Jones. Notations by historian Edward S. Milligan confirm that the likenesses of the two Catholic chaplains are based on Gache's description. This image provided, in turn, the likely basis for several faux artifacts (including a kepi, a hat pin, and a Protestant King James Bible with clumsily forged signature) attached to the name of Darius Hubert, which were mistakenly displayed for several years in the National Civil War Chaplains Museum in Lynchburg, Virginia.

3. Katherine Bentley Jeffrey, *Two Civil Wars: The Curious Shared Journal of a Baton Rouge Schoolgirl and a Union Sailor on the USS Essex* (Baton Rouge: Louisiana State University Press, 2016), esp. pp. 20, 36–38, 44–45. Celeste Repp is the "Baton Rouge schoolgirl" of the title, a student and parishioner of Darius Hubert from 1859–61.

4. *Richmond Dispatch*, December 21, 1902, p. 14.

"A perfect man. Always with his regiment. We cannot express what was thought of him."[5]

Such comments only heighten the central challenge already facing a would-be biographer of Darius Hubert—the paucity of primary material, especially war correspondence or papers related to his lengthy pastoral tenure in New Orleans following surrender. For a man the *New York Times* called "one of the most widely-known priests of the South" to have left such a minimal paper trail is as vexing as it is surprising. It is hard to know whether this may have been deliberate or simply a matter of carelessness about his legacy on his own part or that of his religious community. For whatever reason, documents that one would expect to find in one of the Jesuit archival repositories in the United States or France were at some point either lost or discarded. The archive of the University of Notre Dame, where most diocesan correspondence from mid-nineteenth-century New Orleans is housed, includes a scattering of antebellum correspondence to and from Darius Hubert, but nothing from the war years or later. He is little mentioned in retrospective volumes written about Catholicism in Louisiana. And the Jesuit church in New Orleans where he served faithfully for nearly thirty years has no documentary history of his tenure and little apparent interest in his biography, perhaps because of the taint of Confederate association.

Unlike the Redemptorist chaplain of the Fourteenth Louisiana Regiment, Father James Sheeran, Father Hubert kept no written record of his Civil War service. He was not temperamentally self-interested, nor was he as prolix or as inclined to pontification as was Sheeran. And it is clear that his dedication to pastoral care and practical assistance to his men completely preoccupied his waking hours from April 1861 until he returned from Richmond to New Orleans in the summer of 1865. We can be grateful, therefore, that Father Sheeran mentions him as frequently as he does, especially in connection to their shared service with the Second

5. Darius Hubert's service records may be conveniently accessed online on the Fold3.com website, in both regimental and officers' listings. They include not only engagement notations and pay vouchers but official correspondence, some of which is quoted throughout this volume.

Louisiana Brigade from October 1862 to early 1864.[6] The other person who speaks about him with some regularity is the aforementioned Father Gache, a French-born Jesuit like himself and his longtime colleague, in wartime letters to friends in the Order.[7] Gache's relationship with Hubert was obviously complex and somewhat strained; almost every mention betrays a hint of jealousy, condescension, or judgment.

Perhaps a trove of missing documents by or about Father Hubert will one day be discovered, "filed in the wrong place," as one archivist suggested hopefully. May it be so. Until then, the material for this *Life* of Darius Hubert has been gleaned from myriad secular sources (both military and civilian, including notably newspapers in New Orleans, Baton Rouge, and Richmond) as well as personal reflections, letters, and diaries, and brief notes, with varying levels of accuracy, in Jesuit publications and archives.

I have endeavored to interrogate all such accounts with attention to possible embellishment or inadvertent error. A mistaken assertion that Darius Hubert gave the eulogy at Jefferson Davis's funeral in 1889 seems to have entered early into Jesuit records; it is repeated in the brief obituary attached to his name in the annals of the New Orleans Province, even in its most recent version,[8] and was accepted without question by Cornelius Buckley, S.J., in his edition of the Hippolyte Gache papers.[9] Father Hubert did not, in fact, preach the homily that day, but his emotional final prayer—"the most affecting part of the service," in the words of a local reporter—was apparently better remembered than the eulogy.[10] One wartime anecdote that accrued additional color and some incidental error in the retelling relates to Darius Hubert's hastily authorized chaplaincy

6. A new and very welcome expanded edition of Sheeran's journal, with related papers, has been edited by Patrick J. Hayes as *The Civil War Diary of Father James Sheeran, Confederate Chaplain and Redemptorist* (Washington, DC: Catholic University of America Press, 2016).

7. Gache, *Frenchman, Chaplain, Rebel.*

8. Jerome Neyrey, S.J., and Thomas Clancy, S.J., *Southern Jesuit Biographies* (Lafayette, LA: Acadian House, 2015), p. 27; this brief obituary is based on earlier editions of an in-house collection of Jesuit biographies by Father Clancy, titled *Our Friends* (New Orleans, 1978, 1989, and 1998).

9. Gache, *Frenchman, Chaplain, Rebel*, p. 230.

10. See p. 123 below.

to the CSS *Virginia* at Hampton Roads in 1862.[11] Overall, however, the records are straightforward and unadorned, consistently describing the chaplain's heroism in terms of simple dutifulness and courage—qualities that are amply borne out in other areas of his life.

Darius Hubert's prominent role in postwar remembrance in New Orleans and his public identification with Lost Cause ceremony, if not all of its tenets, have to date been virtually invisible to scholars. This is surely in part because their form and tone were unusual: Father Hubert neither wrote pamphlets and essays nor gave speeches, as did Father Abram Ryan, the Irish Catholic "poet of the Lost Cause." He did not, like Baptist chaplain J. William Jones, spend decades defining and defending the Southern Army as a Christian vanguard.[12] Nor did he, like some New Orleans clerics, preach the cause from his pulpit. His public role, as it touched on war remembrance, was to lead in the language of prayer, offering eloquent words of invocation and benediction at local monument unveilings, decoration ceremonies, veterans' reunions, and funerals. Beyond that, he maintained friendships with countless veterans and provided counsel and spiritual direction to many whose lives were shattered by the war and its aftermath. But the Confederacy was not his first love, nor did it define him.[13] He was a priest and a spiritual shepherd

11. See pp. 46–49 below.

12. Charles Reagan Wilson, in *Baptized in Blood: The Religion of the Lost Cause, 1865–1920* (Athens: University of Georgia Press, 1980; 2009), devotes a chapter to Jones, longtime editor of the influential *Southern Historical Society Papers* and prominent memorialist, whom he calls "evangelist of the Lost Cause." Though Jones admired Father Hubert, his own propensity for careless conflation of Christian and Confederate devotion contrasts strongly with the judiciousness of his Jesuit counterpart. Wilson quotes Jones as having once prayed at the University of North Carolina, Chapel Hill: "Lord, we acknowledge Thee as the all-wise author of every good and perfect gift. . . . But we believe Thou will admit the grave mistake in giving the decision to the wrong side in eighteen hundred and sixty-five" (p. 133). Though the anecdote is almost certainly apocryphal, it reflects a tendency in some Lost Cause apologetics to confuse God and idols.

13. There is no record of Darius Hubert having associated himself with the Southern Historical Society, in which New Orleans clergymen, Episcopal Bishop John Galleher and Presbyterian divine Benjamin Morgan Palmer, were both founding members (Palmer the first president).

first, last, and always. When, as he saw it, God determined that the Confederacy should fail,[14] he accepted that judgment unreservedly, and sought to bind rather than to reopen the wounds of factional hostility.

Whatever his convictions may have been about the institution of slavery when he encountered it on American soil, he treated slaves and free blacks as fully worthy of his spiritual care and instruction, and seems always to have had a particular concern for the education of black children. He pastored an interracial church in postwar New Orleans, where Creoles of color and former slaves shared worship with white congregants,[15] and his "universal charity" and "friendship with all races" were routinely acknowledged. It is impossible to know whether his views concerning the social and political status of blacks evolved with those of friends like P. G. T. Beauregard or were simply reconfigured in light of his clear prior understanding of the equal *spiritual* dignity and standing of all people before God. By the mid-1880s he strikingly, publicly affirmed the "perpetual brotherhood" and universal rights of all "children of Adam."

In dedicating a memorial to Stonewall Jackson and the fallen soldiers of the Army of Northern Virginia in 1881, Father Hubert expounded the meaning of such remembrance, which he saw as fully consistent with national healing and social reconciliation: "The gratitude of love is a good and perfect gift. It is not only the cause, but also the measure of a nation's greatness." He then added, with what can seem eerily prescient but is really a commonplace of spiritual wisdom, that no material tributes, even those wrought of marble or bronze, endure forever—or can be compared with an eternal weight of glory: "At what precise hour this shaft, though consecrated with Thy approving smile, will be prostrated in the dust, Thou knowest, O Lord. But Thou knowest also that the name of Stonewall

14. This was the theme of his oft-quoted Stonewall Jackson tribute; see pp. 124–25 and notes.

15. Darius Hubert did not live to see the emergence of distinct African American Catholic churches in the Crescent City; black Catholics themselves "unambiguously opposed segregation" in the 1870s and 1880s. See James B. Bennett, *Religion and the Rise of Jim Crow in New Orleans* (Princeton, NJ: Princeton University Press, 2005), esp. chap. 5, "Interracial Catholicism in New Orleans."

Jackson, and of each one of his comrades, shall live forever, entwined with immortal glory."[16] Few there are who would now so confidently assign such "knowledge" to the Almighty, but for Darius Hubert, this was the most natural of convictions.

I am indebted to many individuals who provided assistance in the course of this project, even when they could not find information that "should have been" in their collections; these include Jay Peterson, director of Museum Services at Beauvoir, the Jefferson Davis Home and Presidential Library; and Gentry Lankewicz Holbert, director of Burke Memorial Library at Spring Hill College in Mobile, Alabama. Joan Gaulene, former archivist of the Jesuit Archives of the New Orleans Province at Loyola University, has long been a patient, helpful, and gracious interlocutor; my favorite email from her, to which were attached several obscure but pertinent documents that she located in a "Miscellaneous" file, began: "The Holy Spirit gets the credit for this one." Ann Knake, associate archivist at the Jesuit Archives & Research Center in Saint Louis, Missouri, where the New Orleans Province papers now reside, has provided a seamless transition in accessing relevant documentation. Dorenda Dupont, in the Office of Archives and Records for the Archdiocese of New Orleans, kindly located and copied for me some crucial antebellum diocesan correspondence. I have enjoyed a lively and fruitful correspondence with Anne Smith O'Brien, a New Orleans researcher at work on a new biography of Margaret Gaffney Haughery, about the relationship between Margaret and her last spiritual director. Several individuals, notably Markham Dossett of Waco, Texas, and Dr. Keldon Henley of Ouachita Baptist University, have kindly shared unpublished materials of relevance to my research.

Drury Wellford, former head of Photo Services at the Museum of the Confederacy in Richmond, made arrangements for the oil portrait of Darius Hubert in that museum's holdings to be photographed for me in 2013; New Orleans photographer Owen Murphy photographed the portrait of

16. "Invocation by Rev. Father Hubert," *Dedication of the Tomb of the Association of the Army of Northern Virginia, Louisiana Division, and Unveiling of Statue of Stonewall Jackson at Metairie Cemetery, May 10th, 1881* (New Orleans: M. F. Dunn and Bro., 1881), pp. 6–7.

Father Hubert held at Memorial Hall on my behalf in 2016. Kemper Sublette, the estimable and inimitable longtime chair of the Memorial Hall Foundation, New Orleans, has been an enthusiastic advocate in a number of important unofficial ways, for which I am deeply grateful.

Several Catholic historians have extended unfailing kindness and encouragement regarding my work on Father Hubert, which I have received with special gratitude as a non-Catholic. Among these I would like especially to thank Father Robert Miller (*Both Prayed to the Same God: Religion and Faith in the American Civil War*), Patrick Hayes (*The Civil War Diary of Rev. James Sheeran, Confederate Chaplain and Redemptorist*), William Kurtz (*Excommunicated from the Union: How the Civil War Created a Separate Catholic America*), Don Beagle (*Poet of the Lost Cause: A Life of Father Ryan*), Father David Endres (editor, *U.S. Catholic Historian*), and especially Father Cornelius M.Buckley (*Frenchman, Chaplain, Rebel: The Civil War Letters of Pere Louis-Hippolyte Gache, S.J.*), to whom, for reasons of immense respect, I dedicate this volume.

S. G. (Sam) Gwynne, author of a captivating, sympathetic, and readable biography of one of Father Hubert's commanders and heroes (*Rebel Yell: The Violence, Passion, and Redemption of Stonewall Jackson*), read an early draft of chapter 4 and offered several valuable suggestions. Terry L. Jones, eminent historian of Louisiana soldiers in the eastern theater of the war (*Lee's Tigers* and *Lee's Tigers Revisited*) graciously agreed to cast his experienced eye over my appendix entitled "Chaplains to Louisiana Infantry in the Army of Northern Virginia." I have also enjoyed the kindness of specialists in several fields, notably Anne Bentley, Bob Fritsch, Patrick McMahon, and Neil Musante, who facilitated my search for an extant copy of the 1876 Savannah Benevolent Association medal that Darius Hubert so treasured.

Rand Dotson and the entire team at LSU Press have been, once again, a pleasure to work with. I am grateful for their confidence in the value of this book and for their partnership at every stage of the publication process.

Most of all, though, thanks are due to my husband, David, who has patiently borne not only my decades-long obsession with the War Between the States but also my affection for a 197-year-old Catholic priest.

It is, in Darius Hubert's own words, the "gratitude of love" that prompts this long overdue testament to an extraordinary pastor and chaplain, whose own greatness was typically disguised in the humble habits of a long obedience. In the pages that follow, he has a modest monument at last. I hope he will forgive me.

FIRST CHAPLAIN OF THE CONFEDERACY

Introduction

Sunday, February 22, 1880, was a day of unsettled weather and charged emotions in New Orleans. Still playing out the prolonged, fractious drama of occupation, military defeat, financial ruin, and political and social reconstruction, the Crescent City was also bedeviled by cronyism, corruption, and contesting prerogatives that perpetually threatened to boil over in violence. It had yet to achieve what historian Justin Nystrom has called the "hard-handed stability" of the late 1880s.[1] The annual carnival season had come and gone earlier in the month in its typically raucous fashion and with the usual eccentric and grotesque diversions from unresolved anxieties and the strictures of social decorum. Today was another parade day, but with an appeal this time to memory rather than forgetfulness: the occasion was George Washington's birthday.

New Orleanians came out in huge numbers to celebrate the Father of America, to whom in the 1860s Southern patriots had claimed unswerving allegiance even as they seceded from the country he founded and entered four years of bloody sectional conflict. Washington's name and memory still evoked deep and complex attachment in the South, and

1. Justin A. Nystrom's *New Orleans After the Civil War: Race, Politics, and a New Birth of Freedom* (Baltimore: Johns Hopkins University Press, 2010) provides a searching and stereotype-shattering analysis of the motives and aspirations of significant players in postwar New Orleans. For a contemporary satirical, and often scathing, portrait of the Crescent City in 1880, see *The New Orleans of Lafcadio Hearn: Illustrated Sketches from the "Daily City Item"* (Baton Rouge: Louisiana State University Press, 2007), with a superb introduction and annotations by editor Delia LaBarre.

wistfulness for the hopeful, undivided nation that had preceded the war.[2] Despite cool temperatures and threatened storms, thousands gathered to observe a colorful military pageant in Washington's honor, "the most brilliant parade of state troops ever witnessed in that city," as it marched along downtown streets to a tumult of hearty cheers.[3]

When the parade was over, both the militias and the citizens crowded onto streetcars for Metairie Cemetery. There, the second act of the day's pageantry took place—the dedication and unveiling of a monument to one of the most venerable and elite military units in the Americas, named for the selfsame president—the Washington Artillery of New Orleans. The Battalion Washington Artillery, as it was sometimes styled, had long predated the Civil War and would long outlive it. But on this day, those whose service was principally being honored were artillery veterans of the Confederate States of America who had fought in sixty battles, from First Bull Run to Mobile Bay—four companies in the Army of Northern Virginia, another in the Army of Tennessee.

The speeches by representatives of the artillery were panegyrical, vivid with allusion to specific soldiers and their "distinguished valor." The lengthy and erudite "featured oration" by Thomas Jenkins Semmes, a local aristocrat and statesman who had served in the Confederate Congress and actively advocated for Louisiana troops in Lee's army, combined eulogy for the dead with a stirring apologia for the ideals and motives of the conquered Confederacy.[4]

2. The Great Seal of the Confederacy, adopted in 1863, featured George Washington on horseback; the date shown on the seal, February 22, 1862, is Washington's birthday—though it is intended also to be linked to the inauguration of Jefferson Davis, which took place several days earlier, on February 18. Four years after the events described here, also on Washington's birthday, the Robert E. Lee monument on Tivoli Circle in New Orleans was formally dedicated.

3. Description of the day's events come from Louisiana newspapers, including the *New Orleans Times-Picayune*, February 23, 1880.

4. See Herman de Bachellé Seebold, *Old Louisiana Plantation Homes and Family Trees*, vol. 1 (Baton Rouge: Pelican Press, 1941), pp. 30–36. It was the Jesuit-educated Semmes who proposed the motto for the Confederate States of America seal, *Deo Vindice* ("With God as [our] Champion"); explicit reference to the deity was a deliberate departure from the US Constitution. Semmes and his family lived near the White House of the Confederacy in

And then, the artillery band having played the popular gospel standard "In the Sweet Bye and Bye," a black-robed priest stepped forward to pronounce a closing prayer. He was nearly sixty, his gray hair thinning, his frame slightly stooped, his gait a trifle unsteady. But there was in his countenance an almost childlike gentleness that belied decades of self-denial and self-sacrifice. Behind round, wire-framed glasses, his eyes looked kindly out over the crowd, then closed as he bowed his head and raised all thoughts toward his first commander:

> God of Battles! Lord of Hosts! Omnipotent and Eternal! Most fervently we implore Thee to consecrate with Thy approving smile the work which we have this day dedicated to the virtues of our departed comrades whose honored names and fame shall ever live in our hearts. Most earnestly we beseech Thee to illumine our minds with a stronger and holier faith, and incline us to raise living monuments to Thy glory, which no splendor can eclipse and no vicissitude desecrate. Teach us, O Father! that the highest human virtue is self-abnegation; a life devoted to the happiness of others the most acceptable in Thy sight; and death in the perilous path of duty the fittest consummation of a Christian's mission on earth. As often as we gaze on this monumental pile—dumb witness of suffering, privation, and courage beyond description—may it awaken in us the memory of those who offered up their young lives by our sides in the dark hours of danger and civil commotion. May their precious blood, so freely shed on the field of battle, cry aloud to us evermore to shun all occasion for strife, and to preserve inviolate the blessings of peace. And may the bonds of fraternal affection and sympathy be cemented and strengthened between the peoples of this great Republic.
>
> Look, O Lord, with fondest predilection upon this our Southern land, clothed as she is with the sackcloth of poverty and mourning. If errors Thy searching eye ever did find in her, when her sons bravely gave their lives, and her daughters not less readily gave the lives dearer to them than their own, has she not by these awful hecatombs sufficiently atoned? And has

---

Richmond during the war and hosted regular house parties, at which Father Hubert was an occasional guest. See chapter 4, pp. 77–78 below.

> she not come forth from among the smoke and carnage of battle revealing a brow unstained with dishonor or complaint? Oh! Let her afflictions draw her nearer unto Thee!
>
> Behold and bless Thy servants here congregated. Touch the cords in our warm hearts that we may rise in the majesty of an intense love, and cheerfully accept from our brothers who sleep on distant battlefields that precious legacy, the care of their widowed wives and orphaned children. By the hallowed memories that hang around us, by this marble destined to perpetuate noble deeds, we solemnly vow that we will never prove recreant to the sacred trust.
>
> And when at last, brother soldiers of the grand old corps, we too shall have finished in double quick time our march through life, and been summoned to cross over Death's dark river, may we all answer to roll call, at the reveille of Eternity, with palms of victory in our hands, and resplendent as the battalions of Eden's sentinels. Amen.

The next day's edition of the *New Orleans Times-Picayune* printed the prayer entire. As was often the case when this man prayed on occasions of public import, reporters ensured that his words were preserved. Something about them affected those present in ways that the stock-in-trade pieties and polished oratory of other clergy did not. Acutely attuned to the collective emotion of a gathering, he was able to elevate it, to move people through his own candid affections and compelling spiritual character to a different and higher place.

It is only because of such journalistic records that his words have survived, for the priest himself took no thought for a written legacy; no memoir, no stash of correspondence or sermons or public addresses remain. He spoke as the occasion demanded, often extemporaneously, and then turned from the crowds to attend to the quotidian duties of all faithful priests—confession, consolation, visitation, spiritual counsel, education, worship, acts of mercy. One of his eulogists, at the time of his passing, said that eloquence was not his gift. It is hard to understand such a comment from this distance, except in the recognition that rhetorical flourish and ornate allusion were never his purpose, nor were they what caused his words to resonate.[5] The eloquence that came through his priestly address, whether to those who attended the churches and schools he served or others in the broad parish of the world, was the eloquence of a wholly consecrated life, animated by hope and love as well as deep Christian faith.

He was, as the newspaper indicated, "an old veteran," a Louisiana chaplain who had left New Orleans with the First Louisiana Infantry Regiment in April 1861 and had not come home until the summer of 1865. By then his health was sorely compromised. But his most daunting work lay ahead, as he returned to "a land clothed with the sackcloth of poverty and mourning," to maimed, traumatized, desolate, and sometimes angry men, and to grieving families in his New Orleans parish. Pointing them past the bitterness of sectional strife to "bonds of fraternal affection and sympathy" and promoting national and racial reconciliation was far harder, he often said, than facing enemy fire on the field of battle. A rare statesman in his time and place, free of the burden to impress or to be elected, he appealed to the best and holiest inclinations of those to whom he spoke. On this February day, tenderly honoring the fallen, whose experience he had shared, and then lifting thoughts past painful reminders of the "civil commotion" that had stolen a generation, he urged those listening to "shun all occasion for strife" and become, themselves, living monuments of self-sacrifice and constructive service in the world. No one modeled such a life better than he.

His name was Darius Hubert.

5. His fellow New Orleans Jesuit, Emmanuel de la Morinière, by contrast, had a reputation for elegant homilies and the florid, neoclassical language favored in public oratory in the South. See his essay "Chivalry," which, in celebrating the reputation of Robert E. Lee, refers also to Darius Hubert and quotes him at some length—almost certainly in a somewhat "improved" baroque paraphrase: *The Louisiana Book: Selections from the Literature of the State*, ed. Thomas M'Caleb (1894; rpt. New Orleans: Cornerstone, 2012), pp. 174–79. Father de la Morinière left the Crescent City to become a professor at St. Stanislaus College in Macon, Georgia, during Darius Hubert's convalescence there (1891–93) and was likely present at the time of his death.

ONE

Toulon, France
1823–1847

The birthplace of Darius Hubert was the Mediterranean port city of Toulon, France. Given its strategic location and crucial military assets, Toulon had been much fought over during the blood-soaked drama of the French Revolution, its population being deeply divided between adherents of the *ancien régime* and those of the new Republican order. In the pivotal year of 1793, marked by the execution of King Louis XVI in Paris and commencement of the Reign of Terror under Robespierre, Toulon was flooded with refugees escaping Republican atrocities in Avignon, Lyon, and Marseille. Royalist elements in the city, in concert with disaffected Jacobins and those anxious to protect their families from the excessive and arbitrary violence of the Republican army, made the extraordinary decision to seek protection from British and Spanish vessels engaged in an offshore blockade. Foreign soldiers manned a series of forts defending the city, raised the *fleur-de-lis* banner, and declared the orphaned eight-year-old Dauphin, Louis XVII, de facto king of France. Toulon's rebellion was short-lived. The Republican army, with an unknown young artillery captain named Napoleon Bonaparte, besieged the city and eventually drove foreign forces to depart the scene, carrying many sympathetic to the old regime on their ships with them. After predictably brutal retributive bloodletting to punish "enemies of the revolution" unlucky enough to be left behind, the new order was firmly established in Toulon.[1]

1. A detailed and readable account may be found in Bernard Ireland's *The Fall of Toulon: The Last Opportunity to Defeat the French Revolution* (London: Weidenfield & Nicolson, 2005).

Whether any of Darius Hubert's near relatives lived through these events in his natal city is not known. There is a record of a Jacques Hubert being executed by guillotine on January 25, 1794, not on the Mediterranean coast but in La Boussac, in Brittany.[2] This was an area of significant counterrevolutionary fervor in the 1790s, especially in response to the French State's de-Christianization policies; it found military expression in the "Catholic and Royal Armies" of Normandy, Brittany, and Vendée, whose emblem was the sacred heart. Though it is impossible to verify a family connection between this victim of revolutionary violence and Darius Hubert's father, who bore the same name, several Jesuit sources mention Brittany or Normandy as the family's ancestral home. And, on the certificate of baptism for Darius Honoré Hubert,[3] witnessed and signed at L'Église Saint Pierre de Toulon on July 21, 1823, his father, Jacques Joseph Hubert, is listed as a forty-three-year-old navy quartermaster from Granville, Lower Normandy, a fortified port town on the English Channel, only forty miles from La Boussac.[4] Born in 1780, Jacques would have lived through the carnage and chaos as a teenager and witnessed many atrocities—not impossibly including the execution of his own father and namesake.

It is unclear when the younger Jacques departed Granville for the busy naval station at Toulon, but he evidently met and married Marie Rose Adelaide Ferrandin after he arrived on the southern coast; her birthplace was La Seyne-sur-Mer, a little village directly across the bay from the French arsenal at Toulon.[5] Her Marian first name, and her association with the parish of the old convent church, Saint Pierre de Toulon, bespeak more than nominal Catholic piety, as does her ensuring that her

2. A roster of more than thirteen thousand individuals killed by guillotine during the French Revolution is now available on the website Ancestry.com (in French).

3. Darius Hubert's namesake and godparent, likely a relative, was Darius Honoré Leonard Sebastien, a native of Soliers, Normandy, immediately adjacent to the historic (intriguingly named) village of Hubert-Folie.

4. Later records have Jacques Hubert as "superintendent of the naval yard" at Toulon.

5. It was at La Seyne that Bonaparte and the Republican forces scoped and launched their campaign to vanquish rebellious Toulon and retake the Arsenal in the fall of 1793. Darius Hubert's mother, Marie Rose Ferrandin, would have been five years old.

son was baptized within days of his birth. She was likely the faith-bearer in the family.[6]

Young Darius was apparently urged (and expected) by his father to take up a "useful" profession such as shipbuilding or naval engineering but, having both conspicuous intellectual gifts and a studious disposition, he eventually prevailed in choosing, rather, a collegiate education. Notwithstanding his academic temperament, he was by his own account a young man of "indifferent piety" until his twentieth year. The event that awakened his spiritual consciousness and effected his conversion took place in late October 1842. Pope Gregory XVI, responding to a request from the bishop of Algiers, honored the revived Catholic Church in colonial Africa by transferring a relic of Saint Augustine from Italy back to the old Roman town of Hippo (now called Annaba) where the fourth-century Church Father had lived out his life. The port of Toulon was the point of departure from which the relic was carried from Europe to Africa.[7] On October 23, following a solemn Mass and stirring sermon delivered by the bishop of Algiers, the reliquary was borne with great pomp through the streets of Toulon; the following day, as church bells pealed and the guns of the forts fired salutes, an escort of bishops, clergy, and religious sailed out of port, bearing the relic back home to north Africa; more than twenty thousand Toulonese gathered on shore to honor Saint Augustine, Darius Hubert evidently among them.

Shortly thereafter he sought entrance to the Lyon Province of the Society of Jesus, a decision that caused great and lasting alienation from his father. The Jesuits had, of course, a notoriously controversial reputation, having been suppressed in France in 1764, and throughout Europe (and the New World) in 1773. Their restoration throughout the Catholic world was effected in 1814, but the Society of Jesus (like other religious communities) was still illegal, and regarded with distrust, in post-Napoleonic

6. Though Jacques Joseph Hubert's name, age, and occupation are listed on the church register, it is noted that he was not present for his infant son's baptismal rite.

7. Johannes Alzog, *Handbuch der Universal-Kirchengeschichte,* 4 vols. [Mainz, 1841], trans. F. J. Patisch and Thomas S. Byrne as *Manual of Universal Church History* (Dublin: M. H. Gill and Son, 1905), vol. 4: p. 325.

France.[8] There was, however, an additional layer of notoriety associated specifically with Jesuit history in Toulon that might have given a young man (and possibly his father) pause. The port city was the site of the most spectacular scandal in the order's tumultuous history.

In 1728 an austere, middle-aged Jesuit priest, Jean-Baptiste Girard, who "radiated virtue," according to some early witnesses, was sent from Aix-en-Provence to Toulon to take up a prestigious appointment as rector to the Royal Seminary, a Jesuit training facility for navy chaplains. Girard's arrival prompted discord among members of rival religious orders in the city and with local clergy who had anti-Jesuit leanings.[9] Much of the suspicion of the order, historically, attached to the way Jesuits insinuated themselves as confessors into the private lives of the wealthy and powerful, but also of women. Father Girard soon gratified his enemies by attracting a small coterie of local female penitents, including eighteen-year-old Catherine Cadière, a shopkeeper's daughter. Catherine showed an early penchant for fervent devotion, visions, and mystical experiences; she was said to have experienced the stigmata (the wounds of Christ) and was prone to prophetic and ecstatic trances as well as occasional blasphemous outbursts thought to be evidence of demonic oppression. Catherine's growing reputation as a "holy woman," at first validated and encouraged by her confessor, intrigued and divided the local population. But in the autumn of 1730 there was an extraordinary and very public falling out between the young penitent and her spiritual director: she accused him of heresy, bewitchment, seduction, and procuring an abortion. He countered that these shocking charges were all lies, crafted as a form of revenge after he confronted her with his conviction that she was a spiritual imposter, fabricating her visions and mystical experiences to

8. Despite official sanction, many members of the order returned from exile and reopened schools and seminaries under the presumed protection of King Charles X. The policy of the Bourbon kings was inconsistent and vacillating, however, and offered little legal security to the Jesuits.

9. There were strong Jansenist elements in Toulon in this period—Jansenism being a reform movement within the Catholic Church that took strong exception to what it regarded as Jesuit corruption. See appendix I.

gain notoriety. No contemporary tabloid exposé could have been more lurid or sensational. Voluminous legal depositions, published in Paris (and translated into English for the benefit of readers across the Channel), eventuated in a criminal trial that caused an uproar all over Europe, dividing whole communities. Anti-Jesuit riots broke out in Marseille, Aix, and in Toulon itself. Equally vociferous crowds declared the priest's innocence and demanded that Catherine be burned as a heretic. After lengthy consideration, the court was deadlocked; since the claims and counterclaims were of a religious character, the judge expediently sent the matter back to ecclesiastical jurisdiction where, ultimately, Girard was cleared of wrongdoing and Catherine sent home to her family.[10] The whole tawdry affair was to leave an indelible stain for many years on the reputation of the order, especially in and around Toulon, and was one of the narratives produced as "evidence" for the necessary suppression of the Society of Jesus thirty years later.

Despite the Jesuits' contentious history and tarnished local reputation, Darius Hubert was evidently undeterred from his clear sense of spiritual vocation. He was to prove, over the course of his long and eventful life, to be a sterling counterexample to all "Jesuitical" caricatures: a faithful, courageous, self-effacing, and self-sacrificing son of the Church, and a trusted friend and colleague not only to Catholics of all parties but to Christians across a broad range of denominational affiliation.

Having determined to join the order despite his father's objections, Darius went on foot to Avignon (some 120 miles) to seek entry to the novitiate there. He was refused admission for reasons unknown and walked back to his native Toulon. Unshaken in his resolve, he undertook seminary studies at the diocesan seminary at Brignoles, just 30 miles north, before transferring to the seminary at Trèbes, 230 miles to the west. He

10. The narrative is recounted in detail in a recent book by Mita Choudhury, *The Wanton Jesuit and the Wayward Saint* (University Park: Penn State University Press, 2015). Among primary sources, various reprint editions are available in English of Jean-Baptiste Girard, *The Defence of F. John Baptist Girard, Jesuit, and Rector of the Royal Seminary of Chaplains of the Navy in the City of Toulon, against the Accusation of Mary Catharine Cadière, Containing his Refutation of the Charge*, originally published in 1732.

entered the Jesuit novitiate at Toulouse in September 1843. When he had completed his initial two-year ascetical training centered upon the *Spiritual Exercises* of Ignatius Loyola and professed vows of poverty, chastity, and obedience, he commenced his philosophical study, embracing with characteristic good cheer the ordinary life of a young scholastic: "a life of strict discipline, a dull routine of duty . . . of unceasing abnegation of self . . . the foundation of the future superstructure of virtue, an interior spirit, a close union with God."[11]

Then, on the brink of another revolution in France—the Third French Revolution (1848), which forced the abdication of France's last monarch, the so-called "citizen king" Louise Philippe—Darius Hubert volunteered for the North American mission. Two previous groups of French Jesuits had already answered the call from New Orleans Bishop Antoine Blanc to help establish religious schools in Louisiana. This third group departed from Marseille in October 1847 on the sailing vessel *St. Ann* for the six-week journey across the Atlantic. In later years, Hubert would recall his emotional parting with his mother, who gave him her blessing through her tears. He was never to see her, or the country of his birth, again.

11. The words are those of Fr. Frederick Garesche, homilist at the Requiem Mass for Darius Hubert, Church of the Immaculate Conception, New Orleans, June 22, 1893.

TWO

Grand Coteau, Louisiana 1848–1853

The *St. Ann* made landfall at Pointe-à-Pitre, Guadeloupe, in the French West Indies in November 1847. From there, after a brief layover, she carried her Jesuit passengers on to Mobile, Alabama, where local Catholics, especially other members of their order, afforded them a generous welcome. The Society of Jesus had just taken over administration of Mobile's Spring Hill College, a school originally founded by the city's first Catholic bishop, Michael Portier, in 1830.[1] The new Jesuit rector of Spring Hill, Father Francis de Sales Gautrelet, had arrived from France only a few months earlier, along with several priests and scholastics with whom Darius Hubert would work closely over the years.[2] Gautrelet himself was to become a close lifelong friend.

Spring Hill College would figure only fleetingly in Darius Hubert's long

1. For a detailed account of the founding of the college and its cession to the Jesuit order in the 1840s, see Michael Kenny, S.J., *Catholic Culture in Alabama: Centenary Story of Spring Hill College, 1830–1930* (New York: America Press, 1931).

2. Gautrelet's travel companions were Frs. Aloysius Roccofort, Frederick Larnaudie, Hippolyte Gache, and scholastics Joseph Lavay and Francis Lespes. See Kenny, *Catholic Culture in Alabama*, 131. Joseph Lavay would work side by side with Darius Hubert in Baton Rouge for several years until an assassination attempt that apparently targeted them both prompted his reassignment; Hippolyte Gache would shadow Hubert in virtually all of his assignments in Louisiana and, like him, serve as a Confederate chaplain during the Civil War, though for a shorter term and with less notoriety. A stern disciplinarian, with little feeling for American youth, Gache was unpopular with students both at Grand Coteau and later in Baton Rouge, where he had to be replaced—in this as in other ways a striking foil to Darius Hubert.

tenure as an educator, however, and not until more than a decade later. After spending the winter in Mobile in the company of fellow priests and brothers, he was assigned to the Jesuit College of St. Charles in Grand Coteau, Louisiana—a hamlet midway between Lafayette and Opelousas in Cajun country, St. Landry Parish.[3]

The fact that Grand Coteau was well off the grid, remote from any major center, had given the society pause a decade earlier when it was seeking a location for its first educational foundation in the American South. But the location was scenic, and lauded by locals as one of the healthiest sites in Louisiana, notably free of the fevers that tended to afflict the populations of Baton Rouge and New Orleans. Moreover, Catholics in St. Landry, many of whom had moved from Maryland (where Jesuits had a lengthy tenure), were solicitous and generous, offering both property and funds for the new enterprise. The Sisters of the Sacred Heart were already well established in the community; the Jesuits' boys college opened in January 1838 with a cohort of French Jesuit priests and brothers—including the eccentric Father Nicholas Point, who served briefly as St. Charles's first president before taking up his preferred apostolate among North American Indians, and Father John Francis Abbadie, who planted avenues of oaks connecting the College and the Academy of the Sacred Heart, still a picturesque feature of Grand Coteau. Among Darius Hubert's colleagues at St. Charles were Fathers James Duffo, Anthony Jourdan, Aloysius Roccofort, Anthony Francis Nachon, and Hippolyte Gache, the latter of whom was, when Hubert arrived in 1848, director, prefect of students, and general manager of the school and its adjacent farm acreage. The agricultural property, cobbled together largely through donations, included cropland in which corn, sweet potatoes, and forage crops were grown, and a livestock operation, with cows, hogs, and chickens; it allowed for the college to be largely self-sustaining but also entailed an enormous extra burden of labor.

It is clear from ministerial diaries at Grand Coteau, recently translated, that the property was tended not only by the Jesuits themselves but by

3. The school was named for the notable Catholic cardinal, archbishop of Milan, and reformer, Charles Borromeo (1538–1584).

paid itinerant laborers (often immigrants) and also by slaves, most of whom were loaned to the college by local Catholic planter families for specific projects but a few of whom were owned by the community for various periods between the late 1830s and the time of the Civil War.[4]

This was Darius Hubert's first experience of living in a slaveholding community and interacting directly with African Americans. If he was unsettled by the peculiar institution, there are no records of his feelings on the matter, and his support for and solidarity with the South during the Civil War would seem to suggest a largely benign and paternalistic view of slavery. Like many of his French-born colleagues, he perhaps saw in the zeal of abolitionists a mirror of the revolutionary passion that had consumed his own country, turning the high-sounding ideals of *liberté* and *égalité* into rationalizations for terror, and the overnight elimination of slavery in the French colonies, without any provision for a stable economic order to replace it, into the "horrors of St. Domingo."[5] But the distinctive warp and woof of community life in St. Landry in the antebellum years doubtless shaped his views as well, for the peculiar institution in southern Louisiana was not as starkly black and white as elsewhere in the South. Louisiana specifically, and St. Landry notably, included a

4. Documentation may be found in the "Minister's Diary Volume 1, 1837–1855," English translation, St. Charles College Collection, New Orleans Province Archive, now located at the Jesuit Archives & Research Center, St. Louis, Missouri. The author is grateful for the opportunity to consult these materials when they were housed at Loyola University in New Orleans, and for the generous assistance of Joan Gaulene, former archivist of the New Orleans Province collection.

5. Thus Stephen Dubuisson, S.J., a refugee from the slave rebellions in Haiti and witness to atrocities in revolutionary France, involved in the American Jesuit mission in the generation preceding Darius Hubert's arrival, regarded instant manumission as dangerous and ill-considered, not least to the black population. See Cornelius M. Buckley, *Stephen Larigaudelle Dubuisson, S.J. (1786–1864) and the Reform of the American Jesuits* (Lanham, MD: University Press of America, 2013), pp. 151–57. A valuable anthology of primary sources may be found in Kenneth J. Zanca, ed., *American Catholics and Slavery: 1789–1866* (Lanham, MD: University Press of America, 1994). And see Michael Pasquier, *Fathers on the Frontier: French Missionaries and the Roman Catholic Priesthood in the United States, 1789–1870* (New York: Oxford University Press, 2010), chap. 5.

surprising number of wealthy planters of color, themselves slaveholders, in the mid-nineteenth century.[6] The small but bustling steamboat port of Negroville (now Washington), Louisiana, just fifteen miles from Grand Coteau on Bayou Courtableau, so named because of its large free black population,[7] is mentioned with retrospective admiration by Booker T. Washington, citing the well-known landscape architect and social critic Frederick Law Olmsted, who visited St. Landry in 1853:

> The little town of Washington, near Opelousas, in St. Landry Parish, was formerly called Negroville from the number of free Negroes living in that village. A number of them, according to Olmsted, were wealthy and thriving. They owned some of the best cotton and sugar plantations. . . . The best house and most tasteful grounds that he had visited in the state had belonged to a nearly full-blooded Negro—a very dark man. He and his family were well educated and, though French in their habitual tongue, they spoke English with a liberal tongue, and were much more eloquent than most of the liberally educated whites. They had a private tutor in their family and owned . . . a hundred and fifty slaves."[8]

6. For a concise statistical overview, see Loren Schweninger, "Antebellum Free Persons of Color in Postbellum Louisiana," *Louisiana History* 30 (Autumn 1989): 345–64. "During the pre–Civil War decade, Louisiana's free people of color remained, by far, the most prosperous group of African descent in the United States, controlling substantially more property than free Negroes in any other state" (p. 346). See also Margaret Gehman, "Visible Means of Support: Businesses, Professions, and Trades of Free People of Color," in *Creole: The History and Legacy of Louisiana's Free People of Color*, ed. Sybil Kein (Baton Rouge: Louisiana State University Press, 2000), pp. 208–22; esp. 215–16.

7. Vulgarly called "Niggerville" according to local newspapers as early as 1849, but also appearing as such on at least two Civil War–era St. Landry maps, dated 1863 and 1864, in the Richard Holloway collection, Alexandria, LA. Historical sources attribute the name to the community that grew up around the plantation of Antoine Lemel, a wealthy black man who owned "a large tract of land and a great number of slaves." See William Henry Perrin, *Southwest Louisiana Biographical and Historical* (New Orleans: Gulf Publishing, 1891), 56.

8. Booker T. Washington, "The Free Negro in Slavery Days," *The Outlook*, September 18, 1909, pp. 107–14. The unnamed individual mentioned here may be Jean-Baptiste Meullion, who farmed 1,240 acres along Bayou Teche, or Adolphe Donato. Other wealthy free blacks

The Jesuits of Grand Coteau had extensive contact with "Negroville," conducting Mass at the local chapel, performing marriages, baptisms, and funerals, as well as providing religious instruction and visiting the sick among Catholic families, including families of color.[9] Parish work across the rest of St. Landry involved regular visitation schedules to particular areas by Jesuits "on supply": as described by Father Theodore de Theux, pastor of St. Charles Church from 1839–1842, their ministry included not only interacting with middle-class merchants and wealthy planters but also visiting poor whites who found it difficult to get to services and "very many slaves."[10]

Ministerial records from the Hubert years mention by first name several slaves who either lived at St. Charles or were loaned by local landowners for various periods of time.[11] One name is recorded with especial frequency, that of Nace, a long-term and evidently trusted servant of the

---

in antebellum St. Landry included the Simien, Guillory, and Lemel[le] families; ninety-six persons of color in St. Landry were propertied in the late 1840s, and most of these owned bondsmen. The new digital collection "Free People of Color in Louisiana" in the Louisiana Digital Library is a valuable addition to already published materials on this subject. And a rich genealogical study by Alex Da' Paul Lee, who descends from both slaves and slaveholders in St. Landry, opens a fascinating window on the context in which the Jesuit mission was established in the parish (www.facebook.com/Alexgenealogy). During the Civil War, property owned by the free blacks of St. Landry was ruthlessly torched by Union troops under Nathaniel Banks: "the road all the way to Natchitoches was a solid flame" (Schweninger, "Antebellum Free Persons of Color," pp. 351–52).

9. Correspondence between St. Charles College and Archbishop Antoine Blanc in New Orleans (housed in the Archives of the University of Notre Dame) frequently mentions free persons of color, as well as slaves, who desire to be baptized, validly married, or otherwise to receive the blessing of the Church.

10. In a letter to his mother in Belgium, cited in Gilbert J. Garraghan, S.J., *The Jesuits of the Middle United States* (New York: America Press, 1938), vol. 3: p. 149.

11. These are listed with first names only. In addition to Nace and Sally, they include: Frank, Ben, Henry, George, Valsin, Scott, Charles, Henry, Augustin, Mirante, Orton, Pheba (Phoebe?), Julia, Celeste, and Modeste. Of these, George, Henry, and Phoebe, along with Nace and Sally, are referred to as "ours"; others, including Ben, Frank, and Julia, "belong to the [Sacred Heart] Convent." Seven unnamed "domestic workmen who have been here for some time" evidently lived at the college during the Hubert years; others were loaned for digging wells, cutting wood, or for cooking or doing laundry: among these are "the [unnamed]

community. Nace frequently accompanied one or more of the Jesuits on trips to nearby towns, was sometimes charged with looking for lost livestock, led work crews in cutting wood or harvesting crops, and was tasked with building projects such as construction of the new entrance gates in front of the college in the summer of 1851. He and his family were often singled out for special benevolence, especially at Christmas. His one apparent vice seems to have been occasional imprudent use of alcohol. He was incarcerated briefly in 1851 (on three successive Sundays, his penalty consisting not of corporal punishment but a diet of bread and water) for drunkenly abandoning a horse-drawn wagon in the woods, resulting in severe injuries to the horses; he shortly returned to his former duties, apparently without further consequence.

Nace came to Grand Coteau, though indirectly, from the Maryland Jesuits, who controversially sold off their plantations in 1838 and sent their slaves to Louisiana planters, with the ostensible assurance that families would be kept together and that religious instruction and access to Mass would be ensured.[12] The "Nace" in question here appears on a manifest of the bondsmen sold from St. Thomas Manor, Port Tobacco, Maryland, the centerpiece of the Maryland holdings.[13] How he came to St. Landry

negress of Mrs. Wells"; Charles, the "negro of the doctor [Millard]"; Mirante, "a negro of Mr. Debaillion"; and "some negroes of Mr. Castille" and of "Mr. Guidry."

12. Details regarding the mass sale of Jesuit-owned slaves, orchestrated by William McSherry, rector of Georgetown College (now University) and Thomas Mulledy, provincial superior of the Maryland Jesuits, in 1838, may be found in R. Emmett Curran, "Splendid Poverty: Jesuit Slave-Holding in Maryland, 1805–1838," in *Catholics in the Old South: Essays in Church and Culture*, ed. Randall Miller and Jon Waklyn (Macon, GA: Mercer University Press, 1983); Thomas Murphy, S.J., *Jesuit Slaveholding in Maryland, 1717–1838* (New York: Routledge, 2001), chap. 7; Edward F. Beckett, S.J., "Listening to Our History: Inculturation and Jesuit Slaveholding," *Studies in the Spirituality of Jesuits* 28.5 (1996); see also Buckley, *Stephen Larigaudelle Dubuisson*, pp. 235–37.

13. This "Nace" should be distinguished from Nace Butler, from the St. Inigoes Plantation, also part of the Jesuit holdings in Maryland; he and his wife, Biby, and nine children were sold to the Louisiana estate of Jesse Batey in 1838, a history recently documented by descendants (www.thehoya.com/bayonne-johnson-my-goal-was-just-to-tell-my-story). The unusual name Nace is a derivative or diminutive of Latin "Ignatius," the name adopted by the founder of the Society of Jesus, Ignatius Loyola. This Christian name was bestowed upon

Parish once in Louisiana is unclear (virtually all the Maryland slaves were sold to plantations in Ascension or Iberville), but he was "bought by the College for $1000" in 1838.[14] Nace and his wife, Sally, and their several children seem to have been informally attached for a time to the household of celebrated converts Pierce and Cornelia Connelly, who taught at St. Charles and at Sacred Heart Academy respectively from 1838 to 1840.[15] Sally named a daughter, born in 1851, Adeline—the name of the Connellys' eldest daughter, whom she had likely known and cared for. Pierce Connelly, in a letter to Archbishop Blanc in 1840, mentions Nace being falsely implicated in an attempted slave insurrection in Lafayette.[16] Despite arrest, torture, and the threat of lynching (a fate suffered by more than a dozen others), Nace never wavered in attesting his own innocence and defending the reputation of the Jesuits—whom some townspeople accused of inciting the rebellion (in part because they had been observed shaking hands and conversing cordially with blacks).[17] After a harrowing

---

a number of young male slaves in the context of Jesuit plantation life; see, for example, Joseph Zwinge, S.J., "The Jesuit Farms in Maryland: Fact and Anecdotes: The Negro Slaves," *Woodstock Letters* 41.2 (1912): 198, 215; see also p. 60.

14. "Father John Abbadie: A Sketch," *Woodstock Letters* 24.1 (1895): 23.

15. The Connellys created a commotion when, having converted to Roman Catholicism and served as teachers at Grand Coteau, they obtained a dispensation to separate in 1844—Pierce to take holy orders (with the blessing of Pope Gregory XVI himself) and his wife, Cornelia Peacock Connelly, to enter a convent at Rome. Father Connelly eventually caused enormous scandal to the church and injury to his family by attempting to reclaim authority over Cornelia and the Order of the Holy Child she founded in England, initiating a notorious lawsuit against her, kidnapping their several children and spiriting them away to Europe. He went on to become a bitter critic of the Roman Church he had so fervently embraced. See Denis G. Paz, *Priesthoods and Apostasies of Pierce Connelly: A Study of Victorian Conversion and Anti-Catholicism* (Lewiston, NY: Edwin Mellen, 1986).

16. "He [Father Abbadie] will tell you also of the horrors that were so near overtaking us from an intended insurrection of the negroes and of our anxiety about poor Nace who was one of those that were taken up [arrested] in our neighborhood . . . a loaded pistol having unluckily been put in his possession by a runaway brother and accidentally discovered in his hands" (Pierce Connelly to Bishop Blanc, September 16, 1840, University of Notre Dame Archives, V-4-k A.L.S).

17. One of the priests was subjected to "insults and curses for having wished to assist the negroes who were hanged. They [local "bigots" and hooligans] wanted to carry their rage to

ordeal that lasted seven days, Nace was exonerated and allowed to return to Grand Coteau.[18]

As minister of the house and keeper of the logbook from 1850 to 1853, Darius Hubert mentions Nace and his family being given, according to custom, warm clothes for the winter and treated, along with the other slaves, with money gifts, fabric for clothing, shoes, and special food treats (including notably chocolate, extra desserts, wine, and whisky) as well as time off from work on feast days, especially at Christmas. He recounts the final festivity of Christmas 1850 as an evening bonfire, to which all were invited, apparently an annual event.

The original St. Charles College complex was a rather primitive facility, of which no images are extant. The main building was far from comfortably livable—either brutally cold or stifling, depending on the season. Students slept in the same rooms in which they studied. The Jesuits themselves were lodged in wooden cabins with less insulation from the elements than afforded by the main building. One complained in an 1849 letter that they were "constructed in such a way as to guarantee that the occupants would roast in the summer and freeze in the winter."[19] A new building was added to the campus in 1852, which became a residence for the boys, allowing the Jesuit fathers and brothers to move out of the cabins and into the original structure.

Following the typical pattern of Jesuit-run lay schools, St. Charles admitted students between the ages of nine and fourteen, and offered a six-year curriculum which encompassed both high school and college courses. Cost, including board, was $150 per year. Core subjects were Latin, Greek, English, French, Spanish, mathematics, science, philosophy, and history; some commercial courses were also available for those who had no aspiration to the professions of medicine or law. Few students

---

the College at Grand Coteau which they wished to demolish or burn because they regarded the Jesuits as instigators of the insurrection of the slaves" (Fr. Peter Beauprez to Bishop Blanc, September 25, 1840, University of Notre Dame Archives, V-4-k A.L.S).

18. "Father John Abbadie," pp. 22–23.

19. See Cornelius M. Buckley, S.J., in the introduction to Gache, *Frenchman, Chaplain, and Rebel*, p. 19.

stayed the course for the full six years, but the school was well subscribed, with upwards of ninety students in some years. Darius Hubert was enlisted as an instructor of Latin and French. He undertook theological and English language study on his own time and became quickly fluent in his adopted language, a skill that would distinguish him from many of his French-born colleagues throughout his long ministry.[20] Sometime in 1848, at the age of twenty-five, he received minor orders.[21]

Though the immediate neighbors of the college were protective and supportive, anti-Catholicism was rife in nearby Lafayette in the 1840s and 50s. Anonymous letters threatened the Jesuits with public whipping, flogging, or lynching if they refused to leave their foundation. Local newspapers published editorial and opinion columns that stirred up suspicion of the order.

These were uneasy times for Jesuits in the South, as elsewhere in America. A nativist, anti-Catholic spirit was rife as immigrants poured into the country from all over Catholic Europe. Writers like Samuel Morse, the well-known inventor, had been inveighing against the influx of Catholics and the "dangerous intrigues" of Jesuits since the mid-1830s, arguing that "Popery is opposed in its very nature to Democratic republicanism."[22] In 1849 a secret society to which Morse was connected, calling itself the Order of the Star Spangled Banner, formed in New York, with membership restricted to Protestant men; their goal was to slow the tide of immigrants through covert political activism. This group and others like it eventually coalesced under the banner of "Know Nothings," since it was their practice to respond to any questions from outsiders with

20. Hippolyte Gache, for example, remained "all but unintelligible in English" his whole life, as did many of his colleagues. See Gache, *Frenchman, Chaplain, Rebel,* p. 24; also John T. McGreevy, *American Jesuits and the World: How an Embattled Religious Order Made Modern Catholicism Global* (Princeton, NJ: Princeton University Press, 2016), p. 153.

21. "Minor orders," marking progress in spiritual formation and advancement toward the priestly office, conferred special duties as porter, lector, exorcist, and acolyte. These were followed by "major (or sacred) orders," culminating in priesthood.

22. Samuel F. B. Morse, *Foreign Conspiracy against the Liberties of the United States* (New York: Leavitt Lord, 1835); *Imminent Dangers to the Free Institutions of the United States through Foreign Immigration* (New York: E. B. Clayton, 1935).

a non-committal "I know nothing." They ran candidates successfully in many political jurisdictions in the mid 1850s until disintegrating over the question of slavery.[23]

Quite apart from these organized political activists, the Jesuits had to confront opposition from other more problematic sources, not least from the likes of the infamous Pierce Connelly, once an intimate of the Jesuits and teacher at St. Charles College but who later publicly renounced the Church and spent his later years writing vicious anti-Catholic, specifically anti-Jesuit tracts.[24]

Another individual provides an equally illuminating case study. Less than a year after Darius Hubert joined the little band of Jesuits at Grand Coteau under the protection and blessing of Bishop Antoine Blanc, a rather mysterious French priest arrived on Blanc's doorstep in New Orleans, having taken a much less direct route than the bishop's Jesuit recruits. Blanc, renowned for his hospitality, welcomed him unreservedly into his own residence.

Father Jean Claudius Pitrat was to have an unsettling effect on the fortune of Jesuit missions not only in Louisiana and Mississippi but throughout the United States. He came bearing letters of introduction from the archbishop of Bordeaux, under whose authority he had briefly served in the mid 1840s,[25] and from the ecclesiastical superior of Guadeloupe, the Caribbean French protectorate where he had spent several months in 1849.

23. For a well-documented study of the nativist (specifically anti-Catholic) movement, see Ray Allen Billington, *The Protestant Crusade 1800–1860: A Study of the Origins of American Nativism* (1938; rpt. New York: Quadrangle Books, 1964). The activities of Know Nothings in Louisiana, especially New Orleans, are chronicled in Roger Baudier, *The Catholic Church in Louisiana* (1939; rpt. New Orleans: Louisiana Library Association, 1972), 379–81. See also Marius M. Carriere Jr., "Anti-Catholicism, Nativism, and Louisiana Politics in the 1850s," *Louisiana History* 35.4 (Autumn 1994): 455–74, and the same author's *The Know Nothings in Louisiana* (Jackson: University Press of Mississippi, 2018).

24. See note 15 above.

25. The Bordeaux document, dated October 4, 1847, indicates that the bearer, "our beloved John Claudius Pitrat," is "a pious and honest priest; that he is not tied by ecclesiastical censures and sentences, hindering him from exercising the ministry in whatever diocese he

Pitrat's biography, for which one is unduly dependent on his own testimony, was much more complicated than he seems to have indicated to Bishop Blanc. He was born into a Catholic family near Lyon; after a youthful period of atheistic rebellion, he returned to the Church, studied theology, and was ordained as a priest, becoming in his own words "so furious an Aristocrat, so strong a believer in Popery, and so devoted an adherent, that I would have killed a Protestant, even a Democrat, as readily as I would have killed a fly, at the order of my Ecclesiastical Superiors." His fanaticism alienated even his devout mother, to whom he remained unreconciled until her death. Pitrat served several parishes in the vicinity of Lyon and then moved, at the invitation of the archbishop of Bordeaux, to that city. It was there, he says, that his "intellectual, moral, and religious emancipation commenced" and he "began to suspect that my intolerance [of non-Catholics] was anti-Christian . . . and that the aristocratical principles which Popery generates are mostly injurious to society. . . . I remained a Roman Catholic but I considered my church as a monstrous compound in which the human elements stifled the Divine institution." His bishop reassigned him in September 1847 to a new parish "very distant from Bordeaux" to rethink his views, but Pitrat, in a daring breach of vows, moved instead to Paris, where in the revolutionary chaos that resulted in the ousting of King Louis Philippe (the third French Revolution) he took up his pen against the Church to which he was still formally attached.

He helped found a daily newspaper, *La Presse du Peuple,* one of nearly five hundred broadsheets that sprang up overnight to spread the gospel of social change and radicalism in France.[26] In one of his editorials he

---

shall visit . . . [and] that he deserves to be treated everywhere as a priest who has obtained from us the permission to leave our diocese." Pitrat's use of it was more than a little disingenuous, since it predated his willful defection from this archbishop and his clerical assignment. This letter, and the details that follow, are included in the self-serving introduction to Pitrat's *Americans Warned of Jesuitism, or, the Jesuits Unveiled* (New York: J. S. Redfield, 1851).

26. Morna Daniels, "French Newspapers and Ephemera from the 1848 Revolution," *British Library Journal* (1998): 219–33.

exhorted fellow priests to "rise as a single man, and with the gospel in our hands and this device on our banner, 'Liberty, Equality, Fraternity' . . . go to the palaces of the Bishops," there to demand freedom from "tyrannical ordinances . . . retrograde and slavish education and instruction of Ecclesiastical schools, with intolerant, immoral, impious, in short Jesuitical principles and teaching!"

In the turmoil that continued through the spring and summer in the French capital, insurgents fought with the more conservative forces of the provisional government, culminating in the bloody June Days Uprising. The archbishop of Paris, attempting to mediate, was himself fatally shot in the back, one casualty among thousands.

By the time an uneasy order was eventually reestablished in France with the election of Louis Napoleon (Napoleon Bonaparte's nephew) in December 1848, John Claudius Pitrat had departed for Guadeloupe, where slavery had just been abolished, with the apparent intention of helping establish there a new national college. Things were not as rosy as he had hoped, however. Abolition had not ushered in "liberty, equality, and fraternity," but a volatile and dangerous racial stalemate. Plantations were abandoned and emancipated slaves, with no prospect of employment and no fear of their former overseers, imported weapons and, in Pitrat's words, "plotted to renew the drama of Haiti."[27]

Pitrat recalibrated once again. With no very encouraging options in Guadeloupe and nothing to take him home to France, he become convinced that "the organization of the Church in the United States would suit him better than in any other country," and made his way via New York to New Orleans. Blanc received him graciously, as did Stephen Rousselon, his vicar general. The version of his life story that he shared with them almost certainly omitted a few important details. Blanc provided him with a placement that would permit him to learn English, to be engaged in ministry, and to earn a modest stipend—sending him to the

27. For Pitrat's description of Guadeloupe in the aftermath of emancipation, see *Americans Warned*, pp. 17–18.

parish of Natchez, Mississippi, under Bishop John Joseph Chanche in late September 1849. He was then entrusted with a small parish at Milliken's Bend, near Vicksburg, in February 1850. In March, Pitrat wrote to New Orleans, asking that his "two trunks and a package of books" be sent to him, since a prolonged stay seemed in order. This was evidently a ruse, however, as he left his charge immediately after receiving his belongings—sending a perfunctory "resignation" letter to Bishop Blanc and heading for Louisville, Kentucky. He had in hand a sensational book manuscript written clandestinely while enjoying the friendship and mentoring of his clerical overseers and occupying the role of priest: *Americans Warned of Jesuitism, or, the Jesuits Unveiled.* It is a lengthy diatribe, retailing all the most damning claims of anti-Jesuit tracts going back to the seventeenth-century *Monita Secreta,*[28] tailored to a specifically American Protestant audience: "O Jesuits, you are now a Cain marked on the forehead with the iron pen of history as the most deadly foes of the human family . . . and if you are not stopped and carefully watched in America you will prove to the United States that they warm in their bosom a snake that will kill them."[29] Pitrat's acquisition of the English language had evidently proceeded much more smoothly than he was letting on.

Bishop Blanc was shattered by Pitrat's betrayal of his trust and kindness, and by his own sense of complicity in foisting an opportunistic imposter on parishioners and clergy under his charge. He wrote directly to Pitrat, appealing to him to consider the spiritual consequences of his apostasy; his only response was to receive an unsigned copy of the offending book when it was published in 1851. Though the clergy in Natchez apparently heard rumors that Pitrat became a Presbyterian (for them a dire enough

28. The typical themes of such literature include allegations of fanaticism and of notorious, ingenious abuse of spiritual position for material and worldly ends. Jesuits are routinely charged with employing casuistry, political machinations, and their role as confessors to gain control over wealthy penitents, undermine familial and social loyalties (including national allegiances), and extend the reach of their global cabal. For a concise overview, see appendix I.

29. Pitrat, *Americans Warned,* p. 148.

defection), he actually moved on rather quickly from anti-Jesuit and anti-Catholic polemicism through the exit doors of Christian affiliation.[30] He became a Universalist, earning a living by writing and lecturing on the origins of all orthodox Christian doctrines as "off-shoots of paganism."[31]

For Jesuits laboring at Grand Coteau and in Spring Hill College in Mobile under already difficult conditions, the publication of scurrilous and sensational attacks by a former French priest whose apparently credible accusations were couched in autobiographical bona fides was a particularly onerous thorn in the side. Clergy lamented to Blanc that Pitrat's infamous volume was the subject of great interest and curiosity, even among Catholics. Newspaper editors were happy to validate Pitrat's self-presentation as a model of good intentions and propriety: "We have no doubt but that his exhibition of Jesuitism in this volume is true, and it will awaken feelings of disgust and horror in those who will read it. Such revelations are necessary, and we wish they could be widely read, for they would show the hatefulness of Romanism, and it principal defenders, the Jesuits."[32]

In such unpromising and turbulent times, Darius Hubert was ordained a priest on September 14, 1850. Thereafter, in addition to his teaching duties at Grand Coteau, he was named "minister of the house" and pastor of St. Charles Church, confessor for students, and prefect of the Sodality of the Blessed Virgin Mary, a role intended to cultivate Marian devotion among devout students. He led retreats at the convent and undertook ministry outside the confines of Grand Coteau as well, notably in April 1851 conducting a "Jubilee" in Plaquemine Brulé (now Church Point) over

30. His second volume, a fictional offering called *Paul and Julia: Or, the Political Mysteries, Hypocrisy and Cruelty of the Leaders of the Church of Rome* (1855) was addressed to "American Protestants." Eventually Protestants too would come under his haughty censure.

31. One of the first "literary notices" concerning Pitrat's volume was published in the *Universalist Quarterly and General Review* 8 (1851): 325–26, which calls it a "Gospel of Diabolism," revealing a Jesuitical "genius for iniquity that is sublime."

32. *Cincinnati Central Christian Herald* (1865), rpt. in the "Biographical Notice" of the third edition of *Americans Warned of Jesuitism* (Boston: Edward W. Hinks & Co., 1855), xi.

the course of several weeks—an immersive mission intended to revive the faithful and to instruct the nominally Catholic, who lacked a local church or priest, in the rudiments of the faith.[33] As the tide of anti-Catholic sentiment continued to rise, his life of intense, varied, and self-sacrificing service was commenced in earnest.

33. Jerome Neyrey, S.J., "St. Charles Borromeo and his 'Daughters,'" *Acadiana Catholic* (October 2016): 30–31; (November 2016): 24–25. According to the Grand Coteau "Minister's Diary" for 1851, Father Hubert was accompanied by Fr. Anthony de Chaignon.

THREE

Baton Rouge
1854–1861

Notwithstanding the success of St. Charles College at Grand Coteau, Bishop Blanc, who became New Orleans's first archbishop in 1850, had long wanted to establish a similar boys' school at Baton Rouge, which was an important center of commerce, readily accessible by steamboat to the archiepiscopal see in New Orleans, and had been designated the state capital in 1846. Blanc himself had served as priest in Baton Rouge from 1826 to 1835, overseeing the construction of the first St. Joseph Church in 1830, and he was optimistic about prospects of promoting Catholic education in that city. The difficulty was always lack of manpower; as the flow of priests from Europe stalled, people were shifted around from Spring Hill College, Grand Coteau, and New Orleans as needs arose, and the eventual decision to establish a boys' college in Baton Rouge initially seemed to require shuttering the school in Grand Coteau altogether, despite local support.

The two projects were something of a study in contrasts. Though there was considerable anti-Jesuit rabble-rousing and vigilantism in Opelousas and Lafayette, especially in the early years, the immediate neighbors of St. Charles College were generally protective of the Society of Jesus and grateful for the local Jesuit presence; this support helped to sustain the college through many trials and for many decades. In Baton Rouge, by contrast, when some prominent local citizens learned of plans for a Jesuit school in the city, they used whatever disruptive means they could to discourage the priests and scholastics—from political maneuvering and harassment to outright threats of violence.[1]

The first significant confrontation occurred in 1848, shortly after land was purchased for the future College of St. Peter and St. Paul—a two-block parcel of unimproved property on the north side of North Street, not far from St. Joseph Church, jurisdiction over which had just fallen to the Jesuits.[2] The foundations for the first college buildings were soon laid, facing south onto North Street. With construction barely begun, a cohort of local Methodists prevailed upon the mayor and municipal council to bifurcate the property by extending a street that currently dead-ended at North Street right through the center of the Jesuits' new purchase. What reasons were given can only be surmised; the partition was clearly capricious and unwarranted. It did not, however, achieve its goal of causing the Jesuits to abandon their project. Father John Cambiaso, then superior of the order, calmly fenced the two squares on either side of the new road, redesigned the overall layout, locating the college buildings on the east property, facing the newly created "Hypolite Street" (now Sixth), and reserving the west block for gardens and a recreational area. When a delegate of the disgruntled Methodist party came to deliver a threat to the priests, saying that the person he represented had bought a revolver with five barrels to "settle the matter for good," he was sent home with the mocking retort that Father Cambiaso had only one barrel in his own gun to protect himself, but that would certainly be sufficient; if anyone wished

1. Local nativist sentiment had a prominent mouthpiece in the *Weekly Comet*, a popular Baton Rouge newspaper published by Know Nothing Party member and advocate George A. Pike, from 1853 to 1855, after which the *Comet* merged with the *Baton Rouge Gazette*. Pike was especially virulent in his opposition to the Jesuits and their prominent role in local education (as may be seen, for example, in his *Comet* editorials of October 30, 1853, and October 1, 1854).

2. According to Francis Leon Gassler, *History of St. Joseph's Church, Baton Rouge, La., from 1789 to Date* (Marrero, LA: Hope Haven Press, 1943), p. 147, the property was bought for $1,800 from a free man of color, possibly a Catholic, Theophile ("lover of God") Bertrand. Those associated with the short-lived and trouble-plagued school would doubtless have laughed at it being mistakenly called "The College of Immaculate Saints" in an essay penned at the time of Darius Hubert's death (*New Orleans Daily Picayune*, June 17, 1893).

to enter the fence to test him, he was welcome. That rather startling answer from a black-robed priest seemed, for the moment, to put a halt to the intimidation.

Shortness of funds dictated a pragmatic and modest initial footprint for the Jesuit school—two identical two-story frame structures separated by a space of about seventy feet, where a brick building was eventually to be constructed.[3] Each of the original houses had four rooms on the main floor; the one closest to North Street had four upstairs rooms, while the other had only two larger spaces on the second floor—to be used for a yet-to-be-constructed chapel and a dormitory for boarders. When Father Gache moved from Grand Coteau to Baton Rouge to take over management of the college, things were far from ready for occupancy: "none of the upper rooms were plastered; there were no blinds on the windows; the door of my room was shut by a blanket suspended in front of it; the ceiling was still *in fieri*, and during the night, from my bed, I could contemplate the stars with great ease."[4]

The school opened in 1849 with twenty-five students. By the third year, that number had doubled and construction on the main brick building had begun. Father Gache, whose somewhat imperious Gallic manner (exacerbated by his inability to communicate well in English) did not sit

3. Many of the details may be found in a letter written by Father Hippolyte Gache, first superior of the school when it opened in 1849; his account was penned at the request of the province nearly fifty years later, when he was living in Philadelphia. This retrospective on "Our College at Baton Rouge, Louisiana," is published in the *Woodstock Letters* 27.1 (1898): 1–5, and reprinted in several local histories. Neither the Jesuit Archives of the New Orleans Province nor any of the Catholic or Jesuit histories of Louisiana have any images of the buildings described by Father Gache. The consensus has long been that none existed. In tracing the later history of the school and property, however, I was able to uncover and identify three images of the College of St. Peter and St. Paul, two of the initial frame buildings started in 1849 and finished the following year, and one of the main brick building built a few years later. The property had a fascinating and complex history during the Civil War, recounted in considerable detail in my *Two Civil Wars*, pp. 27–32; 196–201, with photos. See also "The History and Provenance of a (Frequently Misidentified) Baton Rouge Civil War Photograph," *Louisiana History* 57.3 (2016): 349–58. An image of the main college building is published here for the first time.

4. Gache, "Our College," p. 3.

well with either the boys or their parents, was reassigned to Spring Hill College in 1852, after which a round-robin of priests, scholastics, and lay brothers attempted to keep the project going.[5] Among these was Father Joseph Lavay, whose tenure in the river capital was shared for several years with Darius Hubert.

Father Hubert arrived in Baton Rouge just as the college project was failing. He is listed among the instructors in the final year of operation, 1854–55. The straw that broke the back of the school's short history was not Protestant opposition, but disease. The dreaded scourge of yellow fever descended on the lower Mississippi, including Baton Rouge, in the summer of 1855, taking the lives of several Jesuit priests and brothers as well as Sisters of the Sacred Heart, other religious and lay Catholics attending a nearby retreat, and local citizens.[6] Fathers Lavay and Hubert were on the front lines ministering to the sick in the community, an effort that earned respect from many erstwhile opponents of the order.[7]

They shared other obligations as well for several years—looking after small free schools for both black and white children, fulfilling preaching and liturgical duties at St. Joseph Church, and performing Catholic rites—baptism, marriage, and funerals—in the city and in the surrounding area. Extant correspondence between both men and Archbishop Blanc often involves requests for special dispensation to marry individuals whose circumstances are canonically "irregular" or permission to visit (for example, to perform a baptism for) families unable or unwilling to attend church services within their immediate ecclesial jurisdiction.[8] Father

5. Gache was treated with considerable disdain by the trustees of the church, who in 1852 reduced his annual salary from $800 to $600 without consultation. Not until Archbishop Blanc himself intervened on his behalf was the initial sum restored—though Gache was shortly reassigned to Mobile, replaced by the more conciliatory and patient Joseph Lavay.

6. An earlier yellow fever outbreak in 1853 had already taken the lives of Father Anthony Parrett and Brother Henry Visconte, both active in the service of the Baton Rouge church and Jesuit College. The more virulent pestilence in 1855 had an even more devastating toll.

7. This was the first of many times Darius Hubert would be wrestling with yellow jack throughout his long life. See chapter 5, below.

8. Most correspondence from the relevant years is housed in the Archives of the University of Notre Dame in Indiana, but some few letters may also be found in the Office of Archives and Records of the Catholic Archdiocese of New Orleans.

Hubert, unlike Lavay, was by this time effortlessly fluent in English, and thus able to minister effectively to native English speakers as well as the many Irish and other English-speaking immigrants flowing into the area; as such, he was in frequent demand to make home visits and to provide retreats.

The partnership of Fathers Lavay and Hubert came to an abrupt end as a result of another violent episode, one that is curiously missing from all histories of the Catholic Church in Baton Rouge and of Jesuit tenure in that city.[9] In December 1857, while the two Jesuit Fathers were enjoying dinner in the refectory in company with a local Catholic layman, shots were fired through a glass door by a would-be assassin. Both priests were injured. Father Hubert was struck in the face by flying glass and Father Lavay by a bullet that grazed his shoulder and lodged in his wrist, there to remain; though the wound was not regarded as dangerous, medical removal of the bullet was deemed too difficult to attempt. The perpetrator was never found. Emotionally shaken, Joseph Lavay pulled back from many of his former duties and asked to be reassigned. He soon found refuge in New Orleans, where he stayed briefly before returning to his native France—eager to shake off the dust of frontier ministry in the Americas.

Darius Hubert, as would be repeatedly shown in subsequent years, was not easily intimidated; he chose to stay on to carry the burdens of parish work alone, even against the wishes of his Jesuit superior, Father Aloysius Curioz. His reasons are given in a lengthy letter to Archbishop Blanc several years later and provide an early index of his personality

9. For example, Rev. Fr. Anthony Drossaert, "History of St. Joseph's Church," *Proceedings of the Historical Society of East and West Baton Rouge Historical Society,* vol. 1: pp. 30–33, published in *Louisiana State University Bulletin,* vol. 8, n.s. 8 (August 1917); Gassler, *History of St. Joseph Church.* No mention is made of the incident in Baudier, *The Catholic Church in Louisiana,* or Garraghan's three-volume history, *The Jesuits of the Middle United States.* The event is touched on in a letter written by Father Hubert to Archbishop Blanc and alluded to in veiled fashion by Matilda Victor in a later letter to Blanc; it was reported initially in the *Baton Rouge Advocate* and picked up and reprinted widely in Louisiana (for example, *New Orleans Times-Picayune,* December 23, 1857, p. 1). The journalist seems to have assumed that the specific target was Joseph Lavay, perhaps because his injury was more serious than Hubert's, but the Society of Jesus itself or the Catholic Church more generally was the likely object of the assailant's malice; he was never identified or captured.

and character.[10] If he departed the city, he said, not only would faithful Catholics be without a shepherd, but a very worthy educational project in Baton Rouge would be doomed to failure and its principal to financial ruin. The school in question, St. Mary's Female Academy, occupied the old Jesuit College buildings and grounds which had been shut down in 1855, and as Father Hubert pointed out, the society was implicated in encouraging the headmistress, Matilda Victor, to purchase it, for the considerable sum of $10,500.

Matilda Victor was a Catholic educator with a very unusual pedigree and formation. She was northern-born, from Sandusky, Ohio, and a convert, having entered the Roman Church while studying as a youngster at a convent school in Cincinnati. Her family was shocked by her religious defection, and she found no spiritual solace or encouragement in her immediate environment. She decided that she might have more opportunity for "the enjoyment of her religion" and a chance to exercise her vocation as a teacher in Louisiana.[11] She had not conjured with the fact that her new Church did not regard laywomen as fit instructors for girls. As she complained in a letter to the noted public intellectual (also a Catholic convert) Orestes Brownson, even "rude servant girls" in religious habits, foreign-born and lacking adequate English, were preferred over well-educated American ladies, whose skills and devotion to the faith were above reproach. A single Catholic woman like herself, without a vocation to religious life, was regarded as suspect in the Church's educational mission; at the same time, given widespread anti-Catholic prejudice, secular schools were closed to her as well. Conversion thus commenced, for someone like her, a veritable "life of martyrdom."[12]

10. Rev. D. Hubert, S.J., to Archbishop Blanc, May 19, 1859 (Archbishop Blanc Administrative Records, 1858–1860, Office of Archives and Records, Archdiocese of New Orleans).

11. Her brother Orville James Victor, a well-known New York–based journalist and author, provides some of these details in a letter to Archbishop Jean-Marie Odin (Blanc's successor), May 21, 1861 (University of Notre Dame Archives, VI-2-d *A.L.S.*); see Jeffrey, *Two Civil Wars*, p. 8.

12. Mathilde Victor to Orestes A. Brownson, August 22, 1859 (University of Notre Dame Archives, I-3-o *A.L.S.*, 3 pp.).

Archbishop Blanc, on the strength of a letter of reference from Miss Victor's spiritual mentor in Cincinnati, decided to take a chance on her. Two different religious orders—Sisters of Charity and Sisters of the Sacred Heart—had briefly opened girls' schools in Baton Rouge, but both projects had failed after a few years in much the way the Jesuit College had, and for some of the same reasons; yellow fever had in 1855 alone taken the lives of a third of the Sacred Heart nuns.[13]

Into this unpromising situation, in a season of discouragement and bereavement, Matilda Victor arrived in December 1855 like a fresh wind of Providence. Her energy, panache, and resolve seemed inexhaustible. Within several weeks, she had opened Baton Rouge's third "St. Mary's Academy" in an old, unoccupied convent building, found teachers to assist her, and wooed a host of young girls to come and study with her. By the end of her first academic year, she was the toast of the town, holding commencement exercises for her inaugural class on a canopied stage on a perfect moonlit night. A series of dramatic and choral performances were presented by the girls, after which the governor of Louisiana handed out the academic prizes. It was, pronounced the local newspaper, "a great event in the history of Baton Rouge." In the flush of this early success, Miss Victor undertook the purchase of the old Jesuit College, expanded her staff, and extended her course offerings.

Darius Hubert took an active role at St. Mary's, became a French instructor, provided religious instruction, catechism, and confession, conducted Mass in the school chapel, shared special treats with the boarders at Christmastime, and even took the girls on day trips.[14] The daughters of many prominent Baton Rouge families attended the academy, including notably the well-known diarist Sarah Morgan, her sister Miriam, and her

13. Madame Amelie Jouve to Archbishop Blanc, October 11, 1855 (University of Notre Dame Archives, VI-1-I *A.L.S.*).

14. For details, see Jeffrey, *Two Civil Wars*, pp. 35–45. The titular "Baton Rouge schoolgirl" was a student at St. Mary's, and a devoted spiritual daughter to Darius Hubert. She writes both about and to him in her brief French compositions recorded and translated in that volume.

cousin Mary.[15] If the French journal of St. Mary's student Celeste Repp may be taken as indicative, Father Hubert's kindly affection for the girls was warmly reciprocated.[16]

Father Hubert also ran interference for Matilda Victor with individuals who opposed the school because of its "Jesuitical" connections, with jealous nuns who sniped at her for being improperly employed in the formation of young women, and with Jesuit superiors like Father Curioz, who seemed suspicious of her independence and strong opinions, despite her evidently sincere Catholic devotion.[17] In confronting this clucking disapproval on several sides, Father Hubert evidenced a trait that would mark him for life, a capacity for loyal and principled friendship, often across typical boundaries and very occasionally against the wishes of his immediate superiors. He believed strongly not only in the virtues of Miss Victor's educational project but its vulnerability if local pastoral support was withdrawn: "I remain here for the sake of justice! We invited Mademoiselle Victor here. She plunged herself into a grandiose enterprise in purchasing our college. I know for certain that a few of our Fathers strongly influenced her therein; they were very happy, in leaving the school, to see it thus immediately sold."[18]

There are several noteworthy ironies in Darius Hubert's tenure in Baton Rouge. He began to make significant inroads against the strident anti-Catholic prejudice that had dogged Jesuit efforts in the city. Matilda Victor reported that he developed good relationships with Protestants in town, a view borne out in an unusually laudatory newspaper editorial in the *Baton Rouge Gazette* on December 5, 1858:

15. See Jeffrey, *Two Civil Wars*, p. 12. A partial list, garnered from correspondence and newspaper articles, includes, in addition to the Morgans: Lucrizia Garig, Cecilia Jones, Alice and Carrie Kleinpeter, Matilda, Agnes, Emma, and Fannie Kline, Rosa and Laura Larguier, Henrietta Lauzin, Eleonore Lefevre, Josephine Roberts, Anna Sherbourne, Harriet Smith, and Bella Stuart.

16. Jeffrey, *Two Civil Wars*, pp. 20, 37–38, 44–45.

17. In Matilda Victor's own words, Curioz was "inimical to her."

18. Hubert to Blanc, May 19, 1859 (Archbishop Blanc Administrative Records).

> During the time of his service as priest of St. Joseph's Father Hubert has won golden opinions from all sorts of people, for his strict attention to his religious duties; for his gentlemanly deportment as a citizen; and for his kind ministrations to the sick and afflicted during the late epidemic [that is, yellow fever]. As a defender of the Church to which he has consecrated his life we may say . . . that the most eloquent, impressive, and logical discourse we have ever listened to under the roof of St. Joseph's came from his lips. His merit claims this tribute . . . although we are the antagonists of all his religious views.

The last phrase is, of course, key to the whole. Versions of such sentiments would be published many times, especially after the war years, and featured in the memorials at the time of Father Hubert's death.

While Darius Hubert was able to transcend the entrenched bigotry of religious factionalism and indeed to eschew the anti-Protestant biases that afflicted many of his colleagues in the Society of Jesus (for some, local history seemed to more than justify such a bias), he was never shy about calling out insincere or inauthentic faith within the Catholic fold. Hence his strong repudiation of a "spirit of protestantism"—by which he means impious antinomianism and rebelliousness—among the trustees of St. Joseph Church.[19]

The trustee system was the thorn in the side of many a priest and bishop in this and other jurisdictions in the nineteenth century. It is concisely described in *The Catholic Church in Louisiana*: "Under American law, the Catholic Church was not recognized as a legal entity, hence could not acquire and hold any real property. In order to give the individual parishes of the diocese a legal entity, a corporation was formed, composed of laymen as trustees chosen by the parishioners."[20] Such a system clearly depended on mutual respect for the distinctive roles of laity and clergy, as well as an understanding of the difference between real estate

19. Hubert to Blanc, May 19, 1859.
20. Baudier, *The Catholic Church in Louisiana*, p. 335.

and spiritual estate. But trustees who paid the piper often assumed that they could call the tune, and treated priests as underlings rather than spiritual overseers.[21]

Those who aspired to such a role in the churches were not typically the most devout of the parishioners but rather those who already wielded considerable power in the community, or who aspired to such power. Blanc himself had faced a major confrontation with the trustees (French, *marguilliers*) of St. Louis Cathedral in New Orleans in 1842—a lengthy and unedifying spectacle that included appropriation (or desecration) of the sanctuary for secular purposes and heated exchanges in the press and in other public venues; it was ultimately settled in the bishop's favor by the courts. In this and other similar conflicts across the state in the 1840s and 1850s, a "Voltarian spirit" was seen to be at work, as trustees with no evident respect for church authority or the things of God "used the cloak of religion only to fight religion and her ministers in the most bitter assaults that the Church has ever suffered in the annals of Louisiana, *not excepting the Know-Nothings' bigoted antagonism.*"[22]

As the lone pastor in Baton Rouge after the departure of Joseph Lavay, Darius Hubert was to experience, and sometimes be overwhelmed by, the dysfunction and abuse of his own Catholic trustees. Many of the prominent *marguilliers* leading the revolt in New Orleans had been Masons,[23] and in candid correspondence with his archbishop ("I remained silent; but it is finally time to talk"), Father Hubert indicates that the primary loyalty of some of the most "vicious" and "treacherous" trustees of St. Joseph Church is likewise to various secret societies (the Masonic Lodge

21. Baudier, *The Catholic Church in Louisiana,* p. 335. For a more sympathetic view of the lay trustees' position in light of American republicanism and voluntarism, see Patrick W. Carey, *People, Priests, and Prelates: Ecclesiastical Democracy and the Tensions of Trusteeism* (Notre Dame, IN: University of Notre Dame Press, 1987).

22. Baudier, *The Catholic Church in Louisiana,* p. 334, emphasis mine. This extraordinary assessment of the damage done by faithless trustees is echoed by Darius Hubert in his letter to Archbishop Blanc in May 1859.

23. Baudier, *The Catholic Church in Louisiana,* pp. 339–41; also Michael R. Poll, *In His Own (w)Rite* (New Orleans, Cornerstone Books, 2011).

and the Order of Oddfellows) rather than to the Catholic faith: "They must have appeared to you very accommodating during your last visit here. It was a deception. They do not wish to submit to clerical authority. A priest is needed, it is tolerated, but the priest must be only an instrument which is cast aside and held in contempt as soon as he is no more absolutely indispensable; he must be dependent on the laity; that he be paid *when* they wish and *how much* they wish."[24]

Father Hubert bridles with indignation in this extraordinarily candid nine-page letter, which laments not only harassment and persecution by unworthy individuals on whom his livelihood depends but also the "culpable indifference" of faithful Catholics who permit such abuses to go unchecked. "I know quite well how to fulfill my duties and please the people. I would be left quite at peace were I to content myself to fold my arms and remain a passive spectator of evil minds, the protestant spirit which here makes continual progress. But because, through the children, we sought to regenerate a little the population, troubles ensued. Is there possible a more egregious injustice?" He also laments the lack of support from his Jesuit superior, Father Curioz, especially in the matter of his support of and friendship with Matilda Victor, which he regards as a clear matter of justice and of spiritual obligation.

It was no help that a major building project was ongoing during Father Hubert's entire term in Baton Rouge, one which would have taxed the patience of even an otherwise popular priest or Hubert's fictional alter-ego, the "passive spectator with folded arms." In the early 1850s, the old St. Joseph edifice, running east and west, was slated for replacement with

24. Hubert to Blanc, May 19, 1859 (Archbishop Blanc Administrative Records). There is a curious and unexplained lacuna in the otherwise detailed Book of Minutes kept by the trustees of St. Joseph Church, from the summer of 1856 until well after the Jesuits had left the city. Church historians, mystified by the 88 blank pages that follow an entry of July 1856, surmise that the wardens may have disbanded during that period (Gassler, *History of St. Joseph's Church*, pp. 83–84; 90–102). Clearly they did not, though their actions can only be pieced together from court records, and from such fleeting correspondence as is reproduced here, in the hand of the presiding priest. In another exasperated note, Father Hubert admits to his bishop that he wishes "all trustees could be sent to bathe in the sources of the Nile."

a newer and larger brick facility running north and south on the same property at the intersection of Church (Fourth) and Main streets.[25] Its cornerstone was laid in 1853, but work did not begin in earnest until several years later. When Father Lavay left Baton Rouge, responsibility for oversight of the project fell entirely to Darius Hubert. The internal bickering and power-broking that plagued the congregation's spiritual well-being made the practicalities of construction, and of financing it, endlessly challenging. The initial blueprint for the new edifice was made by Father Cambiaso, who had not only created the plans for the College of St. Peter and St. Paul but also designed the impressive Jesuit Church on Baronne Street in New Orleans (Church of the Immaculate Conception). Cambiaso's initial plan for St. Joseph was deemed too costly, and thus modified; among other changes, the beautiful Gothic steeple envisioned by Cambiaso was replaced by a squat foreshortened tower.[26]

The construction saga that followed, for the better part of a decade, was one of cost overruns, inadequate subscriptions by parishioners, defaults by contractors and suppliers, and burgeoning debts contracted, rescinded, and contracted again—in short, a financial boondoggle that would ultimately, after the Civil War, lead to seizure by creditors and the public humiliation of a sheriff's sale of the church property. Father Hubert had no authority in managing the chaos and could himself have had his salary slashed or withheld on the whim of the trustees. Though he was the face of Catholicism in Baton Rouge, he was treated as a religious functionary, employed merely to perform certain services as the board deemed necessary. After a particularly fractious meeting in 1859, in which the trustees overruled debate or any opportunity for congregational input, Father Hubert insisted that "the proceedings of this meeting be published in the Daily papers of this city, and also that copies of the proceedings be put in frame cases and left in the Church for the benefit of the public."[27]

25. Built by Antoine Blanc when, prior to his ascendancy to the bishop's chair, he served as a parish priest in Baton Rouge.

26. The iconic and photogenic steeple of St. Joseph Church (now St. Joseph Cathedral) was not added until December 1891.

27. *Baton Rouge Tri-Weekly Gazette and Comet*, June 26, 1859, p. 4.

It was a small victory. One of the least of his challenges during these years was simply finding space to conduct Mass and hear confession while the construction dragged on; for a time, he did so at the chapel of St. Mary's Academy.

The new St. Joseph edifice was not completed until 1861. Not long afterward, on May 27, 1862, shells from Admiral David Farragut's Union flagship hit the church's modest tower, causing damage to the slate roof and the interior of the sanctuary that would again prevent St. Joseph from being used for worship. That same day, St. Mary's Academy was closed for good by its long-suffering headmistress; it too had been damaged by the bombardment. Matilda Victor marched down to the riverfront, presented her Northern credentials to Farragut himself, and sought safe passage to New Orleans under Union protection.[28]

By then, her friend and mentor, Darius Hubert, had been gone for more than a year,[29] having exchanged his cassock and the interminable "curse" of parish ministry in the river capital for an officer's uniform and the dangers and travails of honest battlefields.[30] He was to serve as a Confederate chaplain in the Army of Northern Virginia for the entire duration of the Civil War.

28. Jeffrey, *Two Civil Wars*, pp. 196–97.

29. Jesuit documents have conflicting and often inaccurate records about Darius Hubert's whereabouts between 1857 and 1861. Census records and correspondence clearly place him in Baton Rouge throughout this period, apart from a brief stint of teaching at Spring Hill College in Mobile in the autumn term of 1860 and periodic assignments in New Orleans. He was in Baton Rouge for the Secession Convention in January 1861, where he blessed the Pelican Flag, and then returned to New Orleans, where a few weeks later he was named chaplain to the First Louisiana Infantry Regiment.

30. In Father Hubert's last extant note from Baton Rouge, he makes a mordant request to the vicar general of the archdiocese: "I dare hope that if you are destined to blow me up in the air here, you will please have the kindness to give me time to parry the shells" (Rev. D. Hubert, S.J., to Rev. Stephen Rousselon, August 16, 1860, Archbishop Blanc Administrative Records).

FOUR

Army of Northern Virginia 1861–1865

Darius Hubert was the first person appointed as chaplain to any Confederate military unit. Colonel Albert Gallatin Blanchard, in offering his own services for the Southern cause, asked specifically that Father Hubert be attached to his First Louisiana Infantry Regiment. Jefferson Davis approved the appointment and thereafter referred to Father Hubert, with affectionate regard, as his "first chaplain."[1]

The commission came with no job description. Those who took the post of army chaplain were evidently assumed to be expert in the spiritual needs of the men they would be serving and free to determine how they would go about meeting them. Needless to say, not all clergy—even those who were eager to assume the role—proved to be well suited to the military context. A great many of them wilted within months; some resigned to go back to their more comfortable duties in home churches, while others were more or less drummed out by the men. Numerous soldiers' letters mention the early departure of chaplains or their shirking of duty, both of which induced disdain: "We have no preaching. Our chaplain has played out and went home long ago. I wish Congress would con-

1. Father Hubert's original signed commission as chaplain (dated May 2, 1861) and a countersigned copy of the commission confirming his appointment as "first chaplain of the Confederacy" were ceremonially donated to Confederate Memorial Hall on Jefferson Davis's birthday, June 3, 1902 (*New Orleans Times-Democrat,* June 4, 1902, p. 3). For Davis's recognition of Hubert as "my first chaplain," see, for example, *New Orleans Times-Democrat,* June 18, 1893, p. 2.

script every preacher up to 50 and make them shoulder a musket and go into ranks. If they won't preach they ought to be made to fight."[2] A Confederate surgeon made the same case in correspondence with his wife: "If Congress would pass a conscript law bringing the preachers into the army we could have chaplains." Referring to their frequent desertion or early resignation, he made the damning comment that "they have acted worse in this war than any other class of men."[3] For the dutiful, however, chaplaincy was a daunting charge. According to Randolph McKim, a Virginian Episcopalian who was a soldier first and later commissioned as a chaplain, there was no question as to which role was more grueling: "I suffered more in the office of chaplain than I ever did as a private soldier carrying a musket and knapsack." Indeed, "it took a good deal more nerve to go through a fight as a non-combatant than as a soldier."[4] And it was this fellowship of suffering shared by the most conscientious of the chaplains that would ultimately reshape not only the Confederate Army but the spiritual landscape of the South after the war—from a society in which religious affiliation was a mark of social decorum but actual faith was regarded as best suited to women and children to a culture in which Christian profession attained respectability among men and renewed vibrancy as a cultural phenomenon. None of that was foreseen at the outset of the conflict, of course. No one expected the war to last long enough to change them, much less the society they were marching off to defend from Northern aggressors.

2. DeWitt Boyd Stone Jr., ed., *Wandering to Glory: Confederate Veterans Remember Evans's Brigade* (Columbia: University of South Carolina Press, 2002), p. 157.

3. Spencer Glasgow Welch, *A Confederate Surgeon's Letters to His Wife* (Washington, DC: Neale Publishing, 1911), p. 78.

4. *Leaves from the Diary of a Young Confederate* (New York: Longmans, Green and Co., 1910; the edition cited here is edited and annotated by Lucy Booker Roper (Southaven, MS: Booker House, 2013), pp. 210, 192. McKim, who was chaplain to the Second Virginia Cavalry, served briefly as a very popular pastor of Trinity Church, New Orleans (Bishop Leonidas Polk's former church), from December 1886 until December 1888. He and Father Hubert doubtless knew each other, especially given their mutual acquaintance with Rev. Alexander Gordon Bakewell, another former chaplain and prominent churchman in New Orleans.

The First Louisiana, unlike some of the state's more notoriously rowdy regiments,[5] was composed largely of middle-class merchants, clerks, small business owners, and students from New Orleans—many of them drawn from Louisiana militia companies—as well as yeoman farmers (especially from Caddo Parish), laborers, mechanics, carpenters, bricklayers, and so forth. The regiment was certainly not, as Father Gache breezily declared, "composed solely of gentlemen."[6] About a quarter of those whose service records include place of birth are listed as native Louisianans; a third were born in other states (principally, but not exclusively, in the South). The remainder were foreign-born—especially Irish and German immigrants who had poured into cosmopolitan New Orleans in the decades preceding the war.[7]

They left for Virginia amidst the cheers of friends and families, and enjoyed similar "cheering, huzzaing, and waving of handkerchiefs" at every whistle-stop between the Crescent City and the Confederate capital, as well as sumptuous meals and patriotic speeches in several towns. Blanchard's regiment was the first contingent of soldiers to arrive in Richmond from the Gulf states, and received an exuberant welcome there as well. When not engaged in company drill, dress parade, field movement, and picket duty, the soldiers wrote letters home extolling the kindness

5. For a detailed history of Louisiana military units, including the Tiger Rifles of Chatham Roberdeau Wheat's Battalion, George Gaston Coppens's Battalion Jouaves, and the Fourteenth Louisiana Regiment, all of which had a reputation for drunkenness, insubordination, and violence, as well as fierce fighting, see Terry L. Jones, *Lee's Tigers Revisited: The Louisiana Infantry in the Army of Northern Virginia* (Baton Rouge: Louisiana State University Press, 2017).

6. The point of Father Gache's observation, written not long before he detached from active field service with the Tenth Louisiana Regiment, was to draw a (somewhat exaggerated) contrast between his fellow Jesuit's unit and his own: "He is much better situated than I: his regiment is composed solely of gentlemen, among whom there is a considerable number of good Catholics who take excellent care of him. It is quite otherwise with me" (Gache, *Frenchman, Chaplain, Rebel*, p. 138).

7. Michael Dan Jones includes a compilation of service records for this regiment in *The Fighting First Louisiana Infantry Regiment in the Army of Northern Virginia* (St. Charles, LA: CreateSpace, 2016), pp. 252–351. The First's Company E (Montgomery Guards) and Company D (Emmett Guards) consisted primarily of native Irishmen.

of local citizens: "On our arrival here, every house . . . was thrown open to us, and all vied with each other in affording hospitality and civilities. . . . We are visited daily by crowds of ladies and gentlemen, who evince much interest in our welfare, and do all in their power to promote our comfort."[8]

The regiment soon moved from the environs of Richmond to a more permanent settlement at "Camp Vincent" on the Elizabeth River, fronting Hampton Roads. Father Hubert located his own quarters near those of Colonel William C. Vincent, and began in earnest to assume a pastoral role with his men, Catholics and non-Catholics alike. In the recollection of one of the officers in his regiment, "while in this camp the good father became endeared to the men of the different denominations, and . . . became acquainted with all of their names, their habits, and the nicknames that they were known by."[9] This ecumenical spirit, which had also marked his pastoral role in Baton Rouge, would be one of the signal features of Darius Hubert's military chaplaincy. He was not only revered by the soldiers, regardless of creed, in his own regiment but became eventually, at least by reputation, "known and dear to every man in the Army of Northern Virginia."[10] He also formed a good working rapport with Protestant chaplains serving alongside—an especially rare and notable phenomenon during the war.[11]

8. Letter from an unnamed member of the Caddo Rifles, part of the First Louisiana Regiment, published in *The Standard* (Clarksville, TX), June 15, 1861, p. 2.

9. From a recollection by Captain Thomas Rice of the Montgomery Guards in the First Louisiana Regiment, published in the *New Orleans Times-Democrat*, May 4, 1896, p. 8. Captain Rice was prominent in directing the Battle of the Rocks at Second Manassas; see below.

10. John Dimitry, in the Louisiana volume (vol. 10) of *Confederate Military History*, ed. Clement Anselm Evans (Atlanta: Confederate Publishing, 1899), p. 234. In a recently edited collection of wartime letters, an Ursuline nun in Columbia, South Carolina, recounts (July 28, 1862) a visit to her convent of a soldier from the First Louisiana who, though a Protestant, surprised her by speaking "so highly of Revd Father Hubert, SJ" (*For Church and Confederacy: The Lynches of South Carolina*, ed. Robert Emmet Curran [Columbia: University of South Carolina Press, 2018]).

11. His friendship with Methodist chaplain of the Second Louisiana Regiment Robert Hardie is discussed below.

We owe a description of the newly minted chaplain of the First Louisiana to Father Hippolyte Gache—his Jesuit superior at Grand Coteau, predecessor in the pastorate at Baton Rouge, and fellow Confederate chaplain—who was more than mildly scandalized by Hubert's decision to wear an officer's uniform rather than his Jesuit cassock. In a letter written in late November 1861 he reports tartly:

> I met Father Hubert on the road to Norfolk. He was traveling with the pastor of Lynchburg [Oscar Sears][12] on the way to Manassas, in western Virginia, to attend some social function. I almost had to be told who it was. . . . Imagine, if you will, a young dandy: his hair elegant, his beard splendid; gold-braid festooned upon his blue kepi and embroidered upon the sleeves of his high-collared frock coat; the golden buttons of his waistcoat emblazoned with the Louisiana pelican; his gold-filleted trousers falling neatly into a pair of comely boots. This dazzling sight was none other than Father Hubert himself! . . . I regard it as only natural that Protestant ministers should disguise themselves in such a get-up, but that . . . Jesuits should do it—well, I have a hard time believing it, much less approving of it![13]

What reasons Father Hubert would have had for eschewing his priestly vestments can only be guessed at. Whether there was indeed a touch of vanity and "putting on of airs," as Father Gache saw it, he seemed from the outset intent on identifying with the company he served in all respects

12. Father Oscar Aloysius Sears was a Catholic convert, ordained in 1857 and serving as pastor in Lynchburg during the war; he undertook informal ministry to locally stationed Confederate troops as time allowed, as did other priests. He died in 1867. See appendix II.

13. Gache, *Frenchman, Chaplain, Rebel*, p. 60, 61–62. Father Gache's description lies behind an image of "Confederate Army Chaplains, 1861" (plate #808) produced by the Company of Military Historians in 2003. The Redemptorist priest, Father James Sheeran, was often similarly attired during the war and sometimes mistaken for an officer by local citizens, which greatly amused him. See *The Civil War Diary of Father Sheeran*, for example, pp. 113–14, 126–27. No "chaplain's uniform" (or rank) was ever formally approved for the Confederacy; such details were generally decided at the regimental level and as a result were somewhat ad hoc.

save carrying a weapon.[14] Within a year of this encounter with Gache, that identification meant that all traces of sartorial elegance were gone; he was not only, in the words of fellow chaplain James Sheeran, generally "disguised in Confederate mud";[15] he apparently gave away his frock coat to someone who needed it more, and what was left of his uniform was in such tatters that he was reduced to scrounging for makeshift and hand-me-down garments. He sometimes marched barefoot, as did many in his regiment; the "Fighting First" was a gaunt and ragged company when it entered the fall campaign of 1862, by which time the peevish Father Gache had been detached from his own regiment (the Tenth Louisiana Infantry) to a much more comfortable apostolate in the hospitals of Lynchburg.[16]

As prepared and confident as the Louisiana boys seemed for war, they were less ready for the first enemy to stalk the camps. Adjusting to close quarters, poor sanitary conditions and unfamiliar cold weather presented unforeseen dangers during the fall and winter months. Though the men received shipments of warm and lovingly prepared garments from the home front, exchanged tents for log cabins in the winter, and enjoyed better and more plentiful food than they would for the remainder of the war years, many succumbed to illness (notably measles, pneumonia, dysentery, and chills and fevers of various kinds, including typhoid) before they ever had a chance to take up their weapons against the Yankees. It

14. Some Confederate chaplains apparently took up arms, and a few were even credited with killing Union troops; Darius Hubert was not among them. For the stories of some of the South's "fighting parsons," see Herman Norton, *Rebel Religion: The Story of the Confederate Chaplains* (St. Louis, MO: Bethany Press, 1961), pp. 81–88.

15. *The Civil War Diary of Father Sheeran,* p. 61.

16. Father Gache found the rigors of marching and the austere conditions of camp to be too much for him by April 1862, noting that it would be "imprudent on my part to spend the nights as one must on these marches—that is, out in the open exposed to the cold, and even, often to the rain" (Gache, *Frenchman, Chaplain, Rebel,* p. 102). He was hospitalized several times in the spring and early summer, observing laconically to a correspondent at Spring Hill College in Mobile that "it is not exactly a pleasant one, this military life, especially under General [Stonewall] Jackson" (p. 127). By August he was expressing "grave doubts as

was an unusually melancholy duty for a chaplain to attend the sickbeds of these young men who had been denied the heroism they aspired to, officiate at burials, and send the painful news to families at home.

Colonel Albert Blanchard, who had organized the regiment and arranged for Darius Hubert to serve as chaplain, was promoted to brigadier general in September 1861; his old regiment became part of Blanchard's Brigade. He was never to lead his Louisianans in combat, however; though present at the Battle of Seven Pines (May 31–June 1, 1862), they were held in reserve. Shortly thereafter, when Robert E. Lee took command of the Army of Northern Virginia, he released Blanchard from field duty and turned the brigade over to General Ambrose Ransom ("Rans") Wright of the Third Georgia.[17]

The only significant military engagement to which Darius Hubert was connected during the entire first year of deployment was offshore—the famous naval battle and clash of the ironclads at Hampton Roads on March 8–9, 1862. Many members of the First Louisiana Regiment were spectators;[18] others were more directly engaged, having volunteered

---

to whether I will be able to stick it out," and in the fall he was assigned to Lynchburg, where by his own admission "the Catholic hospital chaplains . . . are in no danger of being crushed by the burden of overwork" (p. 146). Though some sources suggest that Gache was "present in all the important battles" of his unit, his army chaplaincy actually ended in August 1862; his last engagement was the Battle of Cedar Run. See appendix II.

17. Reasons were not given, but Lee, who knew Blanchard from West Point, seems not to have thought him able for field command in his army; Father Gache's contention that anti-Catholic bigotry was a factor (Gache, *Frenchman, Chaplain, Rebel*, p. 196) is baseless. When Blanchard lost his command he was shuffled around in various administrative jobs. While posted in northern Louisiana (December 2, 1862) he sent a request to the War Department that Darius Hubert be named his "brigade chaplain" and sent from Virginia back to his home state—a request curtly denied. Blanchard moved with his family to the Carolinas in 1864, where he formed a reserve brigade in the final stages of the war. While there, he sent a poignant appeal directly to Father Hubert, asking him to relocate to Raleigh ("I hope you will come, for I need you"). See below, p. 83.

18. One of these, Private Julius Lisso, provided a "graphic and racy description" of the action that was published back home in his local newspaper, the *Natchitoches Union*: "The Combat of the 9th," April 3, 1862, p. 1.

for navy service aboard the CSS *Virginia* (formerly *Merrimack*).[19] Darius Hubert, who knew his way around a naval yard from his childhood in Toulon and who was intent on maintaining spiritual oversight of all the men in his charge, sought and received a commission as navy chaplain to the *Virginia*, since no such provision had been made for the hastily gathered crew. He apparently joined the throng of military and civilian observers on the waterfront on March 8 as the *Virginia* created havoc among the conventional wooden ships of the Union Navy, sinking both the *Cumberland* and the *Congress* and disabling the *Minnesota*. He may also have watched again the following day as *Virginia* and its ironclad nemesis *USS Monitor* fought for four intense but inconclusive hours to a stalemate that both sides claimed as a victory. At some point Father Hubert actually demanded to board *Virginia* to be with the men—an incident that achieved legendary status after the war. This is the way it was reported in the *Richmond Dispatch* years later:

> Father Hubert had in him the element that goes to make the hero—perfect fearlessness in the discharge of duty. The crew of the renowned *Merrimac* were under his chaplainship. When she had her famous fight with the *Monitor*, Father Hubert was on shore. Immediately after the fight Father Hubert sent word to the commanding officer, Admiral Buchanan, that he wished to come aboard and attend to those who needed his services. Admiral Buchanan came ashore and said: "Father, I do not wish you to come aboard. We expect to engage the Monitor again tomorrow, and it will be no place for you." "My place is with the wounded and dying," answered the brave priest. "But, father, listen," returned the admiral. "We are in a very disabled condition, and if the *Monitor* returns tomorrow I shall blow up the *Merrimac*, with all on board, for we are in no condition to fight and will never surrender. Remain on shore." "As I said before, my place is with

19. A complete list of the Louisianans, including members of the First, assigned to duty on *CSS Virginia* may conveniently be found in John V. Quarstein, *The CSS Virginia: Sink Before Surrender* (Charleston, SC: History Press, 2012), appendix VI.

> the wounded and dying," replied the father. "If it is necessary, I wish to die with the men."[20]

The same story in its essentials shows up in Jesuit sources, including an essay based on the letters of a Jesuit Union chaplain, Father Peter Tissot, who met Darius Hubert while he was under house arrest briefly in Richmond in June 1862.[21] In recounting this meeting, the author digresses on the famous story of Father Hubert and the *Merrimack*. In his version Buchanan is more vernacular in his initial refusal: "We're to have another go at it tomorrow and the boat is no place for you." And when the admiral adds that "if on the morrow I see I must surrender I shall blow up the *Merrimac*," Father Hubert's response is simply "Let me aboard tonight, then," upon which "the Chaplain and Commander mounted the gangplank together."[22]

Though the story shows signs of retrospective imprecision and conflation, Albert Blanchard, Father Hubert's commanding officer and eyewitness to the events at Hampton Roads, confirms that "Rev. Father D. Hubert, Chaplain of the 1st Regiment Louisiana Volunteers . . . was in

20. "Chaplain on the Merrimac: The Death of a Priest Who Was a Hero in the Confederate Army," *Richmond Dispatch*, August 5, 1893. This account has been cited in virtually every printed reference to the Confederate chaplaincy in which Father Hubert is mentioned, without comment on several problematic details. Admiral Buchanan was severely injured on March 8, so he could not have "come ashore" for the purported conversation. And while Buchanan was the undoubted hero of March 8, he had no part in the clash with *Monitor* the following day; that responsibility fell to Catesby ap Roger Jones. Moreover, the injuries and death on *Virginia* all occurred on March 8; the famous battle with *Monitor* was neither as costly nor as demanding of priestly duties to the Confederate ironclad.

21. Father Tissot describes his meeting with several Southern Jesuits, including Father Hubert, in his war diary as well as letters. He frequented the cathedral during his time in Richmond, where he was dismayed to find Bishop John McGill and other clergy to be strong partisans of the Southern cause. The men were for the most part content not to talk politics, though the presence of "Yankee priests" in the Confederate capital caused some consternation among local citizens. See "A Year with the Army of the Potomac," *Fordham Monthly* (1900): 535–37; 644.

22. *Woodstock Letters* 43.2 (1914): 170–71.

the *Virginia* during the fight of the 8th and 9th of March."[23] Lacking further detail, one assumes that the chaplain came to Sewell's Point on the evening of March 8, knowing there were dead and wounded aboard, and insisted on fulfilling his obligations as chaplain. Whether he negotiated directly with the seriously wounded Buchanan or a proxy, the importunate priest was eventually permitted to board ship to pray with and give spiritual solace to the crew before the wounded were put ashore in the early morning hours and *Virginia* steamed back out for the action of March 9. It would have been natural for him then to accompany some of the injured to nearby hospitals and to make arrangements for burying the dead. Sadly, those details are lost.[24]

For most of the rank and file of the First Louisiana Infantry the war began in earnest with commencement of the Seven Days Battles, Robert E. Lee's decisive and forceful response to George B. McLellan's advance on the Confederate capital of Richmond. Young recruits who had longed to be in the fight for more than a year soon found that their naive visions of a swift and heroic defeat of the Federals (letters home typically predicted only modest dangers, since "the Yankees cannot shoot")[25] were somewhat premature. At King's School House (June 25, 1862), fighting alongside several regiments from Georgia, the Louisianans showed their mettle and won great praise from their brigade commander, Ambrose Wright, for "a gallantry and impetuosity which has rarely been equaled and certainly never excelled since the war began." When ordered to charge, they did so with cries of "Butler!" and "New Orleans!" and managed to capture the battle flag of Daniel Sickles's Excelsior Brigade (comprised of several

23. *New Orleans Times-Picayune*, July 16, 1878, p. 5.

24. In a modest, one-paragraph, self-penned obituary that he asked not be opened until after his death, Father Hubert himself confirms that he was "detailed for duty as Confederate States navy chaplain on the famous *Merrimac*." An unpublished remembrance by a Jesuit colleague, John Logan, written shortly after his death recounts the story in brief, and Father Hubert's eulogist at the Requiem Mass held in New Orleans likewise recalled how he "insisted on treading the deck of the doomed *Merrimac*."

25. McKim, *Leaves from the Diary*, p. 27.

New York infantry regiments), one of three brigades that opposed them in the field.[26] But their conspicuous bravery exacted a very heavy price, for it turned out that the Yankees could indeed shoot. The First Louisiana had the highest casualty toll not only of Wright's Brigade but of the entire division on the field that day.[27] An admiring reporter heralded their persistent valor, noting that "every second man fell!" Of the 328 deployed, 22 were killed, 109 wounded, and 4 listed as missing. Regimental commander Colonel William R. Shivers was among the severely wounded; he was carried out of the line of fire by a twenty-seven-year-old private named James H. Henderson. Darius Hubert, who was with his men on the front, went to Shivers's side under a heavy fire of musketry and stayed with him until he could be safely moved to the rear by the ambulance corps.[28] Captains James Nelligan and Charles Cormier were also injured, though less severely. Captain Michael Nolan, an Irish-born shopkeeper from New Orleans and close friend of Father Hubert, took over command of the regiment.

The "Fighting First," as the regiment came to be known, was given several days' respite before being called on again on the last of the Seven Days Battles—July 1, at Malvern Hill. For the chaplain of the First, the days between these two bloody engagements would have been filled with care for the wounded, legal and executorial arrangements for the dead, and spiritual encouragement for the shell-shocked young men who had lost friends, family members, and their innocent exuberance. Battlefields

26. The Catholic chaplain to the Excelsior Brigade, Joseph O'Hagan, S.J., was later called by Darius Hubert his "dear friend" (see p. 87 and note below). Whether their acquaintance preceded this fateful meeting on opposing sides of the battlefield is unknown. Father O'Hagan was captured with Father Peter Tissot two days after the Battle of King's School House and served a house arrest of sorts at the cathedral in Richmond during the summer of 1862 before returning to the field (see note 21, above). He resigned from the army in September 1863 but reenlisted the following autumn. When Richmond fell in April 1865, O'Hagan accompanied Union troops into the city (see Gache, *Frenchman, Chaplain, Rebel*, pp. 221–22).

27. For further detail, see Jones, *The Fighting First*, p. 55.

28. Captain Thomas Rice, in a *New Orleans Times-Picayune* retrospective, August 8, 1886, p. 3. Shivers never returned to field service during the war.

strewn with bloated corpses of men and horses, and the intolerably putrid smell of festering flesh, were henceforth to become familiar, almost ordinary: the scene was set for a prolonged and brutal conflict that would test the spiritual as well as physical and emotional resources of any pastor in the field.

At Malvern Hill, the First suffered 79 casualties: 8 killed, 40 wounded, and 31 captured or missing. The Army of Northern Virginia as a whole had over 20,000 casualties in the Seven Days Battles, including more than 3,000 killed and nearly 16,000 wounded. But Richmond was secure, and would remain so for the duration of the war. Robert E. Lee was proving to be the commander the South had been looking for and that troops would willingly, in the words of his greatest general, Thomas J. ("Stonewall") Jackson, "follow blindfold" into the fray.

After the Seven Days Battles, the First was folded into the newly formed Second Louisiana Brigade under General William Starke, along with the Second, Tenth, and Fifteenth regiments and the First Zouave Battalion. Informally known as the "Pelican" Brigade, to distinguish it from the "Tigers" of the First Louisiana Brigade of General Harry Thompson Hays (including variously the Sixth, Seventh, Eighth, Ninth, and Fourteenth regiments),[29] they would soon, with their fellow Louisianans, become part of Stonewall Jackson's Division. As such, they would become used to long and rapid forced marches and savage combat at close range against long odds in some of the most famous and bloody battles of the Civil War: Second Manassas, Sharpsburg (Antietam), Fredericksburg, and Chancellorsville. And in those months, the deep and lasting respect of the South's first chaplain for Lee and Jackson would bloom in proximity. Whether Darius Hubert ever spoke directly with the famously enigmatic and taciturn Jackson, whom he would one day memorialize in an arresting and frequently quoted Lost Cause tribute, he and Robert E. Lee shared a high mutual regard that Father Hubert called friendship,

29. The First Louisiana Brigade had accompanied Jackson on the brilliant and audacious Shenandoah Valley Campaign in the spring of 1862 before joining Lee's forces in the defense of Richmond.

and the general reportedly nodded to him deferentially when they met on the field of battle.[30]

Whether they had done so before, the men of the First began to take up the rebel yell in earnest during these campaigns, reveling in the "maniacal maelstrom of sound" that so rattled Union forces.[31] It had been Stonewall Jackson's idea for his undermanned troops to "yell like furies" as they assailed their enemies. Though the First Louisiana Regiment was not with Jackson at Manassas, where he made the order for the first time in July 1861, Nolan's troops had perfected their own version of the famous yell. According to a rare contemporary description, a "brave, indomitable soldier" named James "Brocky" Gallagher from Brockville, Ontario, a small Canadian village on the St. Lawrence River, led the yell for the First Louisiana "in innumerable victorious and soul stirring charges," starting with his "deep sonorous bass voice" and culminating in "a high-pitched and penetrating "Yi! Yi! Yi!!!"[32] An embedded reporter for the New Orleans daily, the *Times-Picayune,* echoes that "it starts deep and ends high, . . . rises into three increasing crescendos and breaks with a command of battle." While some Federals contrasted the rebel yell disparagingly

30. Emmanuel de la Morinière, S.J., in a speech on "Chivalry" delivered in New Orleans in April 1893, quotes his colleague Darius Hubert's emotional tribute to Lee, "the chieftain whose hands often met mine in the warm grasp of friendship, and who, even at the head of a charging column, always paid me, the humble minister of Christ, the courteous homage of a reverential bow which a king might well envy." Printed in *The Louisiana Book,* ed. M'Caleb, p. 179. Redemptorist chaplain James Sheeran likewise recalls Lee's generous salutation, to different effect (*The Civil War Diary of Father Sheeran,* p. 169).

31. The words are those of Colonel Keller Anderson, of the Kentucky Orphan Brigade.

32. These notes come from the service records for the Canadian native, accessible online at Fold3.com. James "Brocky" Gallagher was, with many of his mates in the First Louisiana, captured at Spotsylvania on May 20, 1864, but managed to survive the war. He may be the same "Brocky Gallagher" who became a notorious horse thief in Montana in the 1880s, eventually caught and lynched in 1884 by a group of vigilantes led by pioneer rancher Granville Stuart. See R. K. DeArment, "Gang Crackdown: When Stuart's Stranglers Raided the Rustlers," *Wild West Magazine,* June 7, 2007; also *Forty Years on the Frontier as Seen in the Journals and Reminiscences of Granville Stuart* (1925; rpt. ed. Paul C. Phillips [Lincoln, NE: Bison Books, 2004]), p. 206.

with the "vigorous manly cheers" of their own troops, its shrill and eerie ferocity was unsettling. Stonewall Jackson once called it "the sweetest music I ever heard."

The air was thick with such music at the Second Battle of Manassas in late August 1862, a brutal affair that, in the understated words of Private Thomas Phifer of the Second Louisiana Infantry, "cost many precious lives." Phifer's company went in with twenty men and came out with four; the eighteen-year-old private was consoled to think that "hundreds of Yankees fell before our [Starke's] Brigade."[33]

Starke's Louisianans more than lived up to their billing as hard fighters at Manassas. And the commander of the First Regiment, Lieutenant Colonel Michael Nolan, was credited that day with one of the more memorable underdog tactics of the war. When his men ran out of ammunition at Deep Cut, a strategic position near the unfinished Manassas Gap Railroad line, Nolan demonstrated audacity and improvisation worthy of General Jackson himself—rallying his men to hurl rocks and construction debris at the enemy, some of whom were indeed only a stone's throw away. They laid down their muskets and did just that, furiously pelting the advancing bluecoats, and lobbing other projectiles up over the embankment, seriously injuring many of the startled troops huddled there. In so doing, they managed to hold their position until reinforcements reached them. Father Hubert's fellow chaplain, James Sheeran, a Redemptorist priest attached to the Fourteenth Louisiana, recorded in his journal that after the battle many unfortunate Yankees were "found on the field with broken skulls."[34]

While the unorthodox Battle of the Rocks was ongoing, Major Andrew Barney of the Twenty-Fourth New York Infantry rode gallantly to the top of the railroad embankment to observe the action and was killed

33. Thomas H. Phifer Civil War Letters, excerpts of which are online at www.countygenweb.com/desotoparishla/phifer.html. This young soldier from Mansfield, Louisiana, was dead by the time his father received his letter—one of the myriad casualties at Sharpsburg. I am indebted to Keldon Henley at Ouachita Baptist University, who shared with me his transcription of the unpublished Phifer papers, including letters and diary.

34. *Civil War Journal of Father Sheeran,* p. 16.

instantly with a bullet to the heart;[35] his terrified horse, a fine bay that all the Southern boys admired, ran into Confederate lines and was captured. It became the favorite mount of Lieutenant Colonel Nolan. When Nolan died at Gettysburg, the men gave the war horse to Darius Hubert, out of affection for both. The priest protested, but was ordered by his superiors to keep it. Under his patient and kindly care, the steed retired at last from the front lines.

Second Manassas was memorable in other ways for Father Hubert. At some point during the fray, an enemy bullet found his kit, narrowly missing him. Though he was frequently in the line of fire (despite Stonewall Jackson's stern admonition to chaplains that in the heat of battle "the rear is your place now, and prayer your business"), this was the closest he had come to personal injury; he kept the bullet as a souvenir and reminder of having been providentially spared that day. After his death, the bullet was donated to Confederate Memorial Hall in New Orleans—one of several Hubert relics in the museum's holdings.

Darius Hubert was up all night after the battle, tending to the wounded at an adjacent field hospital. Father Sheeran was surprised to find the weary chaplain washing up in the muddy shallows of Sudley Ford as he rode by in the predawn darkness the next morning.

The Second Battle of Manassas was, despite its drastic casualty toll, a significant Confederate victory. Robert E. Lee decided to press his advantage, leading his battered army into Maryland, where he hoped to attract new recruits, and then to invade Northern soil for the first time. After yet another exhausting march, the rebels arrived in Frederick, Maryland, on September 5 and 6, a ragged and depleted horde of half-starved war-

35. A remarkable exchange of letters between a Federal private captured that day and Captain Thomas Rice of the First Louisiana, the officer who captured him, was printed in the *New Orleans Times-Picayune*, May 23, 1886, p. 14. The two men, at more than twenty years' distance, compared their memories of the battle, with Rice observing that "no incident of the war affected me more acutely than the heroic death of Major Barney, commanding the Twenty-Fourth New York Regiment," who fell from his horse "just about the point in our lines where you were taken captive." The two correspondents extended invitations to each other to visit and share hospitality (and war reminiscences) with their respective families.

riors, whose three-month campaign had decimated their ranks: "Many were without shoes, their uniforms so tattered they barely held together, their slouch hats so riddled with tears and holes that their greasy hair protruded from them at odd and comical angles. They stank so badly—many had not even removed their clothing in weeks—that it was said that you could smell the vaunted Army of Northern Virginia long before you could see it. The most striking thing about the men was their *gauntness*, the startling hollowness of eyes and cheeks and chests."[36]

In Frederick, only 121 members of the First Louisiana were present and fit for duty. Father Hubert was among them, although he too was reduced to so threadbare a state that he had to resort to mendicancy: "[his] clothes were in such a tattered condition dangling from him like so many rags—but honorable rags—that the good old man was forced to beg new apparel from the people of the town, as he knew that the soldiers were too poor to furnish it."[37] And his health, which had never been robust, was faltering. He enjoyed in Frederick a timely and merciful respite in the local Jesuit novitiate, where a visit to the bathhouse and sleep in a proper bed must have seemed otherworldly after long marches and exposure to the elements and nonstop, spiritually sapping duties of shriving the dying and aiding the wounded on battlefields and in makeshift hospitals. For weeks the screams of artillery and the screams of its victims had merged in a nearly perpetual unholy cacophony: the serene quiet of a house of prayer, and the consolation of the sacrament, was doubtless restorative of both mind and body.

Father Sheeran, similarly soul-weary and likewise covered in Confederate mud, also enjoyed hospitality at the Jesuit house, as did many Louisiana soldiers, for whom the Fathers and novices prepared bountiful meals and maintained an "open house at all hours during the three days of our

36. S. C. Gwynne, *Rebel Yell: The Violence, Passion, and Redemption of Stonewall Jackson* (New York: Scribner, 2014), pp. 451–52. Gwynne's masterful narrative brings the reader into intimate contact not only with its titular subject but with fellow officers and common soldiers.

37. A soldier's remembrance of Father Hubert, published in the *New Orleans Daily Picayune*, June 15, 1893.

sojourn in Frederick."[38] The townspeople, more wary than thrilled with the arrival of this throng of shabby and famished men, nonetheless had goods to offer that the troops badly needed. "Boots that would cost twenty five Dollars in Richmond were bought here for four or five," wrote one young private from the Second Louisiana to his sister.[39] The two chaplains apparently found fresh shirts to put on after they experienced the luxury of warm water and soap.

Father Sheeran followed Jackson's men on September 12–15 as they circled back to capture the Union garrison at Harpers Ferry under orders from General Lee. There, unconditional surrender was effected quickly and with few Confederate casualties, after which Stonewall's forces started toward Sharpsburg, where the entire Army of Northern Virginia was massing to meet George McLellan's Army of the Potomac. Father Sheeran was incensed at the stragglers who lagged behind as Jackson marched his men back to Maryland, and would later blame their default of duty for that battle's outcome, and for thus "prolonging this barbarous war."[40] Despite the harshness of his criticism, Sheeran was himself a little slow in reaching Sharpsburg; he made it as far as the bluffs overlooking the battlefield from the Virginia side of the Potomac by midafternoon on September 17 and watched the "sanguinary contest" for more than an hour before repairing to nearby Shepherdstown, where many of the wounded had been evacuated.

Darius Hubert, de facto pastor to the whole Second Brigade, was the only Confederate Catholic chaplain on the field at Antietam. It is hard to conceive what his mindset would have been on the evening of September 16 as he heard confessions and did the rounds among tents and bedrolls, speaking quietly to young men whose names and habits and nicknames he had known since Norfolk, and who would be called upon to charge and fight and die in the morning. Sleep would have been fleeting at best, prayer his only sustenance against the dread of what lay ahead.

38. *Civil War Journal of Father Sheeran*, p. 29.

39. Phifer Civil War Letters.

40. *Civil War Journal of Father Sheeran*, p. 32.

Stonewall Jackson's corps, to which both Louisiana brigades were attached, fought in the morning hours on the Confederate left flank, giving and enduring a murderous fire until the mingled dead in blue and gray lay so thickly carpeted in a flattened cornfield that had been seized and lost and seized again, that the ground was scarcely visible. By noon, their battle was over; the battle in the center, under Jackson's brother-in-law D. H. Hill, was commencing. At the little whitewashed Dunker Church, Stonewall Jackson sat on his horse looking out over the field and, in his peculiar and inimitable way, saw past the human carnage to signs of providential blessing. His outnumbered troops had staggered and fallen in their thousands, but had held the ground they were asked to hold, despite the bluecoats having "done their worst." He was proud of his men, and he was grateful: "God has been very kind to us this day."

It is well known that the Battle of Sharpsburg/Antietam, waged in three successive waves on September 17, 1862, produced the largest casualty count of any single-day battle in American history. It was also the first Civil War battlefield whose horrors were recorded by a photographer and then displayed to a shocked public—not the fighting itself, which people were accustomed to reading about in highly sanitized and partisan news reports, but its actual human toll. Alexander Gardner's images, which were featured in Matthew Brady's New York gallery in October under the title "The Dead at Antietam," were taken two days after the fighting had ended. By then, most of the Federal dead had been buried; many of the Confederate dead had not. Retreating Confederate forces had neither the means to carry them out with them nor the time to provide them graves;[41] most were buried by Union details or local citizens, while others were callously cast aside to rot next to Union burial mounds. Many of the most famous images of "The Dead at Antietam" are of the mangled and bloated corpses from the Second Louisiana Brigade, Darius

41. One young Confederate officer, Lieutenant Paul Newton, whose body was retrieved from behind Federal lines under a flag of truce, was later found abandoned with several other dead Southern officers. There was simply no means to transport them. See "From the Lab: Civil War Blood," September 28, 2016 New-York Historical Society Museum & Library, blog.nyhistory.org/from-the-lab-civil-war-blood/.

Hubert's brigade, along the Hagerstown Pike fence. It had been known as Starke's until that morning, but William Starke was himself among the dead—mortally wounded in a mounted charge early in the day. Hardly an officer had escaped unscathed; Michael Nolan was among the fortunate few whose wound was not life-threatening. When he fell, command of the First devolved to charming and popular eighteen-year-old Lieutenant Hardy Gill, possibly the youngest officer to command a regiment on a Civil War battlefield.[42]

The dead do not need a priest. Nonetheless, withdrawing from a bloody field in which the remains of boys he loved were unburied and exposed must have been agonizing for their chaplain. But the demands of the living were pressing; from the makeshift field tent thrown up near the battlefield, where Father Sheeran found him on September 18, "attending to the spiritual and physical wants of his many wounded children," to the hospital facilities in Richmond where care could be improved and sustained, he stayed with the injured and helped them heal. Gibbes Morgan, brother to Baton Rouge's famous teenage diarist Sarah Morgan, was eventually sent home on furlough to recover from an ugly Minié ball gash in his shoulder suffered at Sharpsburg; when there, he recounted a hospital visit from Father Hubert, who informed him, among other things, that his brother George had come through the battle safe. Until that moment, Gibbes had not known that his own sibling had been in the fight that day.[43]

The one major battle that remained in 1862—fought between December 11 and 15 at Fredericksburg, Virginia—was, despite long odds, the most lopsided Confederate victory of the Civil War. Lee's dug-in forces behind a stone wall at St. Marye's Heights withstood the attack of fifteen

42. Gill survived the war and returned home to Lake Charles, Louisiana. His likeness was chosen to top the Confederate monument in that city, a likeness that in a winsome dedicatory speech (June 3, 1915) he argued lacked only an apt epithet to the humble valor of those with whom he fought: "They always done their derndest." Gill's speech is reprinted in Jones, *The Fighting First*, pp. 249–51.

43. Sarah Morgan, *The Civil War Diary of a Southern Woman*, ed. Charles East (New York: Simon and Schuster, 1992), p. 293. Gibbes served in the Seventh Louisiana Infantry Regiment, George in the First. Neither survived the war.

brigades of charging bluecoats, whose persistence and valor in an effectively suicidal assault caused admiration even among the men whose guns were turned on them. On the right flank, Stonewall Jackson's repulse of two effective but unsupported Union assaults at what came to be called the "Slaughter Pen" sealed the Confederate victory. In the aftermath, Robert E. Lee famously observed, "It is well that war is so terrible, or we should grow too fond of it."

The First Louisiana regiment, still assigned to Jackson's corps, was only lightly engaged at Fredericksburg; most of its casualties were suffered during skirmishing and picket duty, though the unit was commended for bravery and alacrity in responding to orders. This was the first major engagement in which Darius Hubert was not present with his men. When Albert Blanchard appealed (without success) to have his friend reassigned to the west after Sharpsburg, he noted that Father Hubert's health had lately "broken down," which may explain why the chaplain was "ordered to Richmond" from September 28 through December 16, 1862. By this time he was conspicuously the "longest on duty" among the Southern Catholic chaplains, having been continuously at his post since April 1861.

By Christmas he was back in camp, feeling restored. Campaigning having ended for the year, the Louisiana troops, with the rest of Jackson's corps, had dug in for the winter at the small, strategic, and much-contested village of Port Royal, Virginia, twenty miles southeast of Fredericksburg along the Rappahannock. On Christmas morning Father Hubert and Father Sheeran took turns conducting six Masses, all of which were well attended. Afterward, they enjoyed an ample feast with their boys, consisting of beer, pork, turkeys and geese, as well as spiked eggnog. It was, says Sheeran "truly a happy Christmas in the camp of our brigade."[44]

The flush of victory at Fredericksburg was on them, but the devastating human losses of the year's battles weighed heavily too, now that there was time for reflection. For many, reflection took spiritual form as Protestant

44. Sheeran's Fourteenth Regiment had in October been transferred from Hay's Brigade into Starke's Second Louisiana Brigade; he and Hubert were thus in the same brigade for the first time.

chaplains and visiting pastors and missionaries encamped with the army led worship services, prayer meetings, and collective thanksgivings, and talked privately with the soldiers. And thus, says Methodist Episcopal chaplain William Bennett, "began one of the most powerful revivals witnessed during the war."[45] It was to continue, in greater or lesser intensity, for the rest of the conflict, sometimes with and sometimes without the direct aid of clergy. A soldier in a Richmond Howitzer battery later recounted the unexpected conversion of one of the men in his command at a "simple prayer meeting" and its effect on the rest of the company: "John Wise, one of the best and bravest in the Battery, loved and respected by everybody, quietly stood up and said, 'I think it honest and right to say to my comrades that I have resolved to be a Christian. I here declare myself a believer in Christ. I want to be counted as such, and by the help of God, will try to live as such.'" This startling statement had a marked effect on even hardened and irreligious soldiers, who began to make inquiries about faith. "We had no chaplain to handle this situation but men would seek out their comrades who were Christians and talk on this great subject with them . . . until some sixty-five men, two-thirds of our whole number, had confessed their faith and taken their stand, and in conduct and spirit, as well as in word, were living consistent Christian lives.[46]

As news of such incidents and of the general revival spread, Bibles, prayer books, hymnals, and tracts found their way into the camps in abundance, despite the lack of printing facilities in the South and despite the Union blockade. A Christian Association was formed, with a simple Trinitarian statement of faith based on the ancient Apostles' Creed familiar to Roman Catholics as well as Protestants in liturgical churches; its only variants were the omission of the phrase "He descended into hell" and the substitution of "the Holy Catholic Church" with the "Church of Christ":

45. William W. Bennett, *A Narrative of the Great Revival Which Prevailed in the Southern Armies During the Late Civil War Between the States of the Federal Union* (Philadelphia: Claxton, Remsen & Haffelfinger, 1877), p. 251.

46. William Mead Dame, *From the Rapidan to Richmond and the Spottsylvania Campaign: A Sketch in Personal Narrative of the Scenes a Soldier Saw* (Baltimore: Green-Lucas, 1920), pp. 49–52.

> I believe in God, the Father Almighty, Maker of heaven and earth; and in Jesus Christ, his only Son, our Lord, who was conceived by the Holy Ghost, born of the Virgin Mary, suffered under Pontius Pilate, was crucified, dead and buried; the third day he arose again from the dead; he ascended into heaven and sitteth on the right hand of God the Father Almighty; from thence he shall come to judge the quick and the dead. I believe in the Holy Ghost; the Church of Christ; the communion of saints; the forgiveness of sins; the resurrection of the body; and the life everlasting. Amen.[47]

It was, in short, a creed that not only Robert E. Lee, the evangelical Episcopalian,[48] and Stonewall Jackson, the austere Calvinist, could agree on; it was unobjectionable in its central tenets to a priest like Darius Hubert.

This does not mean, of course, that Catholic priests were as a rule comfortable with this new wave of religious zeal in the army. Father Sheeran dismissed the chaplains as so many "humbugs" and heretics, accusing them of "haranguing" the soldiers and mocking their "nasally hymns" and "plaintive lamentations"; when invited to attend one of their meetings, he replied that "I am sure those Chaplains could do me no good, and I think I could not help them."[49] While very happy to preach to Protestants, he had no interest in listening to them. Father Hippolyte Gache, who encountered revivalism in the hospitals, enjoyed lighting fires with gospel tracts and compared one Protestant pastor who had the temerity to visit his hospital to "a fox raiding a chicken coop." About a Baptist minister who "truly treats me as a brother," his less than gracious response was to "take advantage of every occasion to tell him and the others of his ilk that I don't see them under any other aspect than as gentlemen, but that certainly I don't consider them as ministers of the Gospel."[50]

47. The creed adopted by the Christian Association for the "army church" in the trans-Mississippi was markedly different. Though briefer, and somewhat ecumenical, it seems intentionally to exclude Catholics; it bears no connection to the Apostles' Creed and has a strongly Reformational flavor. For a text, see Bennett, *Narrative of the Great Revival*, p. 358.

48. Robert E. Lee's Christian formation and character are admirably documented in R. David Cox, *The Religious Life of Robert E. Lee* (Grand Rapids, MI: Eerdmans, 2017).

49. *The Civil War Diary of Father Sheeran*, pp. 224–26.

50. Gache, *Frenchman, Chaplain, Rebel*, p. 95.

The Catholic Bishop of Richmond, John McGill, evidently concerned about the revival's effects on nominal or indifferent Catholics, prepared his own "Catholic Devotionals for Confederate Soldiers" to rival the evangelical tracts and Bibles that were pouring into the army.[51] And Father Sheeran thought it prudent, following Fredericksburg, to fight fire with fire; he and Father Smulders gave a "little mission to the [Catholic] soldiers" to remind them whose church they belonged to.[52] Yet the good effects of the revivals on both morale and morals in the camps were hard to dismiss, even for the cynical Sheeran. Masses were better attended, and the lines at the confession tents were longer as religious apathy was replaced with the active practice of faith. When Father Sheeran rather importunately demanded an audience with Col. Henry Forno of the Fifth Louisiana to "make a motion that there shall be no more profane swearing among the officers," he was informed by the amused Forno that his petition came too late—that he had already curtailed such language, apparently as a result of the evangelicals' zeal in cleaning up profanity (as well as drinking and gambling) in the camps.[53]

Devout Catholic soldiers were ambivalent about the revivalism. Though it was alien in its experiential emphasis and non-sacramental character, it clearly had a transformative effect on some of the coarse and godless men in their regiments. Moreover, it was actively supported by generals they revered, notably Robert E. Lee and Stonewall Jackson, and sometimes led

51. He doubtless knew of stories such as one recorded by a chaplain in the Northern Army, where a lifelong Catholic, encountering the simple biblical message of the Protestant chaplains and reading one of their pocket testaments (despite his Catholic chaplain's warnings), embraced evangelical faith. See Robert R. Mathisen, *The Routledge Sourcebook of Religion and the American Civil War: A History in Documents* (New York: Routledge, 2013), pp. 201–2.

52. Later in the war Sheeran would sternly upbraid a Catholic officer for missing a Mass that he conducted and attending instead a Protestant service (*The Civil War Diary of Father Sheeran*, p. 328).

53. *The Civil War Diary of Father Sheeran*, p. 170. Sheeran mistakenly has "Furnow" here, and places him variously in the Fifth and Fifteenth Louisiana; there was no one in the Fifteenth with that or a similar name, and no other colonel with a similar name in the Louisiana brigades.

by chaplains they respected.[54] John Dooley, of the First Virginia Infantry, mentions the chaplain of the Eleventh Virginia as among the exemplary Protestant chaplains who is "held in high esteem by all," regardless of their religious affiliation, for both bravery on the field and zeal in ministry. In describing the revivals, Dooley writes that "the parsons taking advantage of the period of calm are indefatigable in their efforts to draw the soldiers together to sing psalms and assist at prayer; hundreds and thousands respond to their call & the woods for miles resound with the unscientific but earnest music of the rough veterans of Lee's Army." He describes both the "enlivening notes of the initiated" and the more plaintive chorus of the penitent "mourners" whose conversions are a daily occurrence. With admirable restraint, Dooley acknowledges that "there is something very solemn in these immense choruses of earnest voices, and there are, I am sure, hundreds of these honest soldiers truly sincere in believing that they are offering their most acceptable service to God; for they have never heard of the True Church, or if they have, their attention has not been sufficiently drawn to the right which She alone has of teaching mankind the only true mode of Worship."[55]

Dooley adds an interesting footnote about his own regimental chaplain, Methodist pastor Joseph Edward Martin, whose aestheticism would lead him into high-church Episcopalianism after the war. He was, says Dooley, not much for the revival *or* for the hard realities of military life: "Our parson has precious little to do for there are but a few scattering members in our regiment who feel religiously disposed, and our chaplain is not the man to allure converts. He likes good living but very little

54. In Jackson's corps, soldiers were invariably summoned to kneel and to offer prayers with their chaplain before each battle commenced.

55. *John Dooley's Civil War: An Irish American's Journey in the First Virginia Infantry Regiment*, ed. Robert Emmett Curran (Knoxville: University of Tennessee Press, 2012), pp. 60–61. The chaplain of the Eleventh Virginia was John Cowper Granbery, bishop of the Methodist Episcopal Church, who lost the sight of an eye at Frazier's Farm and continued on in his zealous and fearless chaplaincy until the end of the war. Dooley also praises the chaplain of the Seventh Virginia, Florence McCarthy, who was widely revered for good preaching and exemplary devotion to duty and to his men. McCarthy served briefly also with the Ninth Louisiana (see appendix II).

work." As a result, "our regiment at night, instead of reviving themselves with prayer meetings, are serenaded by Bill Deane's troupe . . . with all the old negro songs."[56]

Dooley himself was an Irish American, educated at Georgetown and ultimately headed for the Jesuit priesthood. He had stopped in at the Jesuit house at Frederick at the same time as Father Hubert in September 1862, to visit former teachers; he doubtless shared meals and fellowship with the chaplain of the First Louisiana.

He would also, later in the war, make the acquaintance of one of Father Hubert's unlikely protégés, a young Protestant chaplain attached to the Second Louisiana Infantry by the name of Robert Hardie (spelled "Hardy" in Dooley's journal). The circumstances of their meeting were not pleasant; captured at Gettysburg, they were imprisoned together at Fort McHenry, the stark and overcrowded "Baltimore Bastille." In listing his fellow captives, Dooley mentions "Capt. Hardy, a handsome young fellow, Chaplain of the 2nd La. Inf."[57] A twenty-year-old Methodist from Caddo Parish, Hardie was appointed chaplain in 1863 at the suggestion of the regiment's commanding officer, Jesse Williams.[58] Though captured multiple times, he always returned to the ranks. In this particular instance, sharing a cell with the Irish Catholic Dooley and numerous other unaffiliated and irreligious men,[59] he dutifully preached on the Lord's

56. *Dooley's Civil War*, pp. 60–61.

57. *Dooley's Civil War*, p. 185. Robert Hardie, though attached to the Second Louisiana Regiment, would have known many of the men in the First as well, since one of its companies, the Caddo Rifles, was raised from his home parish.

58. After Chancellorsville, where Brigadier General Francis T. Nicholls was removed from active service by injury, Jesse Williams become the de facto commander for the whole Second Brigade, though he was never formally promoted to a brigadiership. Brigade command passed briefly to Alfred Iverson and then to Leroy A. Stafford; when General Stafford was killed in the Wilderness Campaign in early 1864, Colonel Zebulon York replaced him. Jesse Williams was himself killed on May 12, 1864, leading his regiment.

59. Executive orders in both Union and Confederate armies declared that captured chaplains, as noncombatants, should be "immediately and unconditionally released," though this did not always happen; in August 1863, following Gettysburg, twelve Southern chaplains at Fort McHenry (Hardie among them) were informed that "they were considered and held as prisoners of war" (*The War of the Rebellion: A Compilation of the Official Records of the Union*

Day and prevailed upon Dooley, the only man in the room who knew a hymn-tune, to help them in singing "Jesus, Saviour of My Soul" ("a hymn with a twang," as Dooley styles it, referring to its evangelical origins, and which he evidently learned in camp).[60] A reluctant Silas to Hardie's Paul, he thus intoned the plangent lyrics:

> Jesus, Saviour of my soul, to thy care and love I fly,
> While the waves of trouble roll, while the tempest still is high;
> Hide me, O my Saviour, hide, till the storm of life be past;
> Safe into the haven guide, oh, receive my soul at last.
>
> Other refuge have I none; clings my helpless soul on Thee,
> Leave, ah, leave me not alone, still support and comfort me;
> All my trust on Thee is stayed, all my help from thee I bring;
> Cover my defenseless head with the shadow of thy wing.

The resilient Hardie, captured and paroled several times, served until the end of the war, as solicitous of the welfare of his men as was Darius Hubert, who apparently took him under his wing when he stepped out of the soldiers' ranks to become a chaplain. "They were devoted friends; indeed, the young man looked upon Father Hubert more in the light of a father than friend. He counseled with him about all matters of importance, and after obtaining the Rev. Father's approval of his idea, immediately put it to use. Father Hubert, when speaking to him, would say: 'My son, so and so.'"[61]

It is impossible, without his own written testimony, to know Father Hubert's response to the religious awakening that occurred in Lee's army from 1863 to 1865. But given his history of respectful and amiable relations with non-Catholics prior to the war, and a habit of forming chari-

and Confederate Armies, ser. 2, vol. 6: p. 250). Though Confederate chaplains were typically housed with officers rather than their men (Union officials hoped, by depriving POWs of their spiritual succor, to rob them of the will to fight), Hardie was in this instance clearly housed with the general prison population.

60. *Dooley's Civil War*, p. 188.

61. *Richmond Dispatch*, December 21, 1902.

table and ecumenical friendships during and after the conflict, a quality that drew comment routinely after he returned home to Louisiana, it is impossible to imagine him sharing Sheeran's "humbug" or Gache's supercilious refusal to characterize earnest pastors as "ministers of the gospel." A faithful son of the Church, unwavering in his Catholic convictions, he nevertheless recognized Christian statesmanship in the non-Catholic leaders of the Confederacy and Christian faithfulness in its humbler foot soldiers.[62] Many years later, J. William Jones, a Southern Baptist pastor and one of the principal memorialists of the revivals (notably his 1887 volume *Christ in the Camp*), would reciprocate, recalling with admiration "Father Hubert, the brave Catholic priest."[63]

March 27, 1863, was appointed by Jefferson Davis as a day of fasting, humiliation, and prayer, and was observed throughout Lee's army with unusual solemnity. Immediately thereafter came Holy Week and Easter Sunday, which in the camps of the Louisiana brigades arrived with a heavy snowfall. James Sheeran, who had been in Richmond since the turn of the year, returned to find his men undeterred by the weather from taking their Easter communion; they stood knee-deep in the snow, hats off, and then knelt in the cold as the Mass was observed. It was, he said, "one of the most consoling sights" of his life.[64]

Jackson's corps emerged from winter quarters a few weeks later, ready to take the battle to the Yankees once again. This time, however, the Yankees had the jump on them. Major General Joseph Hooker, with nearly 160,000 men, had daringly crossed the Rappahannock and Rapidan and marched undetected around Lee's flank to a little crossroads called Chancellorsville, ten miles from Fredericksburg, where he established an impressive, apparently impregnable position, and confidently awaited

62. Thus Thomas Markham, chaplain in the Army of Tennessee: "A Catholic by faith, rearing, and conviction, he yet gave the right hand of fellowship, his heart in his hand, to men born and bred in other communions" (*New Orleans Times-Picayune*, June 24, 1893, p. 12); and see the Coda, below.

63. *Daily Times* (Richmond, VA), May 22, 1888, p. 4.

64. *The Civil War Diary of Father Sheeran*, p. 146.

a Confederate force that he knew numbered only 55,000. Savoring the prospect of snaring Lee and Jackson at last, Hooker could not resist boasting about his tactical and numerical advantage, assuring his men that "the operations of the last three days have determined that our enemy must either ingloriously fly, or come out from behind his defenses and give us battle on our own ground, where certain destruction awaits him." To his officers, he declared emphatically, "My plans are perfect."

The remnant of the First Louisiana (a mere 125 men) broke camp on April 28 and moved with the rest of their brigade toward the Wilderness to meet Hooker and his bluecoats. Whether they knew the odds against them or not, they were by now so used to being outnumbered and outgunned and so trusting of their leaders that they had ceased to fret about such details. And experience had taught them that even the "perfect plans" of their enemy were subject to falter and fail, especially when Stonewall led them, and laid hold, in his inimitable manner, on providential aid. The song "Stonewall Jackson's Way," composed and set to music in the autumn of 1862, and by now a kind of unofficial anthem of his corps, included a stanza devoted to Jackson's special connection with the Almighty:

Silence! Ground arms! Kneel all! Caps off!
Old Blue Light's going to pray;
Strangle the fool that dares to scoff;
Attention; it's his way!
Appealing from his native sod,
In *forma pauperis* to God—
"Lay bare thine arm; stretch forth thy rod;
Amen." That's Stonewall's way.[65]

65. The song, recounting Jackson's heroic Shenandoah campaign, celebrates his almost mythic qualities, including his habit of prayer before battle and his rendering praise to a benevolent Providence after each victory. "Lay bare thine arm" derives from Isaiah 52:10, where God figuratively demonstrates his insuperable power to all the nations; "stretch forth thy rod" echoes Exodus 14, where the rod of Moses opens a miraculous path of deliverance from the Egyptians.

Darius Hubert accompanied his regiment to Chancellorsville, as did young Robert Hardie, the newly appointed chaplain to the Second. This was Hardie's first engagement with the Louisiana Brigade, his appointment having been formalized only weeks earlier; priest and pastor likely commiserated as they prepared the men in their respective regiments, by now a much depleted and tightknit fellowship, for the coming battle. Father James Sheeran, the Redemptorist chaplain of the Fourteenth Louisiana, was once again a little late in getting to the battle, blaming a broken-down horse and logistical complications for his failure to reach his men before their audacious, silent, fifteen-mile march around Hooker's right, where they scattered and routed the shocked troops of the Union Eleventh Corps and shattered Hooker's perfect plans. The vastly outnumbered Confederate force had divided *itself* in order to conquer—an unthinkably dangerous tactic—and in the late afternoon of May 2 stunned the unsuspecting bluecoats (whose scouts had assumed the movement they glimpsed along a narrow wooded lane was actually a retreat to Richmond).

Father Sheeran's lengthy journal entry on Chancellorsville provides several cryptic observations that shed light on his Jesuit colleague. Sheeran joined Father Hubert in doing the rounds in the makeshift field hospitals, along with a "horde of Protestant chaplains" he regarded as redundant and worthless. He disparages them as "poor deluding and deluded creatures" with "no sacraments to administer, no graces or consolation to dispense." Even the "kind-hearted" ones were in his mind without any genuine spiritual resources, and frequently resorted to calling Father Hubert or himself to the bedsides of the dying.[66] That all of the non-Catholic chaplains at Chancellorsville were as incompetent as Sheeran suggests is of course highly doubtful, and that there was a need for their pastoral care for non-Catholic soldiers is obvious. The good, even heroic, labors of Protestant chaplains and ministers among the sick and dying in the Wilderness and elsewhere is well documented by this stage of the war, when most of the shirkers had been weeded out. But Sheeran was proud of his prejudice and disinclined to charity in such matters.

66. *The Civil War Journal of Father Sheeran*, pp. 162–63.

Sheeran recounts that he attended also to the wounded Catholics among the captured enemy, always "leaving Father Hubert in our own hospitals during my absences." This is a telling division of labors, and in some measure portends the direction of their lives after the war. Darius Hubert, for whom the "hordes of Protestants" would not have been such an affliction, could not easily be pried away from his men, whatever their creed, throughout the long conflict; nor would he leave them once the guns finally quieted in the spring of 1865.[67] He lived and breathed a pastoral rather than a merely ecclesial priestly vocation, one for which both the affection of a kindly, cheerful, and generous heart and the virtue of *stabilitas* were central. As dutiful a priest as Father Sheeran was, one cannot imagine him lingering long at the bedside of a young man beyond the formalities of liturgical consolation and the administration of Last Rites; this would to him have seemed more like what the Protestants offered—a mere affiliation of sentiment rather than the efficacious and mystical rites of the Church.[68] And his duty lay, as he saw it, with Catholics exclusively, Confederate principally, and Union when they came under his purview (he liked to shame the latter concerning the misguided and tyrannous cause they served).[69] But the devoted affection of Darius Hubert, a deep and unstinting "love of those to whom he was God-given," was what distinguished him from many of his confrères. He was a physician of souls, in whom the soldiers sensed the presence of Christ.

The hospitals were full, and moved repeatedly as the lines of battle shifted at Chancellorsville. The dramatic actions of Jackson's Corps on

67. Like most Roman Catholic priests who served the Confederacy as chaplains, and despite his bellicose Southern rhetoric during the war, Father Sheeran was to spend most of the remainder of his life in the North, confirming Fr. Cornelius Buckley's observation that "the future for the Catholic Church seemed part of the spoils that belonged to the victor" (in Gache, *Frenchman, Chaplain, Rebel*, p. 233). See appendix II.

68. Father Sheeran seems to have acknowledged this himself when, after the Second Battle of Winchester, he was asked to oversee care of the wounded but deputized Fr. Giles Smulders, saying that he would be "a much better nurse" (*The Civil War Diary of Father Sheeran*, p. 183).

69. He also officiously chastised the laxity of Union surgeons in caring for their wounded after Chancellorsville, demanding that their orderlies gather materials for bandages from the haversacks of the fallen and carry water to their suffering men.

May 2 were followed by several more harrowing days, in which the Second Louisiana Brigade suffered horrific losses, until Hooker's whole Army of the Potomac finally retreated back across the Rappahannock River.

It was yet another extraordinarily improbable victory for the Army of Northern Virginia, though won at almost unthinkable cost. In Father Hubert's own, already drastically depleted First Louisiana regiment, 13 were killed and 27 wounded; in the Second Louisiana regiment, in which his young Methodist friend Robert Hardie was now chaplain, 15 were killed, 90 wounded. The Tenth (Father Gache's old unit), suffered 26 killed and 57 wounded; the Fourteenth (Father Sheeran's regiment), 4 killed, 60 wounded; and the chaplain-less Fifteenth, 5 killed, 37 wounded. Many of the wounds required drastic surgery: there were more amputated limbs at Chancellorsville than at any previous battle. As if the horrors of combat were not enough, a section of the field where the Louisiana brigades had been the final night of the engagement took fire from the shelling; flames spread throughout the night where wounded men from both armies lay exposed and helpless, burning them alive. The ghastly scene was for one of those who encountered it the following morning "the most sickening sight I ever saw during the war."[70]

The direst loss of all to the Army of Northern Virginia was its seemingly invincible general, Stonewall Jackson, accidentally shot by his own pickets on the night of May 2. Removed to a field hospital and then again to a cottage at Guiney Station, he was initially expected to recover after his left arm was amputated. But on the evening of May 6 he succumbed unexpectedly to pneumonia. In and out of a drug-induced stupor, sometimes lucid and sometimes hallucinating and giving battle orders, he steadily lost ground. Finally, on Sunday May 10, in peaceful, almost child-like acquiescence to the will of God, with his wife at his side, he uttered his remarkable last words: "Let us cross over the river and rest under the shade of the trees."

Notwithstanding another brilliant military victory, the Army of North-

70. John O. Casler, *Four Years in the Stonewall Brigade* ([1893;] Columbia: University of South Carolina Press, 2005), p. 151; see also *The Civil War Diary of Father Sheeran*, p. 166.

ern Virginia was by this loss gripped with sorrow. From Robert E. Lee down through the ranks of officers who had fought alongside him and common soldiers who had idolized him, battle-hardened men wept openly when they received the news of his death—as did those on the home front. In the words of his most recent biographer, "his loss touched the heart of every household in the South."[71]

Darius Hubert, whose ongoing care of the many wounded in his brigade probably prevented him from traveling to Richmond for Jackson's public memorial, was as shattered as anyone in Stonewall's corps. Nearly two decades hence he would be called upon to solemnize Jackson's legacy, when the veterans of the Army of Northern Virginia dedicated their monument, topped with his likeness, in Metairie Cemetery in New Orleans. For now, he simply mourned the man, the leader, the soldier, and the Christian he had revered, and doubtless prayed for his soul.

The Louisiana brigades retired to their earlier camp for a brief reprieve and were then ordered to the Shenandoah Valley as a prelude to the Gettysburg Campaign. Lee wanted the small, much fought-over town of Winchester, Virginia, occupied by Union Major General Robert Milroy, cleared of Federal forces. The entire Second Corps of his army, under General Richard Ewell, advanced on Winchester from several directions in mid-June, while Milroy waited, refusing an order to evacuate, confident that his strong defensive position could hold. His confidence proved misguided. Enjoying favorable odds for a change, and the strategic advantage of detailed knowledge of Winchester's defenses, Ewell's forces won an easy victory—not only retaking the town but capturing nearly 4,000 Union prisoners, 300 horses, 300 loaded wagons, and large quantities of weapons and ammunition, clothing, and other stores. Confederate field hospitals (and their surgeons, nurses, and chaplains) were happily in less demand than at any engagement thus far in the war, an especially welcome change from Chancellorsville. The entire operation resulted in an astonishingly low number of Southern casualties—47 killed, 219 wounded, 3 missing. In the First Louisiana regiment, which was only

71. Gwynne, *Rebel Yell*, p. 557.

lightly engaged, one private suffered a slight wound; there were in fact no fatalities and only a few wounds in the entire Second Louisiana Brigade.

Once victory was secured, Fathers Hubert and Sheeran, with no pressing responsibilities, went into Winchester to celebrate with the Southern partisans of the town who were thrilled at Milroy's departure and the rout of his troops. In a moment of whimsy, Darius Hubert accepted the gift of a handsome sword from an Irish Catholic prisoner held at the fort, buckled on the showy souvenir, and rode about town on his horse, perhaps contemplating roads not taken. His borrowed coat was darker than typical Confederate gray, and he was briefly taken for a Union officer, which must have amused him as much as those who failed to recognize him. The "arrest" was short-lived.

From there, it was on to Gettysburg, though no one knew at the time where that most fateful battle of the war would occur. It is as well that we cannot see the future; the levity following Second Winchester, sprung from a conviction that Stonewall's providential charisma would continue to follow the Army of Northern Virginia even in his absence,[72] was to come to a quick end on a Pennsylvania battlefield. But for the moment, the graycoats were merry and confident, their marching accompanied by patriotic songs and jests.

Somewhere between the Shenandoah Valley and that ominous rendezvous, the First Louisiana was rejoined by its popular commander, Lieutenant Colonel Michael Nolan.[73] He had been away from his men on an injury furlough (following the Battle of Sharpsburg), which was then extended into a recruiting assignment in Mobile, Alabama, where many Louisianans had relocated from occupied New Orleans and Baton

72. One of the Union officers captured in Winchester was in fact certain that the Confederates had lied about Stonewall's death, as no one in either army could have executed so perfect a maneuver in taking the town, save "Old Jack." See Scott L. Mingus Sr., *The Louisiana Tigers in the Gettysburg Campaign, June–July 1863* (Baton Rouge: Louisiana State University Press, 2009), p. 57.

73. Father Sheeran recounts commiserating with him as the regiment entered Gettysburg, where they found Father Hubert already assisting the ambulance corps with wounded troops from the first day's contest. Nolan was "more than usually calm," according to Sheeran (*The Civil War Diary of Father Sheeran*, p. 194).

Rouge. Nolan's wife, Ellen, had also settled temporarily in Mobile, so he came back to his troops much refreshed from his sojourn.

Arriving at nightfall on July 1, with hostilities already underway, the First Louisiana Regiment was not immediately summoned to action. The next afternoon they were ordered, with the rest of Second Brigade, to charge and seize Culp's Hill, a steep and rocky promontory at the top of which Union forces were well dug in. As dusk came on, Nolan himself led the charge, and was almost instantly killed by a twelve-pound artillery shell—his body horribly mangled. He had been back in service less then twenty-four hours. Some of his men managed to remove what remained of his body out of the line of fire; he was buried that evening "with his uniform and a blanket for a shroud and coffin" in a shallow grave in a nearby orchard. Shortly thereafter, through the kindness of a pious Catholic woman, Isabella ("Belle") Gubernator, and the intervention of Father Hubert, he was reinterred in a makeshift coffin (one account says a piano case) and buried clandestinely in consecrated ground at a Jesuit church twelve miles from the front, the Conewago Chapel of the Sacred Heart of Jesus. Despite the horrific circumstance of his demise, his death was thus solemnized with a dignity accorded to very few in the chaotic charnel house of Gettysburg—where hundreds of Confederate dead, including officers, were cast haphazardly and callously into anonymous mass trenches. The mortal remains of Michael Nolan would rest under the shade of the trees in the Conewago cemetery until the war ended.

Nolan's gallant charge and pitiless death in the first instants of his engagement were in some ways emblematic of the fate of all Louisianans at Gettysburg. The First ("Tiger") Brigade fought tenaciously at Cemetery Hill, the Second just as tenaciously at Culp's Hill. Both were repulsed with huge losses, despite conspicuous courage and resolve—what Shelby Foote called "the simple virtues of duty." But it was General George Pickett's doomed charge across a mile of open ground on July 3, in which every second combatant fell and entire regiments disappeared, that decisively and calamitously ended the Pennsylvania campaign. The long tide of improbable Confederate victories had come at last to a harrowing halt, with Stonewall Jackson only seven weeks in the grave. Robert E. Lee confided bleakly to General James Longstreet, "It's all my fault. I thought my men were invincible." Weeks later, he would offer his resignation to Jefferson Davis, urging his belief that "a younger and abler man than myself" should be given command of the Army of Northern Virginia—an offer Davis politely and firmly declined. For now, shocked and saddened by his failure to win a decisive victory at Gettysburg, Lee sent the long wagon columns back toward Virginia under guard of a cavalry brigade, accompanying his infantry by a different and shorter route. The sweltering summer weather had suddenly changed, and the march of the men and the suffering of the wounded in lurching ambulances and rickety forage wagons—most of whom had not received even minimal medical attention, and many of whom had not eaten for days—was made more miserable by drenching rain and a road that had become a virtually impassable sea of mud.[74]

More than 3,900 Southern combatants were killed in Gettysburg; five times that number were wounded. Many of the dead lay unburied for days, decomposing horribly, covered with vermin and maggots, fed on by hogs. Others that had been buried hastily in shallow graves were uncovered by heavy rains that swept in over the battlefield on the night of July 4, creating a ghoulish spectacle. Hundreds of severely wounded men, left behind when Lee's army retreated, succumbed to a lingering, torturous death while waiting for medical attention. Even Northern observers found their circumstances unspeakably cruel. More than two weeks after the battle, they could still be found all over the area lying upon the bare ground, without any cover: "Day and night, rain or shine, cold or hot, there they lie. Hour by hour they die off, are carried to the trenches, a foot or two deep, in which they are to lie . . . and remain there in con-

74. A graphic description of the suffering of the wounded during retreat is recorded by John W. Imboden, "The Confederate Retreat from Gettysburg," *Battles and Leaders of the Civil War* (1887), vol. 3: p. 424. A member of the Washington Artillery describes the surreal movement of an army so exhausted that those on horseback and those slogging through the muck were often asleep while on the march, "as if under enchantment or a spell." See Napier Bartlett, *A Soldier's Story of the War, Including the Marches and Battles of the Washington Artillery and of Other Louisiana Troops* (New Orleans: Clark & Hofeline, 1874), p. 195.

tinually increasing groups until the parties whose duty it is come around to tend to their interment. It is awful, it is terrible, it is horrible beyond expression."[75]

Those lucky enough to be treated by the surgeons in one of the provisional hospital facilities in town—such as John Dooley of the First Virginia, shot through both thighs—were soon shipped out and joined the swelling population in Federal prisons. Amputated limbs from these various facilities were piled together and buried *en masse*. The bloated corpses of some five thousand horses and mules were burned in reeking pyres. The horrors of Gettysburg in the aftermath of battle, as often and as powerfully as they have been described and depicted, still beggar imagination.[76]

Darius Hubert was himself wounded in the arm at Gettysburg. The nature and cause of the injury is unclear, but it was evidently not serious enough to prevent him from withdrawing with his battered regiment.[77] The emotional toll of personal bereavement (when Father Gache, in Lynchburg, heard of Michael Nolan's death, he called it "a great loss for Father Hubert!") exacerbated the overall burden of horrifying casualties in his brigade, as he retired from yet another battlefield. One wonders if he was beginning to question the costs of a war that was felling a generation of young men before his eyes and casting a grim and dehumanizing pall over the living. He was also by now severely debilitated by chronic pain and fatigue and a racking, and often bloody, cough. He was forty years old, but had aged greatly over the course of two years of constant field duty and exposure to the elements, as well as the unrelenting spiritual demands of conscientious ministry. When Father James Sheeran

75. Robert P. Nevin, in a dispatch to the *Pittsburgh Evening Chronicle*, July 18, 1863, cited in Gerard A. Patterson, *Debris of Battle: The Wounded of Gettysburg* (Mechanicsburg, PA: Stackpole Books, 1997), p. 200.

76. In addition to Patterson, *Debris of Battle*, see Gregory A. Coco, *A Strange and Blighted Land: Gettysburg: The Aftermath of a Battle* (Gettysburg, PA: Thomas Publications, 1995), and *Wasted Valor: The Confederate Dead at Gettysburg* (Gettysburg, PA: Thomas Publications, 1990). For a magisterial study of the grim toll of the American Civil War, see Drew Gilpin Faust, *This Republic of Suffering: Death and the American Civil War* (New York: Knopf, 2008).

saw him in camp along the Rappahannock on October 20, 1863, just before leaving, himself, on a four-month furlough to Alabama, Georgia, and South Carolina, his Jesuit colleague was, in his words, "quite sick."

The only battle fought by Father Hubert's regiment in the remaining months of 1863 was Mine Run (Payne's Farm), in Orange County, Virginia—Major General George Meade's attempt to "mop up" Lee's depleted army that he had soundly defeated but failed to pursue after Gettysburg. It was another bloody and inconclusive affair, commencing November 27 (immediately following Lincoln's first national Thanksgiving Day) and lasting until December 2, when Meade finally tired of the stalemate and retired to winter camp, as did Confederate forces. The First Louisiana Regiment lost 28 of the 125 men engaged; the Second Brigade as a whole was comparably reduced. General Lee commended his battle-hardened but poorly provisioned troops, "thousands of whom are barefooted, a great number partially shod, and nearly all without overcoats, blankets, or warm clothing," in the highest terms: "Nothing prevented my continuing in his [Meade's] front but the destitute condition of the men. . . . I think the sublimest sight of the war was the cheerfulness and alacrity exhibited by this army in the pursuit of the enemy under all the trials and privations to which it was exposed."[78]

It was here, as he stayed behind with the severely sick and wounded, that another notable incident of Hubert's chaplaincy occurred. Sometime during the night after both armies had withdrawn, a woman's screams were heard at some distance from the hospital tents. Summoning several attendants, Father Hubert followed the sounds to a house where four Federal stragglers were ransacking property and terrorizing the female occupant. In a fury of righteous indignation, he "stopped them in their villainous work, and hurled them from the premises."[79] This was a side of his character not frequently on display, but those who knew him during

77. The injury is sometimes said to have happened during Pickett's Charge, though it is doubtful that he would have been in that part of the field on July 3; the Louisiana brigades were not engaged there.

78. *War of the Rebellion*, ser. 1, vol. 29, part 1: p. 408.

79. Recounted in *Richmond Dispatch*, Dec. 21, 1902, p. 14.

the war years saw in such moments the "perfect man" they revered as much as the priest they loved.

As was his custom, Father Hubert spent Christmas 1863 with his regiment—hearing confessions, celebrating Mass, sharing an austere holiday meal with his men, commiserating with and cheering them. He was the only Catholic priest encamped with the Louisiana brigades for Christmas that year, possibly the only priest on duty in Lee's army.[80] Though the cost of meats and holiday fruits and sweets was by now exorbitant, the men were adept at producing a simple feast, complete with whisky-laced eggnog. There were toasts to honor their many fallen companions and their leaders, though the tone was more subdued than in either of the two previous Christmases in camp. There had been a creeping tide of desertions, often into enemy lines rather than toward home, where the risk of capture, public ignominy, and execution was great. For those who remained faithfully and dutifully at their post, the cavalier spirit of 1861 had been replaced by quiet and studied resolve, despite evidently increasing odds and constantly decreasing food, clothing, and other provisions. The pull of nostalgia for their "dear Southland" and those they had left behind was ever strong, especially on such occasions: as the evening wore on, men typically "clustered round the blaze / To talk of other Christmas days, / And softly speak of home and home."[81]

Later in the week, Father Hubert left for Richmond. He had been invited to share a New Year's dinner with the Semmes family, whom he knew from New Orleans. Thomas Jenkins Semmes was a member of the Confederate Congress, and during the war lived with his family less than a block from the Confederate White House in a splendid and capacious home.[82] He and his wife were generous hosts and gave frequent, lavish parties for officers and soldiers and local belles. As they were later to re-

80. Sheeran was away on furlough; Smulders was in North Carolina.

81. From the wartime poem of William Gordon McCabe, who served with the Richmond Howitzers, "Christmas Night of '62."

82. His brother, Alexander Jenkins Semmes, Louisiana brigade surgeon, was also well known to Darius Hubert. A. J. Semmes was ordained to the Catholic priesthood in Savannah, Georgia, in 1878, exchanging a successful and demanding medical career for care of souls.

count, in a long retrospective newspaper interview, "We had great times in the first years of the war, when our cause seemed so sure of success and our boys were fighting so bravely. . . . Many a group of handsome officers danced the night away and went forth to fight on the morrow and were buried in the evening shadows on the battlefield."[83] The dinner to which Darius Hubert was summoned, on January 1, 1864, was one of the last notable gatherings in the Semmes's Richmond home. In contrast to many earlier and more sumptuous affairs, it featured a modest meal, since "money was worth nothing, and provisions were high. We had our expensive Confederate turkey [which cost $110], and vegetables and game, and good bread made at home, and nice dessert." The small company of guests included "Mr. Stephens and General Sparrow and Mr. Garland, from our home, and Bishop McGill and dear old Father Hubert."[84] In the Semmes's recollection, "we all tried to be gay, but our hearts were inwardly sad. There was the usual visiting . . . but the old brilliancy and fire were fast ebbing away."

In a year of many devastating losses, one particular loss still entailed unfinished business for Father Hubert. A few days after muted New Year's festivities at the Semmes home, he was granted a thirty-day leave in order to fulfill his duties as executor for the estate of Michael Nolan. Arranging for another cleric (unnamed) to attend to his men's spiritual needs during his absence, he spent part of the month in the Confederate capital, then traveled to Mobile, where Nolan's widow continued to reside until the end of the war. Nolan had penned a brief and straightforward will before leaving New Orleans in April 1861, bequeathing all of his worldly belongings to his wife, Ellen (nee Hackett); it was probated within ten weeks of his death, in late September 1863. The opportunity to bring spiritual solace as well as practical counsel to Nolan's grieving widow proved also a timely respite for Father Hubert from the field and camps of the war.

83. "Richmond in War Times: A Talk with Judge T. J. Semmes—His Recollections," *Richmond Dispatch*, January 30, 1898, p. 2.

84. Alexander Stephens, vice president of the Confederacy, General Edward Sparrow, and Augustus Hill Garland, a Confederate congressman and then senator from Arkansas, were all boarders at the Semmes residence.

It did not, however, restore his health. He was by this point seriously and chronically ill. When he returned to Virginia his furlough was extended as a sick leave. It is unclear when he was admitted to St. Francis de Sales Hospital, a small private Catholic hospital in Richmond overseen by the Sisters of Charity. But on March 9, his physician, D. William Thomas, wrote a note certifying that "I have frequently attended Rev. D. Hubert . . . and here state that he is the subject of Phthisis Pulmonalis [tuberculosis] attended by constant and harassing cough, severe pain, and frequent hemorrhages and general debility. I have no hesitation in saying that he is entirely unfit for the active duties of the field and therefore recommend that he be assigned to post duty where he can receive the protection and comforts of home."[85] Regimental commander Lieutenant Colonel James Nelligan supported the doctor's recommendation in an affidavit: "He has been through many campaigns and is one of the most faithful officers in discharge of his duty it has ever been my good fortune to know," but the officer acknowledged that he "has been unfit for service for some months, having suffered much from a constant cough with much emaciation and debility."

Darius Hubert had served continuously and unstintingly for three years, and could certainly have retired from his chaplaincy at that point and returned to the Jesuit house in Mobile, if not to occupied New Orleans. But his sense of obligation to the troops made such an option unthinkable. He requested reassignment to hospital duty in the Confederate capital, where the need for pastoral care was overwhelming and where he could carry out such responsibilities as his strength allowed. Having expressed his regret to Major Charles E. Cormier for vacating his place in the camp, Cormier replied that, "in my opinion dear Father, you have already exposed yourself too much in persisting to remain in active duty on the field in cold and biting weather of the winter," adding his hope that "your health will be actively restored and 'ere long grant the men of the old First the presence of their beloved and revered Chaplain."

85. Dr. Daniel William Thomas was associated with St. Francis de Sales Hospital for most of the war, apart from a brief stint in the late spring of 1864 at the Jackson Hospital, where he worked with Dr. A. J. Semmes.

On March 30, 1864, his new orders were formalized: "Rev. Darius Hubert Chaplain . . . is assigned to duty for religious ministration to the Roman Catholics in the various Hospitals in this City and Manchester, and will report to Surgeon W. A. Carrington, Medical Director."[86] From that day until the city fell almost exactly a year later he visited all the hospitals in the Richmond area. Though his assignment was formally to Catholic soldiers, he had never restricted his ministrations to those of his own faith, and it was almost certainly during this last year of the war, in visiting the sick and wounded on daily rounds, that his reputation as a chaplain "known and dear to every man in the Army of Northern Virginia" was cemented.[87]

By mid-1864, the patchwork of hospital facilities across the Confederate capital was extensive and varied.[88] The largest and best-known was the Chimborazo, modified from an 1861 military barracks and winter quarters to a pavilion-style hospital complex that could house more than 3,400 patients.[89] The Louisiana Hospital to which Father Hubert devoted much of his energy, and where he conducted regular divine service, was housed in the buildings of Richmond [Baptist] College; it held upwards of 150 patients.[90] Louisiana troops were also to be found in Howard's Grove,

86. Carrington was chief inspector of the Richmond-area hospitals through the end of the war. His "Inspection Reports," listing the number of sick, wounded, and convalescent in area hospitals—including General Hospital No. 1, Chimborazo, Howard's Grove, Jackson, Louisiana, Robertson, St. Francis de Sales, Stuart, and Receiving and Wayside Hospital (General Hospital No. 9)—provide a window into the crushing burden of medical care toward the end of the war. In one such report he indicates that the care of 10,200 patients was currently assigned to only 131 medical personnel, many of whom had only rudimentary skills.

87. Richmond was a second home to all of Lee's soldiers, and for Louisianans whose home towns were occupied by Federal forces, the place to which they flocked for furloughs and times of respite.

88. A useful overview may be found in Robert W. Waitt Jr., "Confederate Military Hospitals in Richmond," a pamphlet published by the Richmond Civil War Centennial Committee in 1964. See also Rebecca Barbour Calcutt's detailed and informative recent study, *Richmond's Wartime Hospitals* (Gretna, LA: Pelican, 2005).

89. Dave Ruth, "Chimborazo Hospital," *Encyclopedia Virginia*, published by the Virginia Foundation for the Humanities, March 1, 2011.

90. See the wartime pamphlet "The Louisiana Soldiers' Relief Association and Hospital in the City of Richmond, Virginia" (Richmond: Enquirer Book and Job Press, 1862), which

and in the Jackson Hospital, named for Confederate General Thomas J. ("Stonewall") Jackson and opened shortly after his death; it was a spacious facility with forty-nine buildings and extensive gardens, but had a reputation for being short-staffed and poorly managed. In addition to the more than twenty "General Hospitals" were smaller private infirmaries such as St. Francis de Sales [Catholic] Hospital and numerous, often temporary, medical hospices located in hotels, warehouses, taverns, factories, theaters, churches, and private homes. In the last year of the war, Darius Hubert would become a familiar presence in virtually all of them.

He also did the rounds in town among Louisiana and other Gulf Coast expatriates who were "exiled" in the Confederate capital for one reason or another.[91] He preached at St. Peter's Cathedral with relative frequency, heard confessions, visited the sick in the city's civilian population, and generally exhibited a significant pastoral presence well beyond his assigned responsibilities in the military hospitals.

He would later say that the intensity, chaos, and physical dangers of the battlefield were less trying than the spiritual anguish and malaise he encountered in the sick wards during this final phase of his wartime service—especially as hopes for Confederate victory drooped. For what had these wounded and suffering men sacrificed youth and health and vigorous limbs? For what purpose had their friends, kin, and messmates

---

contains a detailed description, roster of medical and administrative personnel, and even a list of current residents, with their rank and regiment, ailments and injuries—including the site of battle wounds and fatalities.

91. The detailed diary of New Orleans clerk Henri Garidel, published under the title *Exile in Richmond: The Confederate Journal of Henri Garidel*, ed. Michael Bedout Chesson and Leslie Jean Roberts (Charlottesville: University Press of Virginia, 2001), mentions Father Hubert's pastoral care and preacherly eloquence during the Jesuit's tenure in the city. Garidel had been expelled from New Orleans for his refusal to sign the Oath of Allegiance after Federal occupation; his wife and family found safe haven in Italy, but he was "trapped" in Richmond from May 1863 through May 1865. In one striking anecdote, Garidel recounts Father Hubert tenderly blessing and anointing Gabrielle Laresche, the young daughter of Garidel's friend, who was sick unto death with typhoid fever—performing the rite of extreme unction surrounded by her weeping family. The devout child, spiritually prepared for death, surprised everyone by recovering: "the sacrament had the desired effect," says Garidel (p. 374).

died? How could these broken men, maimed and sick, contemplate returning home without the prize of victory, the glory to which they so confidently aspired when they marched away under waving banners and stirring music and the fond good wishes of pretty girls? It was impossible for an empathetic shepherd, even one with a wealth of spiritual resources, not to feel keenly the weight of such questions. And it seems that in these months, as unsettling news from the front continued to trickle in, and Richmond itself became an increasingly desolate and impoverished city, that Darius Hubert was wrestling with the possibility and the meaning of a cause lost, prayerfully formulating a new understanding: "Thou knowest, O Lord. . . ."

In early May 1864, the First Louisiana infantry, bereft of their chaplain, fought again in the Wilderness, the site of Lee and Jackson's great victory a year earlier, but at Spotsylvania, where fighting raged for nearly two weeks, Federal forces overran their position, killing or capturing most of the regiment. The casualty count was so high by midsummer that the remnants of the First were consolidated with the Fourteenth. They took part in the Shenandoah Campaign, once again circling back to a place of earlier triumphs, but the old bravado and the old magic were gone. After a series of defeats, Confederate forces under Jubal Early pulled back, and Union General Philip Sheridan ordered the whole Shenandoah Valley—railroads, mills, factories, farms and homes—set ablaze, crops destroyed and livestock large and small killed or seized, a ruthless total war tactic that presaged Sherman's March to the Sea.

Major Charles Cormier, who had so warmly hoped for Father Hubert's soon return to his men, was severely injured and captured during the Shenandoah Campaign; he spent the rest of the war in a Federal prison, and was not released until July 24, 1865. Lieutenant Colonel James Nelligan was also captured, but exchanged and returned to service in late December. Though the First Louisiana Regiment retains his name "Nelligan's" as its last commanding officer, he did not personally lead his men for the remainder of the war; he was on a furlough in Lynchburg until the spring and then on recruiting detail in North Carolina.

Brigadier General Albert Blanchard was also by this time in North Carolina; he had been pushing papers in Louisiana for several years but now had a brigade to lead at last. In March 1865 he sent a plaintive note to Father Hubert, renewing his request to have the priest join him as "brigade chaplain": "My dear friend, I am going to ask of you a great sacrifice, and yet I hope you will grant my request. I have been on duty here since last November, and in that time have been in church but once. There is no Catholic chaplain in this army, and there are many who would be glad to see a priest. It is not necessary to say that I should be delighted to have you with me again." Blanchard pressed him to carry a letter formally requesting the transfer to General [Samuel] Cooper, and then to make his way to Raleigh, North Carolina, adding plaintively, "I hope you will come, for I need you. I have no news from my family since the fall of Columbia, SC. Please present my respects to Bishop McGill and the fathers and ask them to pray for me. If you come, please bring a few books." He signed the letter "your friend and penitent."

There is no record of the "enclosed letter" having being delivered to Cooper; it is doubtful that Darius Hubert would have opted to leave his post in Richmond for even so good a friend as Blanchard. In any case, by the time this missive reached him, the suggestion was moot: it was obvious (despite the misleading propaganda of local newspapers) that the military situation was dire, and the ball was nearing an end.[92] Richmond was the only significant Southern city not in Union hands. On Sunday, April 2, the capital itself was abandoned by Jefferson Davis and his cabinet, followed closely by local troops; even barely ambulatory soldiers in the hospitals rejoined the army in order to avoid being sent to Federal prisons. The men were under orders to set fire to the armory and warehouses on the waterfront and to bridges as they evacuated; unchecked flames, spread by high winds, began to engulf the whole business district and nearby residences by morning. The sudden vacuum of civil authority

92. See Anne Karen Berler, "Unconquerable Defiance: Richmond Newspapers and Confederate Defeat, 1864–1865," MA thesis, Virginia Commonwealth University, 2000.

also prompted a carnival of overnight looting and destruction, adding to the chaos, as crimes of opportunity combined with "retributive justice on the aiders and abettors of treason."[93] Order was not restored, nor were the fires extinguished, until Federal forces under Major General Godfrey Weitzel arrived on April 3 and took over administration of the city.

As Northern officers scouted Richmond, they were apparently surprised to find the hospitals clean, well ventilated, and well managed; many surgeons, attendants, nurses, and chaplains like Father Hubert were dutifully at the bedsides of the remaining sick and wounded.[94] On April 8, Special Order No. 95 authorized the breaking up of all the general hospitals, which were then reassigned as barracks for Yankee troops and wards for their own wounded. All remaining Confederate patients, numbering about four thousand, were moved into the Jackson Hospital until further arrangements for their ongoing care or parole and transfer could be made.

The next morning, April 9, some ninety miles west, the Louisiana Brigade (the old First and Second brigades now amalgamated into one depleted force of only 178 men), which had been part of Lee's defense in the trenches at Petersburg, shared the final, futile charge of the Army of Northern Virginia. General John Brown Gordon would later say that "this last charge of the war was made by the footsore and starving men of my command with a spirit worthy of the best days of Lee's army." But, willing spirits notwithstanding, the game was up. While fighting continued along the lines, a note arrived from General Lee announcing his meeting with Ulysses S. Grant to effect a surrender and to end hostilities. Three days later, among the "thin, worn, and famished" Confederates at Appomattox, Darius Hubert's own First Louisiana Regiment, with only two junior

93. The words are those of Thomas Chester, an African American reporter who, arriving with Union soldiers, viewed the actions of the black-led mob sympathetically. Cited in Nelson D. Lankford, *Richmond Burning: The Last Days of the Confederate Capital* (New York: Viking, 2002), p. 101.

94. "Mr. Theodore C. Wilson's Despatches" from the Spotswood Hotel, Richmond, April 10, 1865, published in the *New York Daily Herald*, April 13, 1865, p. 5. Wilson's man-on-the-street reports provide useful detail about life in the capital in the immediate aftermath of its fall to Federal forces, including abiding local veneration for Robert E. Lee but seething anger toward Jefferson Davis.

officers and eighteen soldiers, passed by the solemn Union ranks, stacked their arms, and started for home.

When Richmond fell, Father Hubert's Jesuit confrère Hippolyte Gache was in the city as well, having been sent with a few nuns from Lynchburg to the Stuart Hospital in Richmond several weeks earlier. Gache was sanguine about the arrival of the "victorious Yankee army" in the capital, greeting Catholic Union officers and chaplains as the "*best* of enemies" and extolling their magnanimity: "I don't know whether the Protestants of Richmond realized to what extent the kindly attitude of the conquering army was due to the Catholicism of its leaders [especially General Edward Ord], and that consequently it is to Catholicism that the conquered are beholden."[95] Father Gache left Richmond for Washington, DC, on Easter Monday, April 17, in company with "many acquaintances," and without much of a backward glance.[96]

Despite Father Gache having "done everything possible to persuade Father Hubert to come along with us," the latter elected to remain in Richmond for several more months. Gache, who seems never to have approved much of what his younger colleague did, found this decision incomprehensible, and pronounced it foolish: "He has been seriously sick since that time and probably would not have been had he come with us. The change of climate, the food and the rest would most assuredly have done him good."[97]

95. Gache, *Frenchman, Chaplain, Rebel*, p. 221. Gache refers specifically to General Edward Cresap Ord ("a Catholic, though he does not practice his religion"), his brother Placidus, and several members of his staff; he notably omits any reference to General Godfrey Weitzel, the first commander of occupied Richmond. Weitzel, a Protestant, was himself regarded as imprudently lenient by Lincoln's secretary of war, Edwin Stanton, partly for failing to impose prescribed loyalty prayers "for the President of the United States" on Roman Catholics and other members of liturgical churches in Richmond. Stanton had Weitzel replaced by Ord on April 13.

96. For more on Gache, see appendix II below. Father James Sheeran, who had been hospitalized in Richmond since mid-January, suffering the effects of long field service and imprisonment, also left the Southern capital for good that weekend, immediately following his Easter Mass.

97. Gache, *Frenchman, Chaplain, Rebel*, p. 222.

Father Hubert gave two reasons for his unwillingness to leave the defeated capital. He had friends in Richmond whom he did not want to leave, and he had plans to attend to that required him to stay on. The "friends" very likely included civilian acquaintances as well as still-hospitalized men awaiting transfer home and soldiers who had drifted back to the capital after Appomattox; his erstwhile contacts from the old Confederate elites, including the Semmes family, had all made their escape, but it was characteristic of him to insist on being present to the bitter end with those he was called to serve. Bishop McGill chose Darius Hubert to preach the sermon at High Mass at St. Peter's Cathedral on Easter Sunday morning, April 16, 1865—a sermon on the Resurrection, spiritual balm for a vanquished city.[98] Then, as other clergy swiftly pulled up stakes, he stayed on both to advocate for his men and to ensure continuity in care, especially with the practical challenges of a new administrative regime in Richmond and the emotional adjustment of his "wounded children," as Father Sheeran had called them, to military defeat, until they could return to families and communities in Louisiana.

As for the "plans," that he mentioned but did not divulge to Father Gache, they evidently involved one particular friend, whose mortal remains lay buried in a Pennsylvania churchyard. Once Father Hubert's "parole of honor" was formalized on Good Friday, April 14, before John Coughlin, provost marshal general of the Department of Virginia, he apparently consulted with Federal authorities about retrieving the body of Michael Nolan and getting it home to New Orleans. All such arrangements would have been complex and time-consuming, not only because of other immediate pressing priorities in Richmond itself, complicated by heightened suspicion and intrigue following the assassination of Abraham Lincoln, but also because of damaged roads, railway lines, and infrastructure around the capital and indeed throughout all of the territory that armies had been clashing over violently for four years. The logistics

98. McGill officiated, with three other priests assisting. The city was briefly awash with clergy returning from war-related field service with both armies; most would be gone the next day, never to return.

were daunting: Nolan's remains, once disinterred from Conewago Chapel cemetery in Hanover, near Gettysburg, would need be taken overland to a coastal port, likely New York, and then borne by ship to the Crescent City. It would take a year before the transfer was effected, but the wheels were set in motion before Father Hubert finally left Richmond.

Toward the end of June, "broken down with fatigue," and convinced at last that his work in the former rebel capital was done, the chaplain determined on a final house call:

> I could not leave Richmond without visiting for the last time our great chief, General Robert E. Lee, who had always treated me with so much consideration.[99] The priests of the cathedral expressed a desire to accompany me and to be introduced to the incomparable warrior. Among them was a dear friend of mine, a chaplain of the Army of the Potomac, Rev. Father O'Hagan, S.J. The interview was most pleasant. In leaving the residence of the conquered chief, I asked my friends to express freely what impression the visit had produced upon them. Speaking in the name of all, Father O'Hagan remarked, "I tell you, Father Hubert, had you not introduced us to General Lee we would have taken that gentleman for one of our grand bishops of the Catholic church; we would have fallen upon our knees at his feet and asked him to impart to us his blessing."[100]

99. Darius Hubert returned the consideration in a variety of public ways in the following years. After Lee's statue was erected in New Orleans's Tivoli Circle in 1884 he always paused to salute his old general when he passed by.

100. The anecdote was handwritten by Father Hubert into a scrapbook kept by New Orleans resident Mary A. Heatherton, "My Last Visit to General Robert E. Lee, June, 1865." See *New Orleans Times-Picayune,* August 4, 1901, p. 18. Mary Heatherton's brother, James Nelligan, was the last commander of the First Louisiana. For more on Father Joseph O'Hagan of the Excelsior (Sickles) Brigade, see William R. Eastman, "The Army Chaplain of 1863," in A. Noel Blakeman, ed., *Personal Recollections of the War of the Rebellion . . . 1883–1891,* 4th ser. (New York: Military Order of the Loyal Legion of the United States, 1912), pp. 346–50. O'Hagan, called "a delightful companion and a true man" by the author, was notably deeply attached to his Protestant counterpart in the brigade, Joseph Twichell (later friend and pastor to Mark Twain). In this capacity for warm ecumenical relations he mirrored his "dear friend" Darius Hubert.

After a brief respite at the Jesuit House in Georgetown, Father Hubert went home at last to New Orleans in July 1865, arriving four-and-a-quarter years after departing with the blithe and optimistic men of the First Louisiana Regiment. The South's first chaplain was also the last to return from the war.

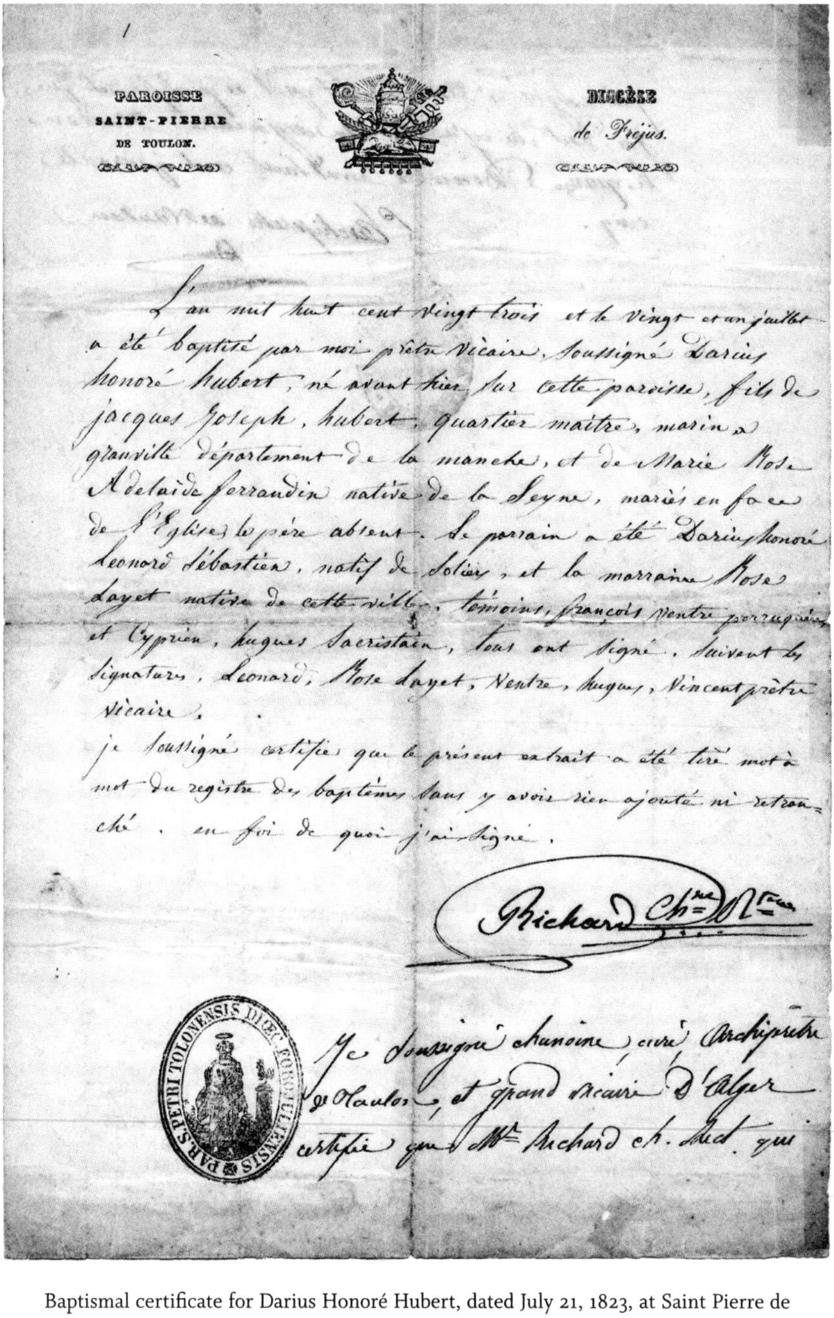
PAROISSE
SAINT-PIERRE
DE TOULON.

DIOCÈSE
de Fréjus.

L'an mil huit cent vingt trois et le vingt et un juillet
a été baptisé par moi prêtre vicaire, soussigné Darius
honoré hubert, né avant hier sur cette paroisse, fils de
jacques Joseph, hubert, quartier maître, marin à
granville département de la manche, et de Marie Rose
Adelaïde ferrandin native de la Seyne, mariés en face
de l'Eglise le père absent. Le parrain a été Darius honoré
Leonard Sébastien, natif de Soliès, et la marraine Rose
Layet native de cette ville, témoins, françois ventre perruquier
et Cyprien, hugues sacristain, tous ont signé. Suivent les
signatures, Leonard, Rose Layet, ventre, hugues, vincent prêtre
vicaire.
je soussigné certifie que le présent extrait a été tiré mot à
mot du registre des baptêmes sans y avoir rien ajouté ni retran-
ché. en foi de quoi j'ai signé.

Richard Ch.ne R.

PAR. S. PETRI TOLONENSIS DIOEC. FOROJULIENSIS

Je soussigné chanoine, curé Archiprêtre
de Toulon, et grand vicaire d'Alger
certifie que Mr Richard ch. Rect. qui

Baptismal certificate for Darius Honoré Hubert, dated July 21, 1823, at Saint Pierre de Toulon parish church in the diocese of Fréjus, France. *Courtesy New Orleans Province Archive, Jesuit Archives & Research Center, St. Louis, Missouri.*

Diabolic caricature of "A Jesuit," published as the frontispiece of the first American edition of the scurrilous *Monita Secreta* (*Secret Instructions of the Jesuits*), 1857. Depictions of Jesuits as seductive religious charlatans were common in mid-nineteenth-century America, as nativist, anti-Catholic propaganda presented an especially sinister view of the Society of Jesus.

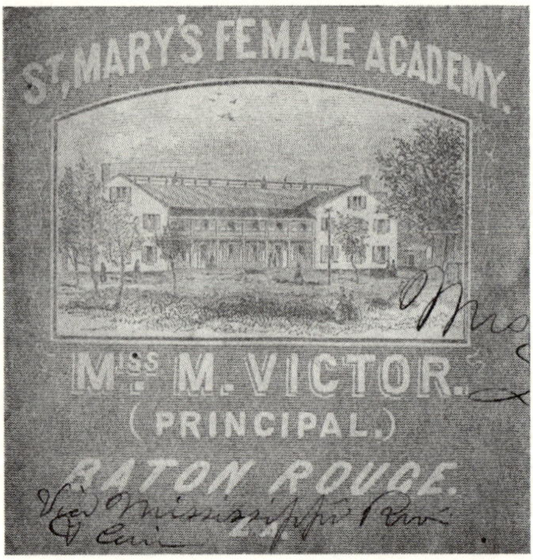

The only extant image of the main campus of the short-lived Jesuit College of St. Peter and St. Paul in Baton Rouge (1849–1855). The college was purchased by Matilda Victor and reopened as St. Mary's Female Academy in 1856; Father Hubert was a teacher and staunch advocate of the school. The image is part of a bookplate, ca. 1859, in a volume of French poetry from the St. Mary's library, "borrowed" during the Battle of Baton Rouge and left in the tent of Union colonel Volney S. Fullam, Seventh Vermont Infantry. *Courtesy Special Collections, LSU Libraries, Baton Rouge.*

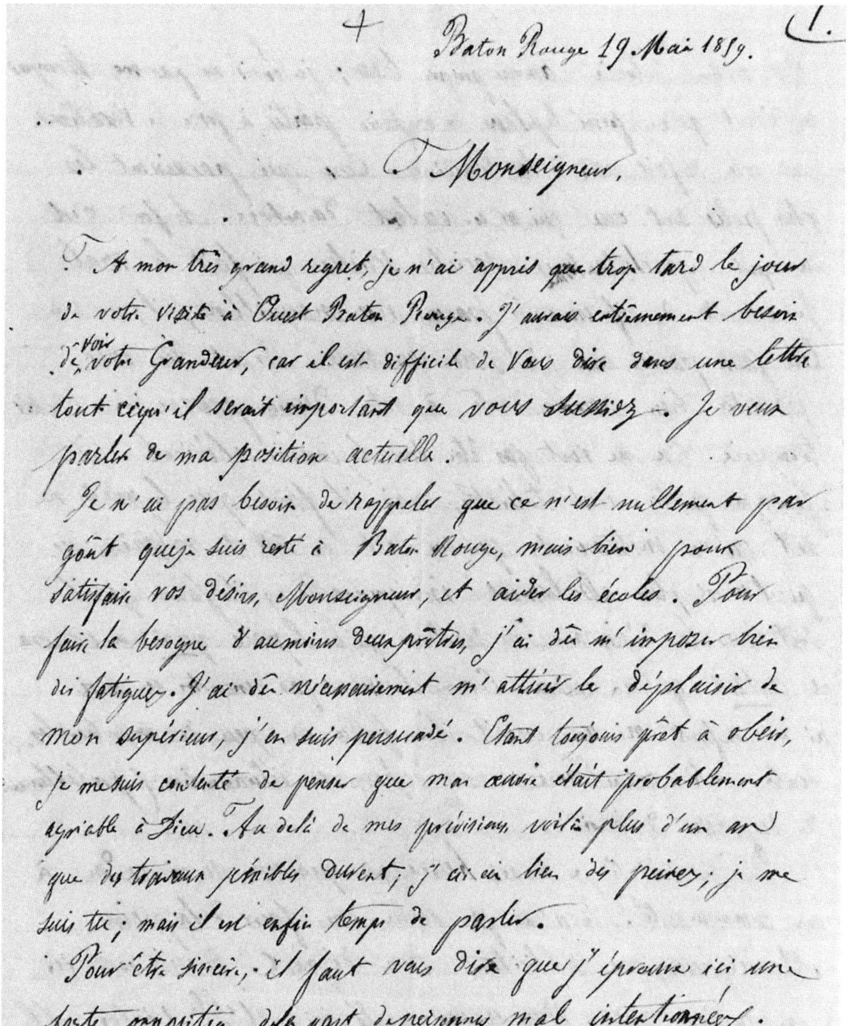

1.

Baton Rouge 19 Mai 1859.

Monseigneur,

A mon très grand regret, je n'ai appris que trop tard le jour de votre visite à Ouest Baton Rouge. J'aurais extrêmement besoin de voir votre Grandeur, car il est difficile de vous dire dans une lettre tout ce qu'il serait important que vous sussiez. Je veux parler de ma position actuelle.

Je n'ai pas besoin de rappeler que ce n'est nullement par goût que je suis resté à Baton Rouge, mais bien pour satisfaire vos désirs, Monseigneur, et aider les écoles. Pour faire la besogne d'au moins deux prêtres, j'ai dû m'imposer bien des fatigues. J'ai dû nécessairement m'attirer le déplaisir de mon supérieur, j'en suis persuadé. Étant toujours prêt à obéir, je me suis contenté de penser que mon œuvre était probablement agréable à Dieu. Au delà de mes prévisions, voilà plus d'un an que des travaux pénibles durent; j'ai eu bien des peines; je me suis tu; mais il est enfin temps de parler.

Pour être sincère, il faut vous dire que j'éprouve ici une forte opposition de la part de personnes mal intentionnées.

First page of a lengthy, stinging letter from Darius Hubert, then parish priest in Baton Rouge, to Archbishop Antoine Blanc, dated May 19, 1859. Father Hubert expresses exasperation with the trustees of his church and anxiety for the fate of St. Mary's Academy, whose mission he strongly supports. *Courtesy Office of Archives and Records, Archdiocese of New Orleans.*

“Confederate Army Chaplains, 1861,” purporting to depict Darius Hubert (First Louisiana Infantry), center; his Jesuit colleague Joseph Prachensky (Third Alabama), right; and Southern Baptist chaplain J. William Jones (Thirteenth Virginia), left. The image, created in 2003, has no photographic precedent, but is based on the description by Father Hippolyte Gache of his fellow Jesuits in an 1861 letter. Father Prachensky, styling himself a major, apparently fancied the sash and plumed officer’s hat of his Alabama regiment; he did not last long in the chaplaincy. Jones, who became a prominent memorialist and Lost Cause exponent after the war, was a whimsical addition on the part of the artist. *Plate no. 808, artist Peter Copeland, “Military Uniforms in America” series, Company of Military Historians. Used with permission.*

Left: Undated *carte de visite* portrait of Darius Hubert, likely taken within a few years of his return to New Orleans after the war. This rare image, by Samuel Anderson of New Orleans (whose photographic partnerships with Samuel T. Blessing and Austin A. Turner had dissolved by 1865), shows a somewhat disheveled and weary priest, with facial scarring and glasses askew. From a personal photo album of the Roman family, prominent antebellum Catholic Creoles. Colonel Alfred Roman (Eighteenth Louisiana) was *aide de camp* to General P. G. T. Beauregard for the last two years of the Civil War and his first biographer. *Courtesy Carroll Delery.*

Right: Undated "cabinet card" portrait of Darius Hubert (ca. 1885) by New Orleans photographer Charles T. Yenni (1860–1909). A well-known local photographer and founder of the New Orleans Photographers Association, Yenni was for many years the manager of the Souby Art Gallery on Canal Street. *Courtesy New Orleans Province Archive, Jesuit Archives & Research Center, St. Louis, Missouri.*

Savannah "Good Samaritan" medal, bronze copy (obverse). In 1877, the Savannah Benevolent Association commissioned gold medals to thank and honor eighteen individuals who assisted during a devastating yellow fever epidemic the previous year. Darius Hubert was one of the recipients, having spent the entire fever season in Savannah, as he had during past outbreaks in other fever-stricken cities. The medal, one of his few cherished material possessions, appears in several portraits. None of the original gold medals is believed to survive. *Anonymous, private collection.*

Statue of Irish-born entrepreneur and philanthropist Margaret Gaffney Haughery in the Lower Garden District of New Orleans. The Carrera marble monument with a one-word inscription, "Margaret," was unveiled in 1884, shortly after the death of the city's beloved "friend of orphans" in 1882, the first publicly erected statue of a woman in the United States. Margaret's passion for the poor, especially the city's orphaned children, was supported and honored by her friend and spiritual director, Father Darius Hubert. *Author's collection.*

Oil portrait of Darius Hubert by noted New Orleans artist Alexandre Alaux, ca. 1885. This large formal oil on canvas painting was apparently commissioned by the Association of the Army of Northern Virginia. It was displayed in the veterans' meeting hall on Union Street from 1886 until 1891, and then moved to the newly opened Confederate Memorial Hall, where it enjoyed pride of place near portraits of Stonewall Jackson and Robert E. Lee. Fifteen years later, a local Confederate Ladies Memorial Association, responding to a request from the Museum of the Confederacy in Richmond, Virginia, sent it there, to be featured in the "Louisiana Room." *Courtesy Museum of the Confederacy, American Civil War Museum, Richmond, Virginia.*

Ca. 1895 "pastel portrait" of Darius Hubert, attributed to Louise Riera. The provenance of this image is not well documented, and its description is somewhat confusing. There are several newspaper references to a "crayon" or "pastel" portrait of the city's famous chaplain a few years after his death in 1893. In 1896, a "fine crayon portrait of the late Father Darius Hubert, S.J.," was donated to a fundraiser in New Orleans by a Mr. J. C. Norton. This is likely also the "handsome portrait of Rev. Darius Hubert, S.J." that was given to the Camp Nicholls Soldiers Home in 1905 and that hung there until the home closed in 1940. This large framed image on glass is photo-based rather than life-drawn, possibly an opaltype; it clearly derives from the photo portrait in Father Albert Biever's memorial volume (see frontispiece to this volume). While the original photographer is unnamed, the likeliest suspect would seem to be Louis Robira, a New Orleans photographer who specialized in studio portraits with props such as appear here, classical columns and a table on which the subject rests his hand. Enlargement (up to life size) and hand coloring of photos was very popular in this period, though a portrait on this scale is unusual. If the attribution to "Louise Riera" is accurate, and not a mistaken reference to Louis Robira, then a young New Orleans woman by that name (b. 1869) may have been the colorist. *Courtesy Confederate Memorial Hall, New Orleans.*

Gravesite of Darius Hubert, Historic Jesuit Cemetery, Spring Hill College, Mobile, Alabama. Though Father Hubert died in Macon, Georgia, his remains were expected, after temporary interment at the cemetery of St. Stanislaus Novitiate, to be returned to New Orleans where his memory could be conspicuously honored. But his remains stayed in Georgia until a fire destroyed St. Stanislaus in 1920, at which point they were moved to Spring Hill College, the site of Hubert's first brief residence in America. His name is modestly marked on one of six large Celtic crosses that cover the burial site of two dozen Jesuits. *Author's collection.*

FIVE

New Orleans 1865–1891

On July 19, 1866, a brief notice appeared in the *New Orleans Times-Picayune*, announcing that "the remains of that gallant soldier Col. M. Nolan, of the 1st Louisiana Volunteers, who was killed at Gettysburg, are now on their way to this city for final interment" and were expected to arrive in about ten days. A funeral took place a month later, August 19, at St. Joseph Church, with Fathers Sheeran and Hubert presiding. Darius Hubert, who through long acquaintance was "well qualified to speak of [Nolan's] virtues," gave the homily in tribute. He then accompanied fellow clergy; Nolan's widow, Ellen; an honor guard of Louisiana veterans; and a host of mourners—the cortege was reportedly more than two miles long—to St. Patrick's Cemetery, where he discharged at last his final pastoral duties to his fallen friend.[1]

This is the first published mention of Darius Hubert following his return to New Orleans, and the first occasion in which he was publicly associated with the remembrance of Confederate dead. In the 1870s and 1880s his voice would be among the most frequently and memorably heard on such occasions, but for now he maintained a low profile as he resumed many of his former responsibilities, quietly stepping back into the traces as teacher and pastor, confessor, and spiritual director—a familiar apostolate in a city that had changed forever during his absence.

1. *The New Orleans Crescent,* August 20, 1866, p. 1. The funeral was also front-page news in the *Times-Picayune* that day.

New Orleans had been occupied by Federal personnel since April 25, 1862, when a fleet of Union vessels under Flag Officer David Farragut sailed largely unimpeded into the Crescent City, hoisted the Stars and Stripes, and established martial law. The initial, draconian regime of Union General Benjamin Butler (known ever after as "Beast" Butler by locals), lasted until December of that year.[2] Butler's replacement, General Nathaniel Banks, leaving behind an ignominious record of military defeat at the hands of Stonewall Jackson in the eastern theater, relished his new role as administrator of a conquered territory. He introduced a more conciliatory tone, quietly reversed some of Butler's unpopular regulations, freed many civilian prisoners, established a labor plan for former slaves, and returned some of the property arbitrarily seized under his predecessor's "carnival of confiscations and auction sales."[3] Meanwhile, the general's wife, Mary Palmer Banks, took it upon herself to inject a note of gaiety into local proceedings, especially through lavish parties for Unionists. In 1864, under President Lincoln's "10 percent plan," Banks reopened the courts, appointed magistrates, and restored many of the trappings of civil society, including state elections—an early experiment in Reconstruction intended by Lincoln to encourage the South to re-

2. Infamous not only for his General Order 28, against the "women of New Orleans," which drew howls from even the *London Times*, but for confiscation of personal property and censoring or shutting down local press outlets, Butler also closed churches, exiled clergy, and shuttered the Free Market, a longstanding charitable institution, through which private citizens aided the city's poor. The market, which provided "no questions asked" food distribution to the needy, was replaced by Butler's United States Relief Commission, which taxed known supporters of the rebellion and used the funds to aid the "deserving poor" according to their political loyalties. See Marion Southwood, *"Beauty and Booty": The Watchword of New Orleans* (New York: M. Doolady, 1867), pp. 77–97. See also the doctoral dissertation of Elizabeth Joan Doyle, "Civilian Life in Occupied New Orleans, 1862–1865," Louisiana State University, 1955, chap. 8.

3. The phrase is that of Grace King, whose family fled New Orleans for Iberville Parish during Butler's tenure. Her vivid recollections of wartime and Reconstruction are contained in her *Memories of a Southern Woman of Letters* (New York: Macmillan, 1932) and *New Orleans: The Place and the People* (New York: Macmillan, 1895). This quotation comes from the latter memoir (p. 154). See also Doyle, "Civilian Life in Occupied New Orleans," chap. 11.

unite peaceably and quickly with the Union. Governor Michael Hahn, a German-born moderate Unionist, who styled himself a "friend of colored people" but emphatically opposed black suffrage, was elected Governor in February 22.[4] The *New York Times* described his inauguration as an "ever-to-be-remembered day—the day that witnessed Louisiana reushered into the Union, a free State, as it were, born anew."[5]

It was to this "newborn" state that ex-patriot Confederate loyalists who had fled occupation and weary, shell-shocked soldiers returned after Appomattox. The city of New Orleans had been spared the physical destruction of Richmond, Atlanta, Vicksburg, or Columbia—its port was busy and its infrastructure largely untouched by shell or cannon—and yet nothing about it was familiar. Black soldiers, policemen, and officials, along with their Union sponsors, were everywhere conspicuous. Streets and shops swelled with ex-Union combatants, Northern entrepreneurs, speculators, fortune seekers, immigrants, and freedmen and women seeking the fruits of emancipation. The demographic makeup of the city had been entirely refashioned, the old social hierarchies annihilated. Afro-Creoles and free people of color saw their own privilege eroding, their unique status diminished under the new rules of black and white social stratification; in the eyes of the law they would come increasingly to share the standing of ex-slaves.

Public schools were overseen by teachers chosen by such prominent Unionists as John Butler Carter and Anthony Dostie, who had introduced national songs and rituals to the classroom, imposed the reading of patriotic texts and celebration of such heroes as "Butler, the indomitable," and "Banks . . . our leader, gallant and strong," and strictly forbade children

4. Hahn proposed anti-vagrancy laws and a "new labor system" for emancipated slaves that were virtually identical to what came to be called the black codes; if such a system could not be enacted, he argued, citing Lincoln's own earlier proposal, freedmen should be resettled in "colonies abroad." See Frank J. Wetta, *The Louisiana Scalawags: Politics, Race, and Terrorism During the Civil War and Reconstruction* (Baton Rouge: Louisiana State University Press, 2013), pp. 70–71. By 1866, the politically adroit and ambitious Hahn would be singing an entirely different, Radical tune (Wetta, *The Louisiana Scalawags*, p. 72).

5. *New York Times*, March 20, 1864, p. 2.

to express any Southern sympathies.[6] At one point, over half of the city's students boycotted classes to protest this heavy-handed indoctrination; Dostie summarily expelled three hundred of those who persisted in their "disobedience."[7] Private schools, less easy to control, continued to be havens of Confederate sympathy and allegiance, despite Banks authorizing clandestine "special police" to make unannounced visits; whenever the monitors turned up any hints of "disloyalty," including even hand-drawn Confederate flags or symbols in students' notebooks, they exacted exorbitant fines from teachers and overseers.[8]

Most of the city's churches had also been "reformed" by activists like Dostie, who ensured that Union loyalists replaced "seditionists" on boards of trustees and Northern men filled the pulpits, preaching a new gospel of solidarity with the Union and leading prayers for the "legitimate authorities" in Washington.[9]

6. Dostie, born in Saratoga, New York, had come to New Orleans in the antebellum heyday to practice dentistry; a prominent Mason, he hobnobbed with members of the city's elite class. His Unionist loyalties prompted him to flee the city when war was declared, but he returned during Federal occupation and became a notorious Radical activist until being mortally wounded in the 1866 Mechanics Institute riot. The only biography is that of his daughter, Emily Hazen Reed, *Life of A. P. Dostie; or The Conflict in New Orleans* (New York: Wm. P. Tomlinson, 1868).

7. Wetta, *Louisiana Scalawags*, p. 64. Dostie's zealous and increasingly "fanatical" efforts to refashion all aspects of New Orleans culture, including even entertainments such as the theater, engendered extreme hostility. It is not unlikely that some among the very students he expelled took their grim revenge on July 30, 1866, where it was widely reported that boys as young as ten and eleven were on the streets, wielding weapons.

8. The Jesuit College, then under the direction of Father Anthony Jourdan, was among the institutions on which a fine was imposed; Catholic schools in the city almost uniformly opposed administrative demands to enforce Union patriotism among their students. A detailed overview of the educational situation in wartime New Orleans under Federal authority may be found in Doyle, "Civilian Life in Occupied New Orleans," chap. 5.

9. Several prominent and popular preachers left New Orleans before Farragut's ships arrived; still others, including Episcopalian pastors William T. Leacock, Charles Goodrich, and John Fulton, were formally deported and imprisoned by Butler for failing to adhere to what he called "loyal Christianity." In a city whose clergy (including the prominent Jewish leader Rabbi James K. Gutheim) had been almost unanimous in support of the Southern

Adjusting to this new reality, where the facade was recognizable but the substance of things was unfamiliar, was far from easy for returnees. And despite the bustle, economic prospects for former rebels were uncertain at best. Severely wounded veterans faced an especially bleak existence; unemployment and indigence would, for many, define the remainder of their lives. Those whose families had been reduced to poverty were dependent for self-maintenance on benevolent societies and churches, who had already a crushing burden of care for war widows and orphaned children;[10] it would be nearly two decades before a Soldiers' Home was built in New Orleans, allowing veterans a measure of comfort, security, and comradeship.[11] But even ex-soldiers and civilians who were hale in body and mind found homecoming more disquieting that they had anticipated: "Everything seems unsettled, & a restless uneasy spirit pervades every quarter. . . . all creation seems turned upside down."[12] For all that, local chronicler Grace King would later reflect, the first year after surrender "was a year of simple existence and endurance of the new condition of things . . . a year of stupor and, as it seems now, of grace."[13]

By the summer of 1866, however, the stupor was ending and grace dissipating, as a sense of thwarted entitlement on all sides became more ominously dangerous. Governor Hahn had resigned the governorship to

---

cause, this imposed "conversion" was drastic and unpopular. It also had ludicrous elements: whereas Butler and Banks forbade observance of days of prayer and fasting, or thanksgiving, announced by Jefferson Davis, they demanded faithful observance of such days when pronounced by Lincoln.

10. An example of the plight of Confederate widows may be seen in the case of Ellen Nolan. Apparently childless, she did not remarry, and seems never to have climbed out of poverty after the death of her husband (Col. Michael Nolan) at Gettysburg. She was (among hundreds of others) cited for default of taxes in 1870, 1872, 1874, 1876, and 1878. Eventually, the city sold her property at a sheriff's sale in August 23, 1879.

11. For a history of Southern veterans' homes, see R. B. Rosenburg, *Living Monuments: Confederate Soldiers' Homes in the New South* (Chapel Hill: University of North Carolina Press, 1993). The New Orleans facility, Camp Nicholls, is discussed below.

12. William Woodson King, in a letter to his wife, cited in Robert Bush, *Grace King: A Southern Destiny* (Baton Rouge: Louisiana State University Press, 1983), p. 14.

13. King, *New Orleans*, p. 156.

seek national office as a US senator.[14] His replacement, James Madison Wells, an aristocratic plantation owner who had opposed secession and the Confederacy was thought a safe bet by local Unionists. But once in office, for reasons of political expediency, Wells forged an alliance with the white planter class, much to the delight of conservatives and ex-Confederates who also won a significant legislative majority in the same election that brought Wells to power.

For most white New Orleanians the continuing presence in the city of Northern interlopers was a constant flashpoint; they had lost the war and were coming to terms with emancipation, but they had no love for self-righteous and meddlesome Yankees in their city and wanted them to go home.[15] They were also intent on reasserting control over newly emancipated blacks, who made up close to half of the city's adult population, many of whom were now rootless and unemployed. In a special session of the new legislature in November 1865, vagrancy laws were passed, by which freedmen who could not immediately furnish for themselves suitable housing and a visible means of support would be "hired out, by public advertisement, to a local citizen."

The fuse was lit. Impatient with the pace and character of Reconstruction under the relatively lenient policies of President Andrew Johnson, furious about Wells's betrayal and the return to civic prominence of unreconstructed rebels (including John T. Monroe, New Orleans's antebellum mayor, now reinstated), as well as the legislature's imposition of discriminatory laws on freedmen, a Radical coalition, including black leaders, now openly pushed the agenda of immediate black suffrage. Moderate Unionists, alarmed at the prospect of alienating white residents and igniting a race war, urged caution, but were shouted down. There was suddenly no middle ground, no capacity for negotiation or compromise, no road to gradual and peaceful conciliation of racial and social grievance. Moderation, the Radicals argued, had only emboldened the old

14. Though elected, he was not seated by Congress, which regarded the state as insufficiently reconstructed.

15. Nystrom, *New Orleans after the Civil War,* p. 61.

white ruling class to believe they could restore antebellum conditions; they needed be reminded, harshly if necessary, that military defeat of the Confederacy mandated a cultural revolution in the South. Wells, having been outmaneuvered, now decided that black suffrage was his personal ticket to political survival, and the only means of achieving "satisfactory political results" in Louisiana. And the formerly equivocating Hahn now attacked the very codes he had once authorized and asserted his desire for immediate franchise and empowerment of black men, declaring provocatively that "I would rather every office in the State was in the hands of colored men than in the hands of unrepentant rebels."[16]

The proposed means of initiating this revolution was to reconvene, on tenuous legal grounds,[17] the Constitutional Convention of 1864, which had been held under Banks's military authority, and through its delegates to override the current legislative status quo. Specifically, the plan was to create a new Louisiana constitution that would strike down the black codes, disenfranchise former Confederates, and provide universal suffrage for black men. For those who had been duly elected, and their supporters, this idea seemed the height of lawless fanaticism; it was, in effect, a proposed coup d'état. That Federal intruders intended to strip local men, especially veterans, of the vote and to give the franchise "indiscriminately" to former slaves would not only upend the natural order, as they saw it, but guarantee illegitimate Republican control of Louisiana in perpetuity.[18]

16. Reed, *Life of A.P. Dostie*, p. 294.

17. For details regarding the claims and counterclaims over legality of reconvening the 1864 convention, see James G. Hollandsworth Jr., *An Absolute Massacre: The New Orleans Race Riot of July 30, 1866* (Baton Rouge: Louisiana State University Press, 2001), pp. 36–42. Hollandsworth's is an even-handed, thoroughly documented account of the context, the event, and the aftermath.

18. Apprehension about "negro supremacy" in the former slave states was regularly featured in the Southern press, but it was also a subject of some anxiety north of the Mason-Dixon line. Even the most ardent supporters of Radical Reconstruction resisted black enfranchisement in their own districts, where the percentage of African Americans was miniscule. Voters in Ohio, Kansas, New Jersey, Wisconsin, Connecticut, Minnesota, Michigan, Pennsylvania, and New York all rejected black suffrage initiatives in their states between 1865 and 1868. Nor did they wish freedmen to migrate north. For many, making

Not everyone on the Union or Republican side was sanguine about the plan. Even the unpopular military commander of the Fifth Military District (Louisiana and Texas) Major General Philip Sheridan denounced the leaders as "political agitators and revolutionary men," and clearly foresaw that civic peace was in jeopardy if they forced the suffrage issue by this means. Several prominent members of the original convention were staunchly and publicly opposed to its being reconvened, refused to cooperate, and predicted a bloodbath if organizers pressed ahead. Yet press ahead they did, without the legally mandated presence of the convention president and with only thirty-nine of the original ninety delegates.

On Friday evening, July 27, 1866, following an impromptu political rally in support of the convention that was scheduled to meet on Monday, A.P. Dostie made an impassioned speech to a large crowd of supporters on the steps of New Orleans City Hall; just how incendiary his speech was would become the subject of much contradictory testimony in later weeks. Several witnesses swore that he urged his hearers to return armed, prepared to seize what had long been denied them and, if necessary, to kill any who interfered.[19] The speech was followed by a torch-lit parade of at least five thousand through city streets: in the words of an admiring supporter, "the steady march and stalwart forms of those composing the procession afforded unmistakable evidence that they had battled for the Union and were determined, if necessary, to fight again for the right of suffrage."[20] Many in the white population regarded the speeches as reckless at best and, at worst, a calculated incitement of race war, encouraging former slaves to turn violently on their erstwhile masters. Local newspapers fueled the apprehension; the city braced for what many regarded as an illegal convention and for the inevitable hostile clash of those who

---

blacks political actors in the South was a means of discouraging them from moving *en masse* out of the former Confederate states. See, for example, Philip Leigh, *Southern Reconstruction* (Yardley, PA: Westholme, 2017), p. 44.

19. The editors of the *Times-Picayune* and *Times-Democrat* dailies both claimed that Dostie's words were intemperate, inflammatory, and a clear provocation to violence.

20. Reed, *Life of A.P. Dostie*, p. 289.

supported and opposed it. Police and firemen were summoned to stations. Military troops were put on alert, but remained at Jackson Barracks outside the city with explicit orders from Sheridan not to give the impression of supporting the convention, and not to intervene "unless necessary."[21]

On Monday, July 30, two weeks before Michael Nolan's funeral, and only a block from where Darius Hubert lived, taught, and served as pastor, New Orleans exploded. "The students in the . . . Jesuits' College, who were just beginning, with the happy ease of youth, to forget their childhood horrors of war," were at their desks.[22] It was a sweltering day, and many windows were open. Officials had urged citizens to avoid the area around the convention, and shops were closed along Canal Street, the usually bustling corridors filled only with idlers and curiosity seekers. Toward midday, the sounds of drums, fife, and singing could be heard first at a distance and then swelling steadily, as a procession of black men, including a nucleus of former US Colored Troops—the Louisiana Native Guard—marched west from the Third District along Dauphin, Conti, Burgundy, and Canal streets toward the Mechanics Institute at the intersection of Canal and Dryades, the temporary state capital where the convention was meeting. They encountered hecklers along the way, and a brief skirmish was broken up by police; upon reaching the institute, within easy sight of classrooms in the Jesuit College on Baronne Street, they were joined by other spectators and convention supporters. There, as a black flag-bearer waved his banner on the steps of the institute, taunts and threats escalated, shots were fired, bricks thrown, and arrests made; still, for a time, the situation remained within check. Fearing a violent confrontation, several members of the convention asked the crowd to

21. Sheridan himself was in Texas at the time of the convention, leaving General Absalom Baird in charge of the volatile situation. No fan of the convention or many of its leaders, Sheridan was perhaps grateful not to have to deal with the day's events; he returned for the mopping up and formal reporting.

22. King, *New Orleans*, p. 157. King mentions the riot in both of her memoirs, noting in both instances the students at the Jesuit College being reluctant witnesses to the chaos and bloodshed.

disperse peacefully, but they refused to leave. A little after one o'clock, things took a deadly turn, with both sides exchanging pistol fire.[23]

Alerted to the eruption of hostilities, firemen as well as police converged on the streets below the Jesuit school and surrounded the institute. Terrorized marchers, most of whom were unarmed, attempted to flee a maelstrom of violence which soon encompassed the convention hall and nearby streets; some delegates managed to escape; others hid; still others were beaten, stabbed, or shot, as were supporters and even uninvolved parties. From inside the Jesuit College, sights and sounds of the unfolding chaos were unavoidable: "Those who ventured to look out saw a wild, infuriated mob in the streets, and heard the cries of a hell in the great ugly building in front, from which negroes trying to escape were climbing out of windows, and over the roof, dropping down wounded, bleeding, dead, in the surrounding court." It was a day that the children, "trembling and anguished," would never forget.[24]

By midafternoon, the bloodshed had ceased but bodies still remained in the streets, including nine at the intersection of Baronne and Common, just outside the doors of the college. Of the more than thirty dead, almost all were black; scores more were wounded, some mortally, and several hundred, black and white, were in jail.[25] Though termed a riot, it devolved quickly into so raw and murderous an affair that it prompted an imposition of martial law and the ouster of both mayor and police chief. Nationally, the events of July 30 in New Orleans, widely publicized in the daily press and in popular journals such as *Harper's Weekly*, induced northern voters to send a super-majority of Radical Republicans to the US Congress in late 1866; the Lincoln/Johnson approach to Reconstruction was dead.[26]

23. A writer for the *Times-Picayune* observed, in the next day's story: "It is useless to endeavor to trace the origins of the [riot]. It had been brewing during the morning and the toss of a feather would have as effectually originated the strife as anything else" (July 31, 1866, p. 1). Hollandsworth holds one of the chief provocateurs, both along the march route and again in front of the Mechanics Institute, to have been a rowdy and intractable white boy.

24. King, *New Orleans*, p. 157.

25. A list of casualties and arrests was reported in the *Times-Picayune*, July 31, 1866.

26. A similarly violent riot had occurred three months earlier in Memphis, May 1–3.

Whatever his private thoughts about the events of that day, Darius Hubert never addressed them publicly. This was perhaps the first major test of his sense of his postwar vocation in a tense and fractured city—to take sides politically or to focus his energies on his priestly obligations and to bend thought, word, and deed toward healing and reconciliation.[27] He chose the latter. In doing so, he chose differently from some of his coreligionists in New Orleans, and from another Catholic priest and sometime chaplain prominently associated with Confederate aspiration and memorial, Father Abram Ryan. Ryan never lived in New Orleans, but he had a significant presence in the city after the Civil War, through his editing of the New Orleans–based *Morning Star and Catholic Messenger* (1872–75), which he used as a mouthpiece for his virulently anti-Northern views and his opposition to racial integration. Ryan inveighed against local Confederate hero (and close friend of Darius Hubert) P. G. T. Beauregard, who in postwar New Orleans promoted an end to carpetbag rule through acceptance of social and political equality for blacks.[28] Ryan also identified openly with the White League, for whose bloody uprising on September 14, 1874, he offered a lengthy, fiery, and full-throated defense at New Orleans's Exposition Hall two months later.[29]

27. Several of the severely wounded among the convention delegates, including Dostie, were taken to the Daughters of Charity hospital, Hotel Dieu, where Father Hubert made regular rounds.

28. For Beauregard's pragmatic advocacy for black civil and political rights in Louisiana, see T. Harry Williams, *P. G. T. Beauregard: Napoleon in Gray* (Baton Rouge: Louisiana State University Press, 1955), pp. 269–72. (Beauregard's first biographer, Colonel Alfred Roman, who served as the general's *aide de camp* during the war, was also close to Darius Hubert; the only known copy of a photograph of the priest taken shortly after his war chaplaincy was recently discovered in a nineteenth-century Roman family photo album. It is published here for the first time. Beauregard left instructions that his funeral should be conducted, if possible, by Darius Hubert. At the time of the general's last illness, however, Hubert was himself in Macon, Georgia, recovering from a stroke. He sent a letter expressing his deep regret at being unable to participate in the obsequies (*New Orleans Times-Democrat*, June 15, 1893, p. 3). The two men died within a few months of each other.

29. Printed on the front page of the *New Orleans Bulletin*, November 20, 1874. The speech was billed as a fundraiser for St. John the Baptist Catholic Church, whose pastor, Fr. Jeremiah Moynihan, had undertaken an imprudent campaign to build an impressive

"I have often been blamed for speaking on political subjects," he intoned, before adding the crowd-pleasing line, "I don't care a straw who blames me, of course." As he did frequently, Ryan intimated more personal familiarity with Confederate service than was warranted, drawing on the patriotic sentiment of those in the hall to make his case against the interminable interference of damned Yankees. And though he was sometimes coy in his discussions of race, his supremacist bona fides were not in doubt that evening: "If there ever comes up a question in the world as between race and race, and the interests of one race against the instincts of another, common human interest tells me, and as religion does not prohibit me, I stand by the white race."[30]

Darius Hubert was no friend of such rhetoric or of political vigilantism. His unwavering clarity about his priestly vocation presents a striking foil to Ryan's often reckless political posturing. Having catechized and instructed black children, both slave and free, and preached and prayed with people of color throughout his entire priestly life, he showed no tendency to "stand by" one race over another. The Jesuit church where he was pastor and eventual rector, like most other New Orleans Catholic churches, had long been a mixed-race worship environment, in which "lips of every shade, by hundreds press with devout kisses the same crucifixes, and fingers of as great variety in color, are dipped in the holy water."[31] Though

---

new edifice. Ryan hinted in his lecture, perhaps facetiously, that Moynihan was not only "in sympathy with the White League," but "in high membership of the same." Despite his efforts on Moynihan's behalf (Ryan had also been homilist when the church was dedicated in January 1872), the church fell into insolvency and Moynihan was forced to resign. For his part, Ryan's intemperate politicking cost him the confidence of yet another bishop and, shortly, the editorship of the *Morning Star and Catholic Messenger.*

30. See also his frankly racist editorial in the *Banner of the South,* in which he counts himself "proud and happy" to align himself "to the last throb of [his] heart" with those who believe "that it is the right of the white man to alone rule this country" (April 4, 1869). For discussion of Ryan's identification with the Confederacy in relation to that of Father Hubert, see Katherine Jeffrey, "The Contrasting Legacies of Confederate Priests Abram Ryan and Darius Hubert, S.J.," *U.S. Catholic Historian* 37.1 (Winter 2019): 1–22.

31. The words are those of an astonished Methodist activist who visited New Orleans in 1874 (cited in Bennett, *Religion and the Rise of Jim Crow in New Orleans,* p. 136). In many local

Father Hubert likely shared the apprehension of many in New Orleans that unlettered freedmen could become the "victims of demagogues" and easily manipulated by their ostensible political benefactors,[32] his focus was on the obligations of practical charity, and spiritual rather than political reconstruction. His friendships, consistent with his sense of religious obligation, crossed color lines as well as lines of creed and party.[33]

As fully as he had devoted himself, as chaplain, to the Confederacy, he now as fully accepted that the failure of Confederate aspirations had been divinely ordained. This permitted him not only to honor conscientiously the loyalty oath he had taken in Richmond but also to retain some detachment from the personal feuds that divided erstwhile comrades over their conflicting interpretations of the war; his warm personal friendship with Beauregard did not intrude on his affection and public honor for Beauregard's "political enemy" Jefferson Davis.[34]

He continued in active ministry to many ex-soldiers and former officers who sought his counsel and ongoing spiritual direction, as well as his benediction upon their weddings and their children's baptisms as they rebuilt their lives. But his energies were also devoted to his students at the Jesuit College, where he taught rhetoric and humanities, to Jesuit

---

Catholic churches during antebellum years half the pews were reserved for free blacks, half for whites; small pews in the aisles were reserved for slaves (Baudier, *The Catholic Church in Louisiana*, p. 365.) As Bennett points out, New Orleans Catholicism was extraordinary in this way; as a result, the push for racially distinct Catholic worship environments came to the Crescent City more slowly than elsewhere.

32. Hubert's friend, the Presbyterian divine Rev. Thomas Markham, in a letter to his mother in 1869, mentions an event at the Mechanics Institute, "noted as the scene of the July riot in 1866, when so many poor negroes fell victim to the delusion and misleading of their false friends" ("The Markham Letters," ed. Frances Sleeper Dossett Swann [1987], an unpublished retrospective, p. 126.) I am indebted to Markham Dossett of Waco, Texas, for kindly lending to me this volume along with "Portrait of a Southern Preacher: Excerpts from Writings of Thomas Railey Markham (1828–1894)," likewise edited by Frances Swann (1978).

33. *New Orleans Times-Democrat*, June 22, 1893, p. 3.

34. Father Hubert was likely among those who encouraged Beauregard's participation in the Davis funeral in 1889. The former general firmly declined: "I cannot pretend I am sorry he is gone. I am no hypocrite" (cited in Williams, *Napoleon in Gray*, p. 318).

novices under his tutelage, and to his congregants in the Church of the Immaculate Conception. His formal duties as preacher, confessor, and catechist extended also to frequent spiritual instruction of children, for whom he had an acutely tender affection. When a social editor from one of the local papers dropped in unannounced to the Jesuit Church to converse with him, she found him engaged in teaching a large group of youngsters—a "dear, courtly man, bending as a father might to the listening faces of his children."[35] He was often in demand for retreats and catechetical instruction outside the immediate bounds of his own parish and city; in the summer of 1868, he provided a week of "indefatigable" religious instruction to a group of thirty-four boys and thirty-six girls, both black and white, at Our Lady of the Gulf in Bay St. Louis, Mississippi—preparing them for their first communion. At the end of the week, in a church "crowded to the galleries," Father Hubert was "directing the young communicants, instructing them and praying with them . . . appealing to mind and heart in terms suitable to their capacity.[36] Such events played out every year, in his home church and others in small towns along the Louisiana and Mississippi coastline.

Beyond the walls of the church, he was a tireless advocate for care to widows and orphans, the homeless and destitute, persons of all stations and all races. The name of Darius Hubert is invariably linked to fundraisers for the city's myriad charitable organizations: orphanages, asylums, and hospitals, many of which were run by Catholic orders.[37] As assiduously as he had tended to the sick and dying on battlefields and in Richmond, he was conspicuous in errands of mercy in the remaining decades of his life. It was he who came when a young prostitute was shot by a jealous lover and lay dying in a squalid hotel room. Roused from sleep

35. *New Orleans Times-Democrat*, March 20, 1881, p. 4.

36. *Morning Star and Catholic Messenger*, August 23, 1868, p. 7.

37. Both Charity Hospital (established in 1736 as L'Hôpital des Pauvres de la Charité) and Hotel Dieu (founded in 1859) were staffed by Daughters of Charity. A useful overview of benevolent societies and institutions in postwar New Orleans can be found in William Head Coleman, *Historical Sketch Book and Guide to New Orleans* (New York: Will H. Coleman, 1885).

at 2 a.m. by one of her acquaintances, he hurried to her side to shrive her and prepare her for death.[38]

In 1876, a different kind of mercy errand took him to Savannah, Georgia. The city had endured unremitting rain through the spring and early summer months, with eighteen inches falling in a two-week period in June. A portion of the city flooded, overwhelming the primitive and poorly managed sanitation system, creating ideal conditions for the spread of disease. By late summer, as temperatures reached the upper 90s, cases of what was initially called "intermittent fever" became suddenly more frequent and more severe, causing widespread panic in the city. Before public officials dared acknowledge it, yellow fever was taking its grim toll—as inexorable and inexplicable as previous plagues. Among its early victims were Father Edward Cafferty of St. Patrick's Church, who survived, and Father J. B. Langlois, a visiting priest at St. John the Baptist Catholic Cathedral, who did not. By mid-September, Savannah was semi-deserted; many who had the means had fled. Businesses were shuttered; laborers had no work and were soon destitute. The city became "a vast hospital."[39] The Savannah Benevolent Association, formed during a previous devastating visitation of yellow fever on the city in 1854, advertised widely for food, money, and medical assistance.[40] Captain John F.

38. The story of Katie Conlan's murder created a sensation locally, not least because the assailant was a handsome, well-regarded police officer (*New Orleans Times-Democrat*, October 6, 1883, p. 3).

39. *Columbus Enquirer*, September 19, 1876. Savannah's population was about 30,000 in 1876, with 16,000 whites and 14,000 blacks; during the epidemic the proportion shifted considerably, as many affluent whites left their households in the care of black caregivers and servants. It was widely believed at the time that persons of African descent enjoyed "racial immunity" or resistance to yellow fever.

40. In an essay for Northern readers, a former Savannah resident explained: "The disease comes on suddenly and almost invariably in the night. . . . The symptoms are intense pain in the head, back, and limbs, and high fever, which lasts twelve hours. At the end of that time the patient is ready either for his cook or his coffin. If the fever subsides without the black vomit appearing, two or three weeks of careful nursing will make him well. A repulse is always fatal. After the black vomit supervenes recovery is rare" (*Democrat and Weekly Sentinel* [Burlington, VT], October 21, 1876, p. 4).

Wheaton, former Confederate officer, three-time mayor of Savannah, and president of the Benevolent Association, organized the relief effort.

Local doctors were soon taxed almost beyond endurance. Dr. Louis A. Falligant reported making eighty house calls per day in the second week of September, ninety the third week, and one hundred the fourth week.[41] Darius Hubert was one of eighteen "good Samaritans" who came to Savannah to help in the harrowing, unremitting work of caring for the sick and dying; among the others were five physicians, four nuns from nearby Georgia convents, a druggist, a judge, and six clergy. "Without ostentation or hope of earthly reward they pursued their labors for months amidst the greatest privations and sufferings, and after the scourge had disappeared they quietly returned to their homes content with the heartfelt thanks of the thousands whom they had succored."[42] For Father Hubert, this was a familiar role. He had earlier ministered to victims of yellow jack in Baton Rouge and New Orleans, and would two years later assist during virulent fever outbreaks in both Vicksburg and Jackson, Mississippi; he was quick to volunteer and did not leave Savannah until the fever season had passed.

This perilous sojourn in Savannah with seventeen other "Samaritans" was recognized by grateful members of the local Benevolent Association with a beautiful gold medal the following year. The obverse of the medal showed a Geneva Cross on which the date 1876 was stamped and an inscription reading "Savannah Benevolent Association," along with the name of the individual recipient. On the reverse was a depiction of the poor man who "fell among thieves" being assisted by his unlikely rescuer, whose donkey stands nearby; the inscription read "I was sick and you visited me," along with its gospel source-text, Matthew 25:36.[43]

41. Falligant recounted his experience in an article for the *North American Journal of Homeopathy* in 1878, which he then reprinted, with addenda for medical professionals, as *A Monograph of the Yellow Fever of 1876: In Savannah, Georgia* (Savannah: Morning News Print, 1888).

42. *Morning Star and Catholic Messenger*, May 27, 1877, p. 1. A complete list of the Savannah "Samaritans" is included in the article.

43. None of the original dozen and a half gold medals are believed to survive. A drawing and description were published in *Frank Leslie's Illustrated Newspaper*, June 23, 1877, p. 277. Several bronze impressions are known to exist, one of which, donated to the Boston Numismatic Society in the 1880s, is in the collection of the Museum of Fine Arts in Boston;

This medallion was one of the few material treasures that Father Hubert cherished; in several extant portraits (dating to the 1880s) he is wearing it pinned to his cassock, alongside his service medal from the Association of the Army of Northern Virginia. He mentions it also in the very brief self-penned obituary composed during his last illness.[44]

Apart from such missions of mercy, and especially after the mid-1870s, Darius Hubert was never far afield from the Crescent City, where his many charitable obligations as well as pastoral responsibilities consumed his waking hours. He was affiliated as spiritual director with the St. Patrick's Convent of Mercy, a foundation of Mercy nuns attached to the oldest English-speaking church in New Orleans.[45] It may have been in connection with the Sisters there that Darius Hubert first met long-time St. Patrick's congregant Margaret Gaffney Haughery. An illiterate Irish woman who was orphaned as a youngster and then, at twenty-two, lost both her husband and her only child to disease, Margaret became New Orleans's most unlikely entrepreneur and most famous nineteenth-century philanthropist. Motivated by her grief to help alleviate the suffering of other widows and orphans, she aligned herself informally with the Daughters of Charity and contributed to their care of orphans from her meager income as a laundress at St. Charles Hotel.

From there, her biography takes on the character of an Irish folktale: she acquired two cows on loan and in a matter of years built a successful forty-cow dairy operation, from which she provided milk for the orphans and raised additional revenue by selling milk, cream, and butter from a

---

another privately owned bronze copy appeared online in 2014 on a popular numismatic website (coincommunity.com/forum/topic.asp?TOPIC_ID=177444). Unlike the gold originals, the copies were engraved with the name "J. F. Wheaton," president of the Savannah Benevolent Association, rather than names of the recipients.

44. The three-hundred-word résumé of his life was sent from St. Stanislaus Novitiate in Macon, Georgia, to his friend Fred Ober, veteran of the Fifth Louisiana Infantry, with instructions that it should remain sealed until after his death. The text was published in the *Times-Picayune* on June 18, 1893; see chapter 6, below. Contrary to rumors that Ober perished on the return trip from the 1888 Gettysburg Blue-Gray Reunion (Jones, *Lee's Tigers Revisited*, p. 387), he lived to a ripe old age in New Orleans; he died in 1913.

45. *Morning Star and Catholic Messenger*, August 24, 1873, p. 5.

handcart that she pushed daily around the French Quarter. She acquired a derelict building to house orphans, and then talked the owner of an airy plantation house into giving it to the Sisters rent free. She also helped to fund a "baby house" (St. Vincent's Infant Orphan Asylum) and a "house of industry" for teenage girls, providing skills that would prepare them to enter society. She supported a home for the aged, run by the Little Sisters of the Poor, and donated generously to Protestant and Jewish as well as Catholic charities, including an orphanage dedicated to black children.

In 1859, she acquired a near-bankrupt bread business, sold her cows and dairy, and built one of the most modern and successful bakeries in the South, which employed dozens of workers and shipped bread and packaged crackers all over the country. "Margaret's Steam and Mechanical Bakery" became a sensation in a city that relished good bread and pastries;[46] it provided baked goods to city orphanages free of charge and became also an informal food bank for the derelict and vagrant, and for sailors who poured off the ships in New Orleans harbor.[47] Plain-looking and plain-speaking, Margaret survived a catastrophic yellow fever epidemic in 1853, faced down Benjamin Butler during occupation, engaged matter-of-factly with whoever was in charge in the volatile political environment of postwar New Orleans, and cajoled her customers and acquaintances ceaselessly to provide for the city's neediest citizens.[48] Despite her lack of education, she was consulted by many in the commercial

46. A constant complaint of displaced Louisianans who found themselves in Richmond during the Civil War was the lack of palatable bread. See, for example, Garidel, *Exile in Richmond*: "What I would give for some bread from New Orleans!" (p. 174; see also pp. 153, 157, 186, 192, 220, 235).

47. Among the many epithets associated with Margaret was "Patron friend of Seamen" (*New Orleans Times-Picayune*, February 16, 1882, p. 9).

48. In an extraordinary gesture for the time, Margaret purchased and presented a ceremonial engraved sword to occupying Northern general Christopher Augur in 1877 to thank him for maintaining order in New Orleans in the dangerous political climate following the White League riots (*New Orleans Daily Democrat*, August 5, 1877, p. 1). Recent attempts to denigrate her legacy by turning her universal charity against her (for example, James Karst, "Friend to Orphans—and White Supremacist Militia," *New Orleans Times Picayune*, March 25, 2018) have not stood up to scrutiny.

district for her uncanny business acumen; despite her rough-hewn background and homespun dress, she commanded the admiration of New Orleans gentry. The children of the city called her simply "our Margaret."

Margaret's longtime advocate, and her pastor at St. Patrick's, Father James Ignatius Mullon, died in 1866.[49] Whether before or after his passing, she went through a spiritual crisis that alienated her from the Church and caused her to absent herself from attendance at Mass for several years. The presenting issue was apparently some word of criticism from a superior that wounded her deeply. She carried on with her usual energy, but her faith was shaken. She found her way to Darius Hubert in the early 1870s, perhaps by way of personal introduction. This improbable relationship between an unlettered Irish peasant woman and a highly educated French-born Jesuit, ten years her junior, was to shape the remainder of her life. Initially, in a "torrent of tears," she unburdened herself of the grievance that had long stolen her peace and barred her from the sacraments. In her candid penitence and the absolution that followed, she experienced a spiritual rebirth and newfound joy in her charitable labors.[50]

Father Hubert, thenceforth her spiritual father and adviser, ceremonially blessed a new seventy-horsepower steam engine in her ever-improving "Steam and Mechanical Bakery" in 1880.[51] Two years later he attended her frequently as she suffered agonizing headaches and debility that confined her to bed in the Daughters of Charity hospital, Hotel Dieu. She had scarcely been sick a day in her sixty-nine years, and the unknown

49. A colorful and beloved character locally, Mullon came to America from Ireland as a young boy and served under Admiral David Porter in the War of 1812. He made his way to New Orleans in 1834 and founded St. Patrick's the same year. During the occupation of New Orleans he famously retorted to a reprimand of General Benjamin Butler for his rumored unwillingness to bury a Union soldier that, "on the contrary, General, I would like to bury the whole lot of you."

50. *New Orleans Times-Democrat,* Feb. 13, 1882, p. 2. This anecdote as Father Hubert recounts it bears an unusually evangelical character: "[that] was the date of a great change in her life. Her charities continued the same, but were now acceptable in the eyes of God, and her heart was happy in the thought, 'I am a child of God.'"

51. *New Orleans Times-Picayune,* May 29, 1880, p. 1. The ceremony attracted five hundred of New Orleans's prominent citizens.

disease that felled her was to claim her life. Father Hubert arranged for a pectoral cross from Pope Pius IX to be given to her, a cherished token that brought her great consolation in her dying days.[52] After her passing he preached her funeral homily to a packed church, admonishing his listeners to move past sentiment and to imitate Margaret in pragmatic ways: "There is an untold amount of misery in our city, and there is a large number of well-disposed citizens who wish to do good but leave to their heirs to distribute their donations. Meanwhile misery goes on increasing and money is hoarded in coffers and in banks, and our heirs will do the same as we have done. Oh, in the name of Almighty God, let us follow the example of this extraordinary woman; let us do good to the poor while we live."[53]

Within days, an article appeared in the *Times-Picayune,* reflecting spontaneous popular desire that a monument be erected to honor Margaret's legacy, and that "Father Hubert, the faithful spiritual adviser of this noble woman, take the initiative. He will find hearty cooperation from people of every race, creed, and nationality in this great city. Let Father Hubert devise the plan . . . [and] the good work will be completed, as it were, by magic."[54] In the end, a committee of prominent citizens devised the plan and raised the funds. Father Hubert was apparently happy to defer to them; his life was consumed with other duties.[55]

52. Many confusions attend the story of the cross, which was mentioned by her frequent visitors and always identified with Pius IX. Since Pius IX predeceased Margaret by several years, he could not have "sent it personally, with his blessing," as has often been attested. It would almost certainly have come from the hands of a previous recipient, possibly Archbishop Napoleon Perche, who traveled to Rome in 1870 to receive the pallium and may have acquired the crucifix at that time. Darius Hubert, Margaret's friend and one of the city's most venerable and influential priests, may have suggested the gift; in any case it was doubtless he who brought the cross to Margaret (not Father Hubert Thirion, as has carelessly entered into many records; Father Thirion, who had a troubled tenure in the diocese, did not know Margaret well enough even to attend her funeral).

53. Margaret's will provided modest bequests to several friends and left the management of her bakery to her longtime business partner Bernard Klotz; virtually all of her considerable estate went to the many orphanages of New Orleans.

54. *New Orleans Times-Picayune,* February 16, 1882, p. 9.

55. The monument to Margaret, unveiled in 1884, was the first publicly erected statue honoring a woman in the United States. It depicts her seated in a plain gingham dress and

He was a pastor to a huge flock, the "chosen confessor of a vast number of the communicants of the city, his kindly manner, uniform courtesy, and excellent counsel winning for him friends by the score."[56] His spiritual advice was sought by many whose names are known only to God; the identity of some found their way into newspapers, usually at the time of their passing. One such individual was Captain Joseph Fry, a former Confederate naval officer, who in October 1873 accepted command of the *Virginius*, an old Confederate blockade runner now being used to supply Cuban rebels seeking independence from Spain. Fry was a member of the Academy of Sciences and an amateur inventor but, lacking any business acumen, had been unable to find sustained employment in postwar New Orleans. His return to naval adventures was undertaken in a desperate bid to provide for his large family. Fry seems naively to have assumed that *Virginius* was American rather than Cuban-owned, and that an American flag and American papers would protect him in the event of Spanish interference. He was fatally mistaken; he and his crew and passengers were captured at sea on October 30 and taken under guard to Santiago. Three days later Fry and thirty-six other were executed by firing squad, their heads severed and paraded on pikes, their bodies trampled by horses. The speed of the proceedings allowed no time for appeal. While awaiting his death, Fry wrote several final letters: to his wife, Agnes Sands Fry, and daughter, also named Agnes; his brother Walton Fry; and his friend at the New Orleans Academy of Science, Dr. Valentine Overton King. He wrote also to President Ulysses S. Grant. And to Father Darius Hubert, his friend and spiritual adviser, he penned a final confession.[57]

---

shawl, with her arm around a child. The Carrara marble monument, with no inscription save the word "Margaret," has recently been cleaned and restored.

56. *New Orleans Times-Democrat,* June 15, 1893, p. 3. The same day's edition of the *New Orleans Daily Picayune* said of Father Hubert that "he officiated at more christenings, marriages, and funerals than any other clergyman in the city."

57. *New Orleans Times-Picayune,* November 20, 1873, p. 1. The contents of the letter were never divulged, being under the seal of the confessional. Father Hubert, in a memorial volume written to raise funds for Fry's widow and children, remarked on Fry's "beautiful affectionate enthusiasm" and semi-mystical apprehension of the spiritual world: "The

The barbarity of the affair caused an uproar especially in New Orleans, where Fry had been resident for years. Despite saber-rattling and calls for a retaliatory war against Spain, a diplomatic settlement was finally reached when the Spanish government acknowledged the illegality of the capture and the executions, and provided $80,000 in reparations. A portion of the money eventually reached the destitute family of Joseph Fry, the "Cuban martyr" as he came to be called. Father Hubert and others in the Crescent City undertook to raise additional funds for their ongoing sustenance.

Among other prominent citizens to whom Darius Hubert was deeply attached was Alexander Dimitry, a scholar, educator, orator, and diplomat, whose personal library ran to fifteen thousand volumes and whose linguistic gifts were *nonpareil.* In his eloquent and emotional funeral homily for Dimitry, Father Hubert did not dwell on his friend's extraordinary intellectual gifts (he was reportedly "the brightest and most thorough scholar that ever left Georgetown College") but his "childlike, deep-rooted Christian faith": "it has often been said that faith and reason are incompatible, that science and religion cannot go together, but here we have a shining refutation of that view."[58] Dr. Thomas Layton, a well-loved New Orleans physician and his French-born wife, Berthe, were likewise devoted spiritual protégés. Berthe, only twenty-four, contracted fever while vacationing with her three young children in Bay St. Louis in 1875 and became violently ill after returning home. Father Hubert was at her bedside for most of the week before she died; his funeral oration was touchingly intimate, addressing her husband as "dearest Tommie" and recounting Berthe's happiness, even *in extremis,* in recognizing her Father Confessor at her side.[59]

Other lesser-known figures were also the object of his concern and dutiful attention when they passed, especially young men who had served

communion of saints . . . was not a mere theory with him." See Jeanie Mort Walker, *Life of Capt. Joseph Fry, The Cuban Martyr* (Hartford, CT: J. B. Burr, 1875), pp. 463–64.

58. *New Orleans Times-Democrat,* February 1, 1883, p. 3.

59. *Morning Star and Catholic Messenger,* October 10, 1875, p. 4.

the Lost Cause in the late war. As he explained to a visitor to his church in 1881, "when a Confederate soldier dies, invited or uninvited, I follow his remains to their last resting place."[60] This commitment to honor the war dead, begun on the fields of battle themselves, became more public in the late 1870s, as Reconstruction ended and memorials and reunions became a regular feature of New Orleans life. Father Hubert's role in such gatherings—decoration days in local cemeteries, gatherings of Army of Tennessee and Army of Northern Virginia veterans, funerals, unveilings of monuments—was always to offer prayers. Though postwar New Orleans had no shortage of pastors noted for their pulpit eloquence,[61] including several who had served as Southern chaplains, Father Hubert was preeminent in offering invocation and benediction on occasions of remembrance.[62]

These prayers, which were often printed verbatim in the local press, are striking in many ways. Though Father Hubert's first language was French, he was effortlessly fluent in his adopted tongue and always conveyed, within and beyond his words, a heart suffused with love of God and neighbor. His words betoken an intimate address to the Almighty, while bearing the weight of priestly intercession on behalf of a gathered people. They do not depend on liturgical formulas, and are generously

60. *New Orleans Times-Democrat,* March 20, 1881, p. 4. Father Hubert's solemn, self-appointed role as spiritual escort to fallen soldiers (presaging in some ways that of military escorts for deceased service personnel) was evidently personal, unofficial, and largely hidden from public view.

61. Foremost among these, on the Protestant side, was Benjamin Morgan Palmer, who could electrify an audience—whether in defense of slavery (November 1860) or in opposition to the Louisiana lottery (June 1891).

62. One notable omission on his résumé is the dedication of the monument to Robert E. Lee on Tivoli Circle, February 22, 1884—which may perhaps be accounted for by the priest's precarious health and the day's violent weather, with torrential rain, that interrupted the ceremony and scattered the crowd before the oration could be read and the statue unveiled. The Episcopal Bishop of Louisiana John Galleher, "in the presence of such persons as were present," pronounced the benediction and adjourned the event; his words were not recorded. See *Ceremonies Connected with the Unveiling of the Statue of General Robert E. Lee at Lee Circle, New Orleans, LA, Feb. 22, 1884* (New Orleans: W. B. Stansbury & Co., 1884).

ecumenical. Their unstudied eloquence frequently mirrors the idiom and cadences of biblical poetry—suggesting thoroughgoing familiarity with the Bible in English translation as well as ecclesial Latin.[63] One of Father Hubert's favorite turns of phrase, "Thou knowest, O Lord," has notable scriptural precedents.

Such memorial prayers were typically not only eulogistic but exhortative. Among the prominent themes: the duty of the living to hold the fallen in grateful remembrance and to care generously for their dependents; acknowledgment of God's sovereignty in the collapse of the Confederacy; and the obligation to move forward as one people in a reunited nation. In a prayer for Decoration Day, 1879, the priest linked honor for heroes with an appeal to national conciliation: "May their bright examples in war nerve us for the nobler works of peace, making us better and worthier citizens of this grand union of States, determined to uphold and obey the laws and to maintain unimpaired the priceless legacy of constitutional liberty."[64] The following year, in a prayer previously quoted in this volume,[65] he implored his audience to listen to the fallen, whose blood "so freely shed on the field of battle" cries out, like that of the biblical Abel (Genesis 4:10): the message is "evermore to shun all occasion for strife, and to preserve inviolate the blessings of peace." In 1890, in yet another Decoration Day tribute, he reminded his hearers that the "Father of all . . . judges the nations not according to the judgment of men, but according to [His] infinite wisdom, overruling all things, drawing good from what we call evil," and enjoined them to worthily emulate the devotion of their fallen loved ones: "Let us now departing on the fields of peace and in the ranks of duty, prove ourselves like them sons of our country,

63. Verbal allusions to the Douai-Reims (1865) translation of the Vulgate are ubiquitous in Father Hubert's recorded prayers. Occasionally, biblical idiom is actually drawn from the King James Version (for example, "good and perfect gift" [James 1:17] in his 1881 prayer at the dedication of the Army of Northern Virginia monument; "bread of idleness" [Proverbs 31:27] in his 1885 prayer at the Cotton Centennial Exposition).

64. *New Orleans Weekly Democrat*, April 12, 1879, p. 5.

65. Introduction, pp. 3–4, above (a prayer on the occasion of the dedication of the Washington Artillery Monument, Feb. 22, 1880).

servants of God, and ever ready for the last taps that soon or late must sound for all."[66]

After the last taps sounded for Jefferson Davis, the Confederacy's only president, on December 6, 1889, "first chaplain" Darius Hubert was several times at the dead president's side as he lay in state in New Orleans, and among the last to look on the deceased's face before the casket was closed and the public funeral commenced at noon on December 11.[67] He prayed "long and fervently" next to the bier and then, "at a quarter to twelve . . . took his soldierly stand at the head of the coffin. An awesome hush fell upon the room as the detail of honor from the Louisiana Field Artillery . . . entered. At ten minutes to twelve . . . the funeral director closed the lid, screwed it down tight. . . . Eight soldiers raised the burden to their shoulders and bore it at funereal pace down the long corridor and out upon the great portico."[68] The aged priest followed with other clergy, and was the last to speak before the more than thirty thousand mourners who had gathered outside in brilliant winter sunlight on Lafayette Square. He did not, as some records state, offer the eulogy; that duty was performed by Episcopal Bishop John Galleher. But it was Darius Hubert's final brief prayer, movingly offered with hands uplifted and "tears in his voice" that touched the crowd and exalted the mood from collective grief to veneration and gratitude. The soldier priest's emotional final tribute to his old chieftain on behalf of his "heartbroken comrades" was, in the assessment of local journalists, "the most affecting part of the service."[69]

66. *New Orleans Times-Picayune,* April 7, 1890, p. 8.

67. Reporters from both the *New Orleans Times-Picayune* and *New York Times* recount that, toward the end of the first day of Davis's lying in state, which saw forty thousand visitors at City Hall, the aged, invalid priest joined the end of a long line of mourners, before being recognized and escorted to the bier by several officials; he fell on his knees in tearful prayer as others watched and waited, and then quietly departed (December 9, 1889).

68. Hudson Strode, *Jefferson Davis, Tragic Hero: The Last Twenty-Five Years, 1864–1889* (New York: Harcourt, Brace & World, 1964), pp. 520–21.

69. *New York Times,* December 9, 1889, p. 1; December 12, 1889, p. 1; *New Orleans Times-Picayune,* December 12, 1889, p. 1; *New Orleans Times-Democrat,* December 12, 1889, p. 1; J. William Jones, *The Davis Memorial Volume* (Richmond, VA: R. F. Johnson and Co., 1890), pp. 527–32.

As momentous and memorable as was the Davis encomium, the single most frequently quoted of all Father Hubert's public prayers occurred nearly a decade earlier, on the occasion of the dedication of the monument to the Army of Northern Virginia in Metairie Cemetery in New Orleans, May 10, 1881. It was the eighteenth anniversary of the death of General Thomas "Stonewall" Jackson, whose image topped the monument. More than ten thousand were present for the unveiling and dedication, including Jackson's widow, Mary Anna, and daughter Julia; Jefferson Davis; General Fitzhugh Lee, nephew of deceased Army of Northern Virginia General Robert E. Lee; J. William Jones, Southern Baptist chaplain and prominent Confederate memorialist; and numerous other dignitaries.

Fitzhugh Lee's lengthy and erudite oration and Jeff Davis's much briefer remarks were bookended by Darius Hubert's invocation and benediction. His invocation heralded, as a part of worshipful obedience, the "gratitude of love" owed to those who perished in the war. It also distinguished impermanent human tributes from immortal glory.[70] But it was the benediction, delivered as the evening sun began to set over the immense gathering, that all remembered afterward—specifically, one trenchant sentence: "Thou knowest, O Lord, that when thou didst decide that the Confederacy should not succeed, thou hadst first to remove thy servant Stonewall Jackson." There may be no more concise and compelling Lost Cause panegyric—expressing the paradoxical connection of passionate allegiance and loving memory with spiritual acquiescence.[71]

The chaplain's words caused an immediate stir and were repeated for decades afterward. J. William Jones cited this prayer of "that brave priest, Father Hubert" (which he had been present to hear firsthand) on more

70. *Dedication of the Tomb of the Association of the Army of Northern Virginia*, pp. 6–7.

71. Father Hubert's "Thou knowest" offers a provocative spiritual recasting of the unanswerable question: "Had Stonewall lived, would the South have won the war?" That God determined the defeat of the Confederacy, and that Jackson—the quintessential Christian knight who of all Southern soldiers exhibited the most wholehearted, almost reckless trust in Providence—needed therefore to be removed, his prodigious military successes cut short, embeds the Lost Cause in an almost incomprehensible mystery, one that depends on a deeply Christian view of history.

than one occasion,[72] and it continued to appear, though often without correct attribution, in the press whenever Stonewall Jackson was memorialized.[73] Presbyterian divine Rev. Thomas Markham, in celebrating the legacy of his Jesuit friend following his death in 1893, reflected on the Jackson tribute, still vivid after twelve years, causing hearts "to burn within."[74]

Father Hubert's role as intercessor-in-chief in postbellum New Orleans extended well beyond events related to his war chaplaincy. He was frequently invited to pray at the opening of state Senate and House sessions. His blessing was sought for the launch of many enterprises, charitable and otherwise: in 1883, he christened a fire truck for the newly formed

72. For example, *Daily Times* (Richmond, VA), May 22, 1888, p. 4.

73. The prayer is cited, with or without accurate attribution, in several hundred newspaper articles in digitized form at the time of writing. The *Atlanta Constitution*, April 29, 1888, p. 6. printed a slightly mangled paraphrase, attributed to "Father Dubert," that was then reprinted by other news outlets all over the country. *The Standard* (London), in a retrospect on General Jackson's life (October 14, 1898, p. 2), cites the "quaint prayer said to have been uttered at the unveiling of the Jackson memorial in New Orleans," without the speaker's name. In a version that appeared on July 19, 1908, in the *News and Observer* (Raleigh, NC), among other dailies, the context and the author are fancifully revised: "While the angels were looking for Stonewall, a Southern clergyman, having heard of the General's death just as he was about to enter his pulpit, said. . . ." Despite the many confusions that attached themselves to Father Hubert's tribute over the years, one can still discover the original words intact and rightly accredited at the turn of the twentieth century (for example, in the *Baltimore Sun*, September 28, 1900, p. 8); more than a decade later, on the fiftieth anniversary of Stonewall's death (though the author is given simply as "a Catholic priest"), the prayer is recalled in many newspapers, including the *Charlotte News* (NC), May 10, 1913, p. 4. In early August 1938, an editorialist named George Tucker ("New Yorker at Large") writing for the *Salamanca Republican Press* (NY) recounts the unveiling of the Jackson statue and the stirring prayer by "an unknown priest," and then adds, "Those were words that Lincoln could have been proud of. I want to see that statue, I want to stand where that priest stood and say a Protestant prayer for his Catholic soul." His column was reprinted in dozens of other papers that summer. The Hubert prayer honoring "thy servant Stonewall Jackson" still occasionally finds its way into newspaper articles (such as the *Monroe, Louisiana News-Star*, January 27, 2011), and online history blogs ("Almost Chosen People," May 4, 2013).

74. Markham's cryptic allusion is to Luke 24:32: "Did not our heart burn within us while he talked with us by the way?"

Metairie Ridge Fire Brigade; in 1890 he dedicated and helped place the cornerstone of the new Young Men's Gymnastics Club facility.[75]

In February 1885, at the opening of the Louisiana Historical Collection, one of the most popular exhibits of New Orleans's ambitious World's Industrial and Cotton Centennial Exposition, Father Hubert, who was in the words of organizers "noted for his piety, patriotism, and his knowledge of Louisiana lore," offered a remarkable invocation: "O Creator and Lord of all things! Hearken to the voice of Thy servants, and look down propitiously on the works of Thy hands. We come as children of Adam to show by the fruits of our toil, that in obedience to Thy command we eat not the bread of idleness but that which cometh of labor and of the sweat of our brow."[76] Extolling the quality and diversity of the exhibits, "the masterpieces of mechanic skill, the genius of art, a world mart of things useful and things beautiful," he praised them as evidence of the Creator's goodness: "It is Thou who enlightenest the human mind; Thou who quickenest the human heart; Thou who givest life and nerve, and cunning, to the hand of man." The entire prayer is a richly textured tapestry of allusions to Scripture as well as *The Confessions* of Saint Augustine, whose public veneration had effected his conversion as a young man: "Oh! Allow not our eyes to be dazzled by the work of our hands. Let not our heart cleave to the perishable goods and splendors of earth, but let them rest in Thee, O truth! O goodness! O beauty! Ever ancient and ever new." And then, in a characteristic turn toward local occasion and a particular audience, he added:

> This day especially, O God, Thy children of Louisiana greet Thee with a mood of praise. Thou hast been with us in the dark hour of adversity. Thou hast

75. *New Orleans Times-Picayune*, July 29, 1890, p. 8.

76. A contemporary and laudatory description of the New Orleans Cotton Exposition may be found in the final pages of a guidebook prepared for visitors to the Crescent City and timed to coincide with the expo's opening: Coleman, *Historical Sketch Book and Guide to New Orleans*. For a detailed account of mismanagement, cost overruns, and financial chicanery associated with the event, see Thomas D. Watson, "Staging the 'Crowning Achievement of the Age': Major Edward A. Burke, New Orleans, and the Cotton Centennial Exposition," *Louisiana History* 25.3 (Summer 1984): 229–57; 25.4 (Autumn 1984): 341–66.

> brought at last the dawn of triumph. Thou hast borne to us by means of our great watercourse the products, the wealth, and the art of this wide continent, nay, of the whole world. Our hearts go out to Thee in fervent accents of gratitude. Our prayer, like Thy mercy, is today universal. Pour down, we beseech Thee, Thy choicest gifts on us and on all who have come to aid us and to rejoice with us. Graciously grant that, gathered together from the four winds of heaven, communicating our good things each to the other, we may cement today a bond of perpetual brotherhood, of equal rights to all, of true civilization, and of Christian greatness. And with all our faculties, with every feeling of our nature, we will ever bless Thy name for Thine infinite goodness. Thine alone be the honor, Thine the Glory, through Christ our Lord. Amen.[77]

Darius Hubert's unaffected delight in the beauties of the earth and the creative industry that flows from the minds and hands of "children of Adam" is as winsome on the page as it evidently was to his original audience. This is the same priest who had accompanied a gaggle of Catholic schoolgirls to the first-ever Louisiana State Fair in Baton Rouge in 1859, enthusing with them over the artful and ingenious displays,[78] and who, two decades later, took immense pleasure in blessing a state-of-the-art steam engine at Margaret Haughery's famous bakery. But his paean of praise is charged with moral content as well; the universal gratitude all owe to their Creator prompts recognition of the universal brotherhood, with "equal rights for all," that the children of Adam, regardless of race, share under his sovereign goodness. Such, as Father Hubert sees it, is the stuff of "true civilization" and "Christian greatness."

This hopeful address to racial harmony and political equality mirrored the optimistic and forward-looking character of the exposition itself, and of the crowds that thronged the exhibits. A northern visitor to the fair, Charles Dudley Warner, longtime friend and sometime collaborator of Mark Twain, expressed astonishment that "white and colored people mingled freely, talking and looking at what was of common interest,"

77. *New Orleans Times-Picayune*, February 20, 1885, p. 8.

78. Jeffrey, *Two Civil Wars*, p. 45.

and that "the colored citizens took their full share of the parade and the honors. Their societies march with the others, and the races mingled in the grounds in unconscious equality of privileges." On "Louisiana Day" an unnamed black pastor "spoke as a citizen of Louisiana, proud of his native State, dwelling with richness of allusion upon its history," and while forthrightly asserting the rights of black men and women, did so in a "spirit of good-will and amity in a common hope of progress" that was warmly applauded by the mixed-race audience. Warner's summary view was that "the feeling between the two races is that of amity and mutual help. This is, I think, especially true in Louisiana."[79] The New Orleans Expo of 1885 was in fact the first ever World's Fair in which African Americans participated fully—showcasing "twenty years of prodigious progress" in a distinct "Colored Department" overseen by former slave and Republican Senator Blanche K. Bruce.[80] The formal opening of the Colored Department on February 23 was hailed by guest orator David Augustus Straker as the "commencement day of the colored American Citizen." In this propitious and precarious cultural moment, in which a multiracial chorus of concordant voices was sounding a new note, alternatives to the Jim Crow future were still viable, waiting to be pursued.[81]

The sheer quantity of Darius Hubert's civic and spiritual obligations in the 1880s (of which only a portion entered into public records) exac-

79. Warner's description of the Cotton Exposition, part of his "Impressions of the South" essay, was published in the September 1885 issue of *Harper's New Monthly Magazine*, pp. 546–51, and later reprinted in *Studies in the South and West* (New York: Harper and Brothers, 1889).

80. For details about black participation in the fair, see Miki Pfeffer, "'Mr. Chairman and FELLOW AMERICAN CITIZENS': African American Agency at the World's Industrial and Cotton Centennial Exposition in New Orleans, 1884–1885," *Louisiana History* 51.4 (Autumn 2010): 442–62. See also Blight, *Race and Reunion*, pp. 368–74.

81. See C. Vann Woodward, *The Strange Career of Jim Crow* (1955; 3rd rev. ed., New York: Oxford University Press, 2002), chap. 2, "Forgotten Alternatives": "In a time . . . when slavery was a live memory in the minds of both races, and when the memory of the hardships and bitterness of Reconstruction was still fresh, the race policies accepted and pursued in the south were sometimes milder than they became later" (p. 65). For the Louisiana context, see esp. pp. 42–44, 45–46, 53–55. Woodward's landmark volume is, among other things, an unsettling and tragic record of lost opportunities.

erbated his increasing physical infirmity. Though robust and athletic as a young man growing up in France (he was apparently a fine swimmer) he had never been fully healthy following his move to the American South. Doubtless the reasons included his disposition to overwork (the "self-sacrifice" that all who knew him attributed to him). But the Gulf climate seems to have wreaked havoc on him, and he fought asthma and other respiratory issues all of his adult life. During the early stages of the Civil War, it was occasionally reported that his health had greatly improved, perhaps a sign that the change of scenery and climate, along with the bracing demands and spiritual fruitfulness of his ministry among the young soldiers, provided unforeseen benefits. But by the spring of 1864 he was chronically exhausted and emaciated, and afflicted with a racking tubercular cough; he spent the last year of the war as a wounded healer in Richmond and returned home an older and tireder man, seeming to many to have aged more than a decade. By the 1880s his chronic asthma was so debilitating that he could not recline to sleep; such fleeting rest as he was able to manage came seated in a chair.

His postbellum schedule, however, included no sabbaticals or vacations. The normal pastoral duties to which he had always assiduously devoted himself had multiplied with the expansion of his de facto flock to include hundreds of army veterans living in the Crescent City.[82] And then as his notoriety grew through his public role, yet more were drawn into his orbit, seeking his counsel and asking his help in their various worthy causes.

Some causes were dear to his heart and needed few efforts of persuasion to enlist him: one of these was the funding and support of a local

82. Among this number were many who fought on the western front, as well as in the Army of Northern Virginia. When Thomas J. Coleman, veteran of the Army of Tennessee, died at only forty-five years of age, Darius Hubert was listed as his "friend and spiritual adviser" (*New Orleans Times-Picayune*, December 17, 1887, p. 4). Father Hubert attended annual reunions of the western army (held every April) with Protestant chaplains Thomas Markham and A. J. Witherspoon as well as those for the Army of Northern Virginia, that took place on Stonewall Jackson's birthday, January 21 (except when it fell on a Sunday, in which case it was postponed by a day in deference to Jackson's sabbatarian views: *New Orleans Times-Picayune*, January 23, 1883, p. 2).

Confederate Soldiers Home. In 1883, an extravagant two-day reenactment, termed a "sham battle," involving hundreds of combatants (most drawn from the ranks of former Confederate and Union soldiers) and thousands of spectators was performed as a major fundraiser for the home.[83] Reprising his old role, at sixty years of age, "conspicuous among the dead and dying was to be seen the faithful and zealous Chaplain, Rev. Father Darius Hubert," the same priest who had "marched with the Louisiana Brigade over every battlefield of Virginia ministering spiritual consolation and physical relief to the sick and dying." When asked about his participation, he responded, "Do not men, at their work or in their pleasures, in all times of life and in the hour of death, always need God? Then as His servant I am here to do my office."[84]

When the Camp Nicholls home opened, Father Hubert visited frequently to say Mass (more than half the old soldiers were Catholics) and to share meals and memories with the men. Later, when he became too ill to visit, and long after his passing in 1893, his presence lingered in a portrait that hung in the capacious parlor of the main building.[85] A women's benevolent society formed in 1894 to support the home and its tenants was named "The Father Hubert Circle"; their intention of building a me-

83. Organizers expressed special gratitude to local members of the Grand Army of the Republic for their support in the pageant and the successful fundraising effort on behalf of the Southern vets.

84. *New Orleans Times-Picayune*, September 17, 1883, p. 1. It was rumored that the chaplain's canteen contained relief in the form of something stronger than water. Camp Nicholls, as the soldiers' home was called, was established in 1882 but not finished and formally dedicated until March 16, 1884; the daughters of Robert E. Lee and the widow and daughter of Stonewall Jackson participated in the ceremony.

85. For a detailed description of the property and grounds and of some of the early inmates of the Soldiers' Home, see *New Orleans Times-Picayune*, February 5, 1893, p. 17. The "portrait" noted here (alluded to also in the *Times-Democrat*, April 11, 1892, p. 3) may have been a photograph. In 1905, a new "handsome portrait"—evidently an artistic rendering—of the Jesuit chaplain was ceremonially presented to Camp Nicholls on Stonewall Jackson's birthday, January 21. The latter was likely the "fine crayon portrait" initially owned (possibly commissioned) by Mr. J. C. Norton and donated to a fundraiser in 1896 (*New Orleans Times-Picayune*, May 25, 1896, p. 6); eventually, when the last veterans died and the home was closed in 1940, this portrait found its way to Confederate Memorial Hall, where it remains in storage.

morial chapel at Camp Nicholls in the chaplain's honor seems never to have been fulfilled.[86]

The increasing frailty of the aging priest did not go unnoticed by his fellow Army of Northern Virginia veterans, who provided a "special chair" (likely a recliner, or "invalid's chair") to allow him a degree of comfort at their gatherings, where he routinely opened proceedings with prayer and offered grace before the meal.[87] They also honored him by commissioning and hanging a large formal oil portrait by noted New Orleans artist Alexandre Alaux in their new temporary hall on Union Street in 1886.[88] The *Times-Picayune* took the unusual step of publishing a laudatory tribute, headed by an engraved portrait, in December 1887: "The kindly smile of the Rev. Father Darius Hubert, pastor of the Jesuits' church, is known to everybody in this community, where he is beloved and honored by people of all creeds and denominations. . . . Words of eulogy are not necessary to express the high esteem and respect in which he is held by everyone. It is sufficient to say that Father Hubert is known only to be loved."[89] Everyone seemed to be aware that he was failing.

But he soldiered on, as the old Confederate veterans had, well past the signs of imminent demise, fulfilling the modest, quotidian obligations of the priesthood—performing the many rites of the Church, especially now the rites of death. His once commanding voice and arresting eloquence were on such occasions reportedly reduced to "trembling tones."[90] The

86. *New Orleans Times-Picayune,* September 14, 1894, p. 3; *Times-Democrat,* September 4, 1894, p. 10.

87. *New Orleans Times-Democrat,* October 10, 1886, p. 3.

88. The oil painting of Darius Hubert mentioned here, by well-known New Orleans artist Alexandre Alaux, was moved into Confederate Memorial Hall when it opened in 1891 and prominently displayed next to a portrait of Stonewall Jackson and directly across from that of Robert E. Lee (*Richmond Dispatch,* Dec. 21, 1902, p. 14). In 1905, it was sent upon request to the Museum of the Confederacy in Richmond, to be featured in its "Louisiana Room" (*New Orleans Semi-Weekly Times-Democrat,* June 27, 1905, p. 5). It still resides in that collection, though it has not been displayed for several decades.

89. December 4, 1887, p. 7. There was no evident "occasion" for the feature; it was not tied to any known anniversary or notable event in the priest's life.

90. *New Orleans Times-Democrat,* December 30, 1890, p. 2.

funeral of Jefferson Davis in December 1889 was, appropriately enough, the last major public event in which he participated. At the end of that grueling day, as the sun set over Metairie Cemetery, people noticed him ("an old man with white hair," in the words of an out-of-state journalist) throwing a small bunch of flowers upon the burial mound, one last tender homage added to the sea of floral offerings.

A month later, notwithstanding his general infirmity, he was reelected by rising vote as continuing chaplain of the Army of Northern Virginia veterans—his friends and colleagues offering an ovation and pledge of their abiding deference to his spiritual guidance.[91] The following year, on the usual day—Stonewall's birthday, January 21, 1891—he was with them again as they met for the first time in their new permanent home at Confederate Memorial Hall on Camp Street. The chaplain's portrait was on the wall, and the menu card for the evening's banquet featured an engraved image of the soldier priest, who expressed regret in excusing himself early from the proceedings.[92] He was, the papers noted, "in very poor health." It was the sixteenth annual reunion of local Army of Northern Virginia veterans, and the last time Father Hubert would sit among them.

On March 25, 1891, while hearing confessions at the Church of the Immaculate Conception, the old priest suffered a severe stroke and had to be carried to his room. He remained in a "helpless condition" for several days and was feared near death. But he rallied unexpectedly and by early April was in stable, if still precarious, health. Doctors warned against undue optimism, given his chronic battle with asthma: "the stroke of paralysis coming at a time when he was already physically weak renders his condition very critical, and it is thought . . . that even at best he will never be physically able to take charge of his work again."[93]

91. At the same meeting, he was called on to speak on behalf of the Army of Northern Virginia in commending the outgoing president, Fred Washington, for his service, after which "three cheers and a tiger were given for Colonel Washington and Father Hubert" (*New Orleans Times-Picayune,* January 22, 1890, p. 8).

92. *New Orleans Weekly Times-Democrat,* January 23, 1891, p. 2.

93. *New Orleans Times-Picayune,* April 8, 1891, p. 4.

Local newspapers published regular bulletins on Father Hubert's health as well as expressions of concern from friends and admirers. An anonymous poem, cast in the form of a rhymed prayer (nicely incorporating the priest's characteristic "Thou knowest"), appeared on April 6 in one of the city dailies. Whatever its literary merits, it ably conveys the devotion of many in the Crescent City to their beloved, ailing priest:

> Lord! Thy vineyard needs his tending, and thy flock demands his care.
> So we pray, though best Thou knowest, spare him, in Thy mercy, spare!
> Though his place in heaven is waiting, though his crown with gems is set,
> Leave him here a little longer, for we cannot spare him yet. . . .
>
> Ease the pain which racks the body consecrated to Thy will;
> Let the hand which oft has blessed us be upraised in blessing still.
> Let his holy life speak for us, our unworthiness forget;
> Souls are waiting for his guidance, and we cannot spare him yet.
>
> Though war's clarion sounds no longer, calling him to scenes of blood,
> Though the ranks are thinned and broken where the hero-priest once stood . . .
> Led by him our way seems clearer, while storms rage and foes beset;
> Leave him, Lord, till we grow stronger, for we cannot spare him yet.[94]

94. *New Orleans Times-Democrat,* April 6, 1891, p. 3.

SIX

Macon, Georgia
1891–1893

By mid-April, it seemed that the poet's prayer had been answered, and that the stricken priest's life would be spared for at least a little longer. Local Jesuits, in consultation with Father Hubert's attending physicians, made the difficult decision to move him, before the "sickly season" came to the Gulf, to a facility where his chance of recovery would be improved and the chronic demands of his life in New Orleans could become mere distant music. So Darius Hubert, greatly incapacitated, unable to walk on his own or to speak clearly, prepared "under orders" to leave his home of several decades for better air, healthier temperatures, and enforced rest at St. Stanislaus College, the Jesuit novitiate in Macon, Georgia.

Many visitors came by to pay their respects, including the state governor and local worthies, soldiers with whom he had served, and congregants and religious to whom he was dear. Tears flowed freely as the Presbyterian divine Thomas Markham, his trusted friend and colleague, met with him in the infirmary at the Jesuit College in early May. For one old chaplain, words were possible; for the other, weeping sufficed. Both seemed to know it would be their last meeting, one final bivouac before each traced the concluding passage of a long obedience.[1]

1. Reverend Markham had several weeks earlier "offered a toast in most feeling terms" to his Jesuit colleague and led a prayer for his recovery at the annual reunion of the Army of Tennessee veterans, which Father Hubert had attended for many years as Markham's guest (*Louisiana Review*, April 8, 1891, p. 4; *New Orleans Times-Picayune*, April 7, 1891, p. 3). Thomas Markham died in March 1894, less than a year after Darius Hubert.

To avoid a crush of "his many friends of all shades and creeds" at the train station on Canal Street, no public announcement was made of Father Hubert's impending departure, scheduled for May 18.[2] Father David McKinery, president of the Jesuit College, went with him to the depot and helped him aboard an early evening train, along with two Jesuit brothers trained in nursing care, assigned to accompany him to Macon.[3] Myra Eulalia Semmes, wife of Thomas J. Semmes, a lifelong friend and his generous host in Richmond during the war years, was at the station to see him off, along with a small company of veterans, men whose names and stories were bone of his bone. From Thomas McPeake, then president of the Association of the Army of Northern Virginia, the departing priest received a note on behalf of his comrades expressing "our heartful feeling and an earnest wish for your speedy restoration."

The overnight Louisville & Nashville line train departed New Orleans about 7:30 and chugged over trestles and bridges through many coastal whistle-stops and towns well known to Darius Hubert in the early hours of his journey—Bay St. Louis, Pass Christian, Gulfport, Biloxi. By midnight it passed through Mobile, Alabama, the port city where his feet had first touched American soil in December 1847, and then turned northeast toward Montgomery. The priest would not arrive at his new residence in Georgia until late the next day.

Set on a rolling forty-two-acre property more than six hundred feet above sea level, St. Stanislaus College had not yet acquired the graceful Victorian collegiate style that marked it after 1898, with tree-lined driveway, ornate cupola, and broad symmetrical staircases leading to its front entrances.[4] When Darius Hubert arrived, the five-story edifice still had a rather plain facade, and lacked the long exterior porches from which later

2. Details after the fact, with this explanation, were published in the next day's edition of the *New Orleans Times-Democrat*, May 19, 1891, p. 3.

3. Elsewhere spelled "McKiniry"; the *Times-Democrat* has "McEnerny."

4. The Jesuits had purchased the short-lived and unsuccessful Pio Nono College in 1883, renaming it St. Stanislaus; they refurbished, expanded, and beautified it during their tenure. On November 7, 1920, the entire college burned to the ground, taking with it art and statuary and a magnificent library of ancient and irreplaceable volumes, as well as countless personal mementos, papers, and artifacts that might well have contributed to this volume.

occupants enjoyed hilltop breezes and long, pleasant views. Nonetheless, in both its elevation and its seclusion, it afforded a striking contrast to his home of nearly three decades in the noisy, crowded streets of downtown New Orleans.

Father Hubert's reputation was well known to the young men at the novitiate, and they welcomed him with a kind of reverential awe. He was provided a quiet room, and permitted a quality of rest, leisure, and freedom from responsibility that, having conscientiously eschewed sabbaticals and vacations, he had never known since entering the Society of Jesus nearly fifty years earlier. Over the next few months, in a way that surprised everyone, including himself, his strength began to return. When Southern Provincial of the Jesuit order Father John O'Shannahan visited St. Stanislaus in September 1891 he was astonished at the improvement in the old priest, who was now able once more to speak distinctly and, with help, to move about the property: "Every day for two or three hours he takes outdoor exercise in the gardens, propelled in his wheeled chair, and has so far overcome his paralysis as to be able to walk a few steps."[5] He greatly enjoyed the fresh air and the company of young scholastics, with whom he conversed feelingly about their theological studies and, at their frequent insistence, recounted anecdotes from his years as a Southern chaplain. Despite his advanced age and the asthma with which he had long contended and that still prevented him from repose in a bed, his brother priests in Macon wondered if something close to a full recovery might be possible.

News of his improvement was carried back to New Orleans, and hopeful talk of the possible return of the beloved priest was occasionally printed in the newspapers. Having regained the use of his hands, Father Hubert wrote brief, cheerful letters to many friends in the Crescent City, some of which found their way to a wider public through those same outlets. He frequently made light of his situation, assuring his correspon-

---

It is likely that Father Hubert's precious Good Samaritan medal vanished in the blaze. The Jesuits lacked sufficient funds to rebuild, and sold the property to a developer in 1926, who retained the "Stanislaus" name for the new upscale neighborhood.

5. *New Orleans Times-Democrat,* September 23, 1891, p. 3.

dents that "I am not in a hurry to go off yet, if it please God." In one such missive, he referenced his old hero Stonewall Jackson's final words: "Now, by no means imagine that I have the least desire to cross the river and go under the shade of the big trees."

Whenever the old soldiers met in Confederate Memorial Hall, their chaplain's designated seat was left empty in his honor. Though he offered to resign his position, the veterans refused him gently but firmly and continued to list him on all programs until his death as "Chaplain to the Army of Northern Virginia." Rev. Thomas Markham, who bore the parallel title of chaplain to the Army of the Tennessee, was among those who regarded Darius Hubert as the indisputable and irreplaceable pastor to the dwindling host of Northern Virginia veterans; he never missed an opportunity, in gatherings of the gray, to rise and toast his old friend with eloquent and stirring words. Father Hubert, in acknowledging the honor and affection he was still accorded, sent a characteristically amiable note: "I am most thankful to my dear comrades to keep me with them as long as I live, and if at any time I *can* be with them, and be able, they will see me at my post. . . . So when you call the rolls, think of me and say in your heart, 'That poor fellow is absent through mere necessity, but we hope not forever.'" To this he added a tender farewell: "Blessing all, from my heart."

Perhaps anticipating that this spell of good health would be brief, Darius Hubert composed a modest one-page résumé of his life (to indicate "what kind of a chaplain I have been") and sent it to the veterans' association in care of his friend Fred Ober. He asked that it remain sealed until after his death, adding—to allay his comrades' worry—that he hoped it would still be in the recipient's possession ten or twenty years later.[6]

Father Hubert's second winter in Macon brought a significant downturn in health as unremitting severe weather kept him confined to his rooms. January 1893 saw a stretch of unusually bitter cold, where for more than two weeks the daily mean temperature was below freezing, and snow, sleet, and ice reduced commerce all over the state.[7] After the

6. This brief self-penned obituary was published, with excerpts from some of Darius Hubert's last letters, quoted here, in the *New Orleans Times-Picayune*, June 18, 1893, p. 3.

7. *Atlanta Constitution*, February 12 and 13, 1893.

respite and improvement he had enjoyed for more than a year, Darius Hubert began to suffer severe arthritic pain and failing eyesight. His hands often shook uncontrollably, a condition he attributed to the cold. In early March he dictated what would be his last correspondence: "I hope in a few days to be quite well again. Thanks to comrades for the anxiety manifested. Fraternally yours," and then slowly and painfully executed his own signature, alongside a self-deprecating parenthesis "(see how nice I write)."

Concern about this reversal was shared with friends in the Crescent City, and the ailing priest was lovingly mentioned several weeks later at an extraordinary event in the precincts of St. Louis Cathedral to celebrate the centennial of the founding of the New Orleans diocese. A huge gathering of dignitaries, clergy and religious, members of all the Catholic parishes across the city, and local citizens was present to hear two orators, the second of whom, US Senator Edward D. White, lauded numerous prominent Catholic leaders in the city's recent history but paused conspicuously over the legacy of Darius Hubert:

> There is a . . . name I would not mention were he here tonight, for I know his sense of modesty would resent it—the name of dear Father Hubert. (Great applause.) How devoted in peace, how true in war. How many of those we love, who sleep upon Virginia's hills, have heard whispered into their dying ears from his dear voice that last word of consolation and hope. . . . His heart knew no fear, his love knew no bounds; his sacrifice knew no limit! Far away in the hills of Georgia, where he is today, I know, as I breathe his name to you, there rises in your heart an emotion of respect and love which I hope may reach him to console and bless his remaining years.

At that, the crowd, twenty thousand strong, erupted into thunderous and sustained applause—as if they did indeed hope and imagine the aged priest might hear it over the long miles.[8]

8. *New Orleans Daily Picayune*, April 26, 1893, p. 3. The ovation for Darius Hubert was reportedly the loudest and longest of the evening—in effect an emotional goodbye from a city that loved him.

Frail and easily exhausted, Father Hubert celebrated the great feast days of Easter and Pentecost with the community at St. Stanislaus. He said his final Mass on Trinity Sunday, May 28, and then retired to his room for the last time. Students to whom he had become a beloved mentor kept vigil, as did his colleagues, around his invalid chair. He was often alert and able to communicate for the next two weeks, at which point he apparently suffered another stroke (an "attack of paralysis"). Sensing that the end was close and sorrowfully aware that he was losing mental clarity, he gestured to the grieving men gathered about him and offered a final benediction. His last words, lucid and tender, were "Good bye my children. I have done my best."

Three days later, June 14, 1893, he slipped the tethers of this life at 11:20 in the morning. He was in his threescore and tenth year, within months of celebrating the golden jubilee of his profession as a Jesuit.

Coda

THE MEMORIALS

That Darius Hubert had been, in his nearly seventy years, much more than "first chaplain of the Confederacy" is clear enough. His five-decade ministry was varied and his parish broad. He was notably a spiritual friend and mentor to women—not only the nuns whose vocations he supported[1] but also secular women as diverse as Matilda Victor, a brilliant and talented Catholic convert who felt perpetually isolated and dispossessed,[2] and Margaret Haughery, an illiterate Irish peasant woman whose charitable industry and genius masked for years her deep spiritual disquiet.[3] His role in their lives was transformative. He was spiritual adviser to the eminent and to the lowly, a favorite of children, a bearer of consoling or of bracing words on occasions of moment for countless individuals. A man of chronically frail health, he was nevertheless a tireless Samaritan in plague seasons in several Southern cities.

1. Darius Hubert was formally attached as spiritual director to Sisters of Mercy in New Orleans. A young student of his in antebellum Baton Rouge, Celeste Repp, became after the war a Mercy Sister in Vicksburg; her devotion to the teaching of black children and heroic steadfastness during a yellow plague epidemic in Pass Christian merited rare commendation and would have delighted her beloved "Père Hubert." See Jeffrey, *Two Civil Wars*, pp. 219–22.

2. Matilda Victor, from the time of her youthful Catholic conversion, was largely disowned by her Protestant family and erstwhile friends and denied employment in public schools; at the same time, she was treated with distrust and jealousy by Catholic religious who thought her unfit to be a Catholic educator. She called it "a life of martyrdom." For her later life, see Jeffrey, *Two Civil Wars*, pp. 200–207.

3. See p. 117, above.

Yet at the time of his passing the eulogists could not help but focus on the four years spent with the Army of Northern Virginia as a window to the whole: the "perfect man, always with his regiment" about whom his admiring, stuttering officer could only say: "We cannot express what was thought of him."

The Civil War and its aftermath had brought this faithful, self-effacing priest—"not particularly conspicuous for talent" or charisma—into public consciousness in a way he never intended or expected.[4] But it had also changed him. It made of him something he could not otherwise have become, revealing depths of character until then largely hidden. In the years leading up to secession, Darius Hubert was a restive man. That someone had shot at him while he was sat at dinner in the priests' quarters in Baton Rouge caused him far less consternation than the consequent departure of his colleague Joseph Lavay, leaving him to manage an impossibly dysfunctional parish without spiritual companionship or assistance. He was indignant with the petty schemes and callous abuse of unworthy men in his own church, angry with Jesuit colleagues who had encouraged an energetic and idealistic woman to purchase their failing school and then "taken the money and run," aggravated with a fault-finding superior who refused to answer his letters. Obliged to obedience by his Jesuit vows, and inclined to fidelity in all aspects of his priestly duties, he was nonetheless frustrated in every effort to do what seemed to him the clear will of God.

Putting on a uniform in April 1861 and accompanying young men to the battlefields of Virginia rescued him from bitterness and self-pity, removed him from petty ecclesial politics, rekindled the fire of his own devotion, and renewed his vocation to the care of souls. As he lingered around the tents with eager, untested soldiers in the spring and summer of 1861—learning their habits and their nicknames, sharing confidences and words of counsel and jests by turn—he knew instinctively how to be the kind of shepherd they needed. The kind of shepherd who could tangle with wolves and endure privation, and who would readily offer his life for those in his care.

4. Fr. John Logan, untitled tribute to Fr. Darius Hubert, S.J. (3 pages), now in the New Orleans Province Archive, Jesuit Archives & Research Center, St. Louis, MO.

At the time of his passing, specific anecdotes arising from his years in the Army of Northern Virginia, many of them recounted in chapter 4 of this book, were told and retold in newspaper tributes and in two large memorials held in New Orleans—from the drama at Hampton Roads, where his chaplain's duties took him aboard CSS *Virginia*, to his healing rounds among the hospitals of Richmond in the months before surrender. The old soldiers had several favorite sayings about their chaplain. One concerned his alacrity and valor on the field: "Had he not been a priest, he could have been a Forrest or a Jackson." The other denoted his presumed influence with the Almighty: "When Father Hubert buries a Confederate soldier, he passes him through the half-way house and sends him straight to heaven." His Presbyterian colleague Thomas Markham was happy to recount the latter witticism, and happy also, as his deceased friend's eulogist at a Mass Meeting sponsored by Confederate veterans of both armies, to add his own memorable summation of Father Hubert's character: "He united the impulsive courage of a Peter to the tender spirit of a John."[5]

Markham was eminently qualified to speak also about what he called Darius Hubert's crowning virtue—his capacity for warm and abiding relationships across denominational boundaries: "A Catholic by birth, rearing, and conviction, he yet gave the right hand of fellowship, his heart in his hand, to men born and bred in other communions." Remarking upon his long friendship with Rabbi James Gutheim, he recounted also Father Hubert's attachment to fellow chaplains A. J. Witherspoon and himself: "Until his failing health forbade, twice each year we walked together in the ranks of the veterans and sat together at the festal board in those annual reunions . . . of the Army of Tennessee and of Northern Virginia. . . . As he walked, one of us on either side and we sat thus at the table, he a Catholic priest and we Presbyterian preachers, as men, as soldiers, and as Christians, we were one, hand grasping hand and heart knit to heart."[6] This quality, universally recognized, had endeared him to the troops from the first days of the war. They always knew—Catholic or

5. Confederate Memorial Hall, New Orleans, held Friday evening June 23, 1893.

6. *New Orleans Times-Picayune*, June 24, 1893, p. 12.

Protestant, churched or unchurched, pious or indifferent—that they were "his boys" and that he loved them with unyielding paternal affection.[7]

At a solemn Requiem Mass at the Jesuit Church where Darius Hubert had labored for decades, homilist Frederick Garesche, S.J., chose as his text John 15:13: "Greater love than this no man hath, that a man lay down his life for his friends."[8] Father Garesche's well-chosen words were born of long friendship and deep understanding, and contextualized the old priest's four-year chaplaincy in Confederate service in spiritual terms: "Not for him the political motive, nor military ardor, hope of warlike fame, nor yet the sacred defense of the hearthstone and the southland, but one only motive there was, worth all these and more, *the love of those to whom he was God-given.*" No better summation was written or spoken in eulogy of Darius Hubert. Such love accounted for his persistence with his men through tribulation and exultation, advance and retreat, his urgent attention to the injured and dying before the smoke cleared from the battlefield, his unflagging kindness to "his many wounded children" in field tents and hospital wards. To the frequent observation that Darius Hubert knew no fear, Garesche offered a gentle disclaimer: "One fear Father Hubert felt, and that fear always—the fear of coming too late to a dying soul." His chaplaincy to his men thus extended well past Appomattox: "When the war-worn, struggling remnants . . . came limping home to desolate hearths, he still clung to hospitals where lay the mangled members of a dead confederacy . . . contending with their conviction of fruitless sacrifice, helpless struggles, hopeless despair. When he had to

7. The veterans, in a formal statement on his passing, observed: "His charity was boundless. It was limited to no creed. Hence, the love he bore for all his companions was strikingly reciprocated" (Special Order No. 1, United Confederate Veterans, June 15, 1893, published in *Weekly Town Talk* [Alexandria, LA], June 24, 1893, p. 2). The epithets most often attached to the name of Darius Hubert are "cheerful," "kind," and "dear"; Father James Sheeran, in his own war diary, almost invariably calls him "good Father Hubert."

8. Held Thursday morning, June 22, 1893. Garesche had also given the eulogy, several months earlier, for Father Hubert's friend Confederate General P. G. T. Beauregard—a briefer and less personal tribute, focused on virtues of honor and patriotism. Quoted excerpts of the Hubert eulogy are taken from the *New Orleans Times-Picayune*, June 23, 1893, p. 3; emphasis mine.

make them strive to live who only asked to die, still worked he in God, with God, for God."

It was through this constancy in "suffering with" that he found his public voice, a gentle, confident voice that bent political animus toward healing and turned collective grief and aspiration into prayer. And lo, observed Father Garesche, "it came to pass, and to many doubtless it was a great marvel, that the old priest, with no eloquence in the pulpit save that which a father's voice has in the ears of loving children . . . became perhaps, the best known, the best beloved of his adopted state."

Another New Orleans Jesuit, Father John Logan, acknowledging rather starkly that "the clergy . . . have not always been what they should have been" and "the young have unfortunately not always found much to attract or admire in our local priesthood," bore tribute to Darius Hubert as one whose example was both compelling to the young and salutary to the lethargic in the priesthood and the indolent in the Creole population at large. In his words, "self-sacrifice is evidently the lesson that Divine Providence wished to give the Society and also the population of New Orleans in the life and death of Fr. Hubert."[9]

The "population of New Orleans," through the voice of its Confederate veterans, asked that the remains of Darius Hubert be returned from Georgia to the Crescent City, to lie in continued proximity to those with whom he had served—in the tomb which he had dedicated so memorably in 1881.[10] Though Father Logan mentions the request and apparently

9. Logan's reflection stands in sharp contrast to Father Hippolyte Gache's assessment that the fortunes of the Catholic Church were "ripening in America" as a result of "educated and intelligent men" in positions of leadership during the war recognizing the intellectual superiority of Roman Catholic dogma over the faith of "poor Protestants" (Gache, *Frenchman, Chaplain, Rebel,* pp. 51–52). It seems rather to have been the selfless dedication and exemplary witness of individual priests, chaplains, and female religious that softened old prejudices and ushered "a new dawn" for American Catholicism.

10. "Resolved, That in testimony of our unfeigned regret at his decease, that his cherished and life-like portrait be draped in mourning, and that we petition his brothers in religion, if compatible with their regulations, to permit his revered remains to be transported hither to rest in our tomb" (*New Orleans Times-Picayune,* June 24, 1893, p. 12). A funeral notice published in the *Atlanta Constitution* two days after his death refers to a "temporary burial"

assumed that it would be honored, the idea seems to have excited debate among the Jesuits themselves, some of whom thought it appropriate to build instead an impressive mausoleum of pure white marble for their famous priest.[11] In the end, neither plan was effected, and the mortal remains of Father Hubert remained in a modestly marked grave at the Jesuit Cemetery of St. Stanislaus College until a fire in 1920 forced their removal to Spring Hill College in Mobile, Alabama.[12]

Failure to bring the old priest home or to establish a tangible memorial to him in New Orleans hastened the time in which his name and legacy would fade from public memory in a city that had cherished and desired to honor him.[13] Once the last of the veterans died and their sons and grandsons began to lose the old stories, the beloved priest who so frequently advocated for perpetual grateful remembrance of the men in gray, was himself forgotten. There was no marker to visit on decoration days, and even his once prominent portraits were removed from the halls of Confederate memory in New Orleans and Richmond—an eventuality he would doubtless have accepted with sublime equanimity: "Thou knowest, O Lord."

---

for Darius Hubert at St. Stanislaus, "as the body will be carried to New Orleans for permanent burial" (June 16, 1893, p. 2). A *New Orleans Picayune* column the same day suggested that the body would be transferred in the coming winter, allowing the people of New Orleans "to display their grief and do honor to the memory of the gentle minister whom all loved and reverenced."

11. *Richmond Dispatch*, Dec. 21, 1902, p. 14.

12. The gravesite there is yet more modest; his name is inscribed on an eight-foot Celtic cross covering a burial plot shared with twenty-five fellow Jesuits.

13. In this he differs from his friend Thomas Markham, to whom an imposing monument was erected at Metairie Cemetery in 1899, and who is prominently featured among the Confederate worthies at Memorial Hall.

Appendix I

ANTI-JESUIT WRITINGS

The Literary Genealogy of *Americans Warned of Jesuitism*

The history of anti-Jesuit polemic is almost as old as the Society of Jesus itself. The first notable example is a clever forgery, the *Monita Secreta* (also known as the *Secret Instructions of the Jesuits*), a Latin pamphlet circulated in manuscript in Kracow in 1612, printed in 1614, and translated into French and English in the 1660s. Though it purports to be written by the superior general of the society, it was almost certainly penned by a disgruntled former Jesuit, discharged after failing his exam in 1611. It is filled with "revelations" that will characterize all such publications in decades and centuries to come: stories of political intrigue and machinations, plots to win favors from nobles, princes, and magistrates and to induce the generosity of rich widows (while discouraging them from remarrying), self-serving manipulation and misrepresentation of the gospel, and use of the confessional as a channel for spiritual and financial leverage over wealthy penitents: "with the Jew they were Jews to gain their object; with the infidel they were sceptics; to the immoral they were the most liberal and indulgent, until they gained the absolute ascendency over them. Hence they found their way into Kings' courts, and Queens' boudoirs."[1]

1. From the preliminary "Historical Sketch" of the *Secret Instructions of the Jesuits* in its first American edition, with Latin and English facing pages (New York: American and Foreign Christian Union, 1857), p. 12, which treats the forged text of the *Secrets* as authentic

Though it is clear that the society's extraordinary early growth was to some degree responsible for the backlash and gossip—an evidence of envy as much as of spiritual scruple—there is no doubt that anxiety about the Jesuit vanguard in Europe was also fanned by the distinctive practices of the society itself. Its formation as a military order (with an exacting hierarchical structure and expectations of absolute obedience) and the apparent insularity and single-minded devotion of its members prompted rumors of its being a powerful secret cabal, seeking global domination. Its internationalism, and its concomitant undermining of local and cultural loyalties, seemed "unnatural" and extreme to many. The remarkable success of Jesuits in becoming confessors to Europe's powerful elites was regarded as deeply suspicious, especially as financial benefits flowed from those relationships. Indeed, the avowed poverty of Jesuits was greatly at odds with the obvious collective wealth of the society within a generation or two of its founding. And the order's penchant for controversial uses of casuistry and "probabilism" made it suspect, especially as it became quickly ascendant in establishing educational institutions and recruiting students.

The initial apostolic mission of the Jesuit Order, as Ignatius of Loyola conceived it, was to take the gospel to the Muslim world, and only secondarily to confront Protestantism. But the Jesuits soon became identified as "enforcers" during the Counter Reformation and as militant defenders of papal authority against all secular or reform movements, including Catholic reform movements such as Jansenism in seventeenth-century France. Jansenism was at one level, like many strains of Protestantism, a religious reaction against notorious institutional corruption in the Roman Catholic Church; it emphasized original sin, human depravity, and the necessity of divine grace for salvation, encouraged personal Bible reading, and identified the "true Church" with the just and the elect rather than with Rome; it was influenced to a large extent by the insights of John Calvin and his followers. In the eyes of many Jansenists, moral laxity,

---

and reliable in its revelations about the order. This text followed publication of Pitrat's *Americans Warned of Jesuitism* by only a few years.

theological deviation, and casuistry (apparent philosophical end runs around moral law) were particularly problematic in the Jesuit order.

One of the most influential of all anti-Jesuit writings was penned in the context of the Jesuit/Jansenist controversy—the pseudonymous *Provincial Letters* (1656–57) of Blaise Pascal, a Jansenist convert. Its brilliantly witty satiric attack on Jesuit casuistry and sophistry are made in the name and on the basis of a principled Christian critique.[2] The popularity of the *Letters* prompted a new round of anti-Jesuit invective, not only from Jansenist publications such as the *Les Nouvelles ecclésiastiques* newspaper but also from the pen of the deistic (though Jesuit-trained) Voltaire, who condemned Jesuits in his *Philosophical Dictionary* for their pride and mocked them ruthlessly in his picaresque satire *Candide* (1759) for their hypocrisy, love of luxury, and indifference to genuine human need.[3]

In the same period, an ex-Capuchin priest, Father Peter Norbert (whose writing appeared under various pseudonyms), published a six-volume anti-Jesuit diatribe, including numerous fabricated documents. By the middle of the nineteenth century, therefore, anti-Jesuit literature was a well-established genre and the "Jesuit myth," as it came to be called, incorporating both mendacious and fraudulent as well as more reputable sources, was a cultural commonplace.

Academic critiques were to add to the literature by the end of the

2. A notable Spanish Jesuit theologian, Antonio Escobar y Mendoza (1589–1669), came under especially scathing attack by Pascal for his casuistry, including his defense of "purity of intention" as sufficient justification for morally questionable actions. In Pascal's view, the ancient aphorism about good intentions proving to be a road to hell, sometimes attributed to Bernard of Clairvaux (around 1150), was more plausibly consistent with Christ's teaching. Some of Mendoza's writings were ultimately condemned by Pope Innocent XI.

3. The specific purpose of the *Nouvelles ecclésiastiques* was to defend Jansenist teaching in the light of a proposed papal denunciation in the apostolic constitution *Unigenitus*. As is so often the case in church history, the condemnations of Jansenism mirrored that which Jansenists leveled against Jesuits: accusations of those who "secretly spread evil doctrines under the guise of piety and introduce ruinous sects under the image of sanctity." The anathematizing of Jansenism was of course closely followed by the suppression of the Society of Jesus itself, though the latter proved temporary.

century. In 1881, the ninth edition of *Encyclopædia Britannica* contained a lengthy scholarly article titled "Jesuits" by the respected Anglican divine Rev. Dr. Richard F. Littledale, which distinguishes the order from all other preceding Catholic societies, including even the military orders, arguing that "not in degree merely, but in kind also," the Jesuit Order is "an institution absolutely unique in history." Referring to charges going all the way back to the *Monita Secreta*, Littledale identifies the Machiavellian principle that "the ends justify the means" as normative doctrine among Jesuits, prompting an observation that "the ordinary secular conscience is a safer guard in morals than a Jesuit casuist.[4]

Though Littledale's carefully reasoned and influential essay consolidated anti-Jesuit arguments and provided critics with a good deal of fodder, the writings and lectures of "celebrity apostates" like Alessandro Gavazzi represented a far more potent form of propaganda. Gavazzi was an Italian ex-friar whose notorious public defection from the Catholic Church was followed by an international speaking tour, which included always a lecture devoted specifically to the evils of Jesuitism. His 1853 lectures in Quebec City and Montreal sparked riots. There, as in in New York, Baltimore, Philadelphia, and other seaboard cities, his overriding intent was "to enlighten the Catholic population to the evils and perversions of the Church of Rome, and to warn the Protestant population of the increasing power of Rome and her Jesuit priests in nations where hitherto Protestantism has been dominant."[5] Know Nothings in New Orleans threatened to bring Gavazzi to the city in the 1850s to undermine Archbishop Antoine Blanc, but the visit never happened.

Memoirs of ex-Jesuits were perhaps the most influential texts of all. Most such autobiographical accounts were sensational and lurid (of the same basic anti-Catholic horror genre as the fabricated bestseller *Maria Monk's Awful Disclosures of the Hotel Dieu Nunnery in Montreal*, published in 1836); all tend to perpetuate a view of Jesuitism in which spiritual, financial, and sexual abuses are inextricably conjoined. Other memoirs

4. Littledale's essay may be found at en.wikisource.org/wiki/Encyclopædia_Britannica,_Ninth_Edition/Jesuits.

5. See *Father Gavazzi's Life and Lectures* (New York: De Witt and Davenport, 1853), p. 105.

were more measured, but nonetheless damning—chief among them the autobiographical *Fourteen Years a Jesuit* by Paul Graf von Hoensbroech, written in the 1890s, which reiterated and lent credence to longstanding critiques of the order.[6] The self-interested shenanigans of John Claudius Pitrat in the archdiocese of New Orleans just as Father Hubert and his Jesuit colleagues were laboring to establish their schools fits comfortably in this well-established lineage.

6. *Fourteen Years a Jesuit* was also published in English translation (London: Cassell, 1911). Another highly influential text, a work of fiction (though purporting facticity) was Eugène Sue's serialized novel *Le Juif errant* (1844), which is largely concerned with Jesuit treachery and abuse of power. It caused a worldwide sensation and sold eighty thousand copies immediately upon its publication in translation in America. See McGreevy, *American Jesuits and the World*, p. 21.

Appendix II

CHAPLAINS TO LOUISIANA INFANTRY IN THE ARMY OF NORTHERN VIRGINIA

There have been many attempts to publish lists of army chaplains who served the Confederacy. All have had to overcome considerable challenges, the first being the dearth of Confederate military records generally, many of which went up in smoke when Richmond fell in 1865. Painstaking efforts to gather such information commenced in earnest in the early twentieth century from available records in home states, as well as in personal diaries and letters and in religious memoirs such as J. William Jones's *Christ in the Camp*[1] and William W. Bennett's *Narrative of the Great Revival*,[2] and, on the Catholic side, David Power Conyngham's until recently unpublished early manuscript (around 1872), "The Soldiers of the Cross: Heroism of the Cross, or Nuns and Priests on the Battlefield."[3] A variety of researchers have drawn on a common store of such records as well as additional local troves of information, with decidedly mixed

1. J. William Jones, *Christ in the Camp: Or, Religion in Lee's Army* (Richmond, VA: B. F. Johnson and Co., 1887).

2. William W. Bennett, *A Narrative of the Great Revival Which Prevailed in the Southern Armies During the Late Civil War Between the States of the Federal Union* (Philadelphia: Claxton, Remsen & Haffelfinder, 1877).

3. Conyngham's memoir, based on sources gathered shortly after the war, focuses largely on Federal and/or Irish Catholics. It has recently been edited for publication by Father David Endres and William Kurtz as *Soldiers of the Cross, the Authoritative Text: The Heroism of Catholic Chaplains and Sisters in the American Civil War* (Notre Dame, IN: University of Notre Dame Press, 2019).

results—as incorrect information has often been repeated from one published roster to the next. The most comprehensive and accurate roster to date appears in *Faith in the Fight: Civil War Chaplains.*[4]

Given the overwhelming preponderance of Protestant clergy serving the troops, especially in the South, the rosters have tended to be especially problematic with respect to the Confederate Catholic chaplains—sometimes omitting them altogether, often getting their names wrong, and/or placing them in the wrong regiments. A lamentable mid-twentieth-century example is Charles Pitts's *Chaplains in Gray,* which lists Father Hippolyte Gache as "Hippolite Farber" and includes Father Darius Hubert twice, but incorrectly in both instances.[5] Fortunately, Father Robert Miller (author of *Both Prayed to the Same God*) is currently at work on an updated study, with roster, of Catholic chaplains North and South.[6]

The most specifically relevant roster to this study in many respects is Sidney Romero's "Louisiana Clergy and the Confederate Army," which lists Catholic and Protestant clergy from Louisiana, including those serving in the western theater, such as the New Orleans Presbyterians

4. *Faith in the Fight: Civil War Chaplains,* ed. John W. Brinsfield Jr., Benedict Maryniak, William C. Davis, and James I. Robertson Jr. (Mechanicsburg, PA: Stackpole Books, 2003). Some wrinkles remain to be worked out even there, including one elaborated below—the failure to distinguish between different military units with similar names—as well as an apparent failure to check some previous erroneous listings against actual service records. James A. God[f]rey, for example, is listed as Methodist chaplain to the Fourteenth Louisiana—the same regiment as Father James Sheeran, which would surely have been an uncomfortable assignment; Godfrey's service records, however, place him in the western theater, with the Fourth Louisiana. This same error (among others) occurs in H. Rondel Rumburg's recent *Roster of Confederate Chaplains* (Owassa, OK: Truth in History, 2018), and there the name is also wrong: Godfrey becomes "Godey."

5. Charles F. Pitts, *Chaplains in Gray: The Confederate Chaplains' Story* (1857; rpt. Penn Laird, VA: Sprinkle Publications, 2003), appendix: "A Roster of Confederate Chaplains." Pitts has "Father D. H. Herbert" as chaplain to the First Louisiana Regiment, and a "Father Hubert" with the Seventh Louisiana. There were no "Herberts" in the Southern chaplaincy and only one "Hubert," the subject of this book, who served with the First Louisiana "Nelligan's".

6. The brief 2010 MA thesis by Gary W. McCall at the University of New Orleans, despite its promising title, "God of Our Fathers: Catholic Chaplains in the Confederate Armies," and its stated intent to focus on Louisiana Catholic chaplains, provides no roster and only a modest overview of familiar sources, principally relating to Fathers Sheeran and Gache.

Thomas R. Markham and Benjamin Morgan Palmer, both of whom were friends of Darius Hubert after (if not before) the war, and Alexander Bakewell, the Washington Artillery cannoneer who was ordained an Episcopalian priest during the war and then became a chaplain in the Army of Tennessee.[7] Bakewell and Markham were eulogists at the time of Father Hubert's death in 1893.[8]

The specific intent of the roster assembled here is to list only those chaplains associated with Louisiana infantry in the Army of Northern Virginia, and who therefore shared ministry, directly or indirectly, with Father Hubert.[9] The chaplain of the First Louisiana doubtless knew and worked with clergy attached to Carolina, Virginia, and Georgia regiments represented in the ANV, but the focus here is on those who directly served Louisianans. In compiling this list, I have corrected some previous published information, and added clarifying detail in several instances, including the brevity of tenure served by some listed chaplains.

It may seem strange to speak of Protestant clergy as "sharing ministry" with a Jesuit priest, especially given that two of Father Hubert's Catholic colleagues in Lee's army, Father James Sheeran and Father Hippolyte Gache, are on record with their outspoken disdain for the Protestant pastors they encountered during the war years, notably those engaged in the revivals.[10] At best, these priests regarded their Protestant counterparts

7. Sidney J. Romero, "Louisiana Clergy and the Confederate Army," *Louisiana History* 2.3 (Summer 1961): 277–300. Romero also lists several chaplains serving with cavalry and artillery units.

8. Father Hubert was also close to Rev. Andrew Jackson Witherspoon, Presbyterian chaplain to the Twenty-First Alabama, who settled in New Orleans in 1873 and oversaw a ministry to sailors called Seamen's Bethel. Witherspoon predeceased Hubert by several years.

9. The Louisiana infantry units that served in the Army of Northern Virginia were: First ("Nelligan's"), Second, Fifth, Sixth, Seventh, Eighth, Ninth, Tenth, Fourteenth, and Fifteenth (organized in July 1862 from companies of the Seventh and Third Infantry Battalions, and in late 1863 consolidated with remnants of the Fifth and Sixth infantries). All other Louisiana regiments, including the First Regulars ("Strawbridge's") and the Third Infantry, served in the Army of Tennessee. Western chaplains sometimes mistakenly end up in rosters of the ANV; Methodist Samuel B. Surratt, for example, who was attached to the Nineteenth (but whose service records indicate a very fleeting tenure) has sometimes been listed with the Second.

10. See chapter 4, above.

with a kind of pitying condescension for what seemed to them a cheap and misleading facsimile of the proper rites of the true Church. While they were on occasion more than happy to preach to Protestants, they were unwilling to reciprocate or even, for the most part, cooperate. Part of the burden of this book has been to demonstrate that Darius Hubert was something of a sign of contradiction in this regard.

Another significant challenge for those compiling rosters is that the definition of "chaplain" is itself problematic and was used quite loosely (and sometimes self-servingly) to cover a multitude of spiritual roles during the war. Ministers who served in the ranks as soldiers, but would occasionally preach or lead Bible studies or prayer groups, were sometimes informally styled chaplains. "Missionaries" or "evangelists" who visited the men in their encampments between military campaigns are sometimes included in "chaplain" lists, as are some local clergy from the vicinity of battlefields in Virginia, Maryland, and Pennsylvania, who assumed itinerant pastoral duties in encampments or in hospitals. Though these often earned the respect and trust of the troops, they certainly had less rapport with the soldiers than those who endured the grueling marches and bloody battles with them.

Even during the "revival" seasons, religious controversialists were not welcome in the Army of Northern Virginia, nor were preachers with strong denominational agendas. Stonewall Jackson was emphatic on this point, asking that denominational distinctives be downplayed by all clergy and that chaplains simply "preach the gospel." The faith statement adopted by the clergy in the ANV, based on the pre-Reformation Apostles' Creed, is a strikingly ecumenical response to this directive.

Military chaplaincy is not for the faint of heart, and even some who enthusiastically embraced formal commission as regimental chaplains wilted rather quickly. Rev. Caleb Dowe, an Episcopalian from Alexandria, Louisiana, was briefly associated with the Ninth Louisiana Regiment, but resigned before the end of 1861—possibly dismayed, or perhaps even afflicted, by disease. (Measles, mumps, and typhoid fever claimed more than a hundred young volunteers before they saw their first battle.) An even shorter tenure can be ascribed to William George Howard (also from

Alexandria, Louisiana), who appears on numerous rosters as having been attached as chaplain to the Seventh Louisiana Regiment. But Chaplain Howard's entire service record consists of a single pay voucher; he departed for home in August 1861, one month after signing on.

Few ordinary clergy, accustomed to comfortable pulpits and polite society, were up to the challenge of dealing with unruly and irreligious men. Although Major Chatham Roberdeau Wheat, of the infamous First Louisiana Special Battalion (the "Tigers," mostly comprised of wharf rats and ruffians from the New Orleans docks), requested from Archbishop Odin a full-time Catholic chaplain for his troops, none was found. Such duties, largely unwelcome by the men, were managed on an ad hoc basis by available chaplains from other units and by priests in Richmond. Material incentives were nonexistent. The chaplains' monthly stipend, reduced from eighty-five to fifty dollars by the Confederate Congress in May 1861, caused a flurry of resignations and several indignant editorials by both denominational and secular newspapers.[11] Overall, turnover among chaplains was extremely high, especially in the first two years of the war, and those who shirked duty, contributed little, took furloughs for trivial reasons, or simply deserted were a source of perpetual agitation throughout the ranks from the common privates to the generals. Very few chaplains were attached to military units for the entire duration of the war.[12]

When Robert E. Lee was asked, following the war, about his recollections of the Catholic chaplains who served his army, his response was that there were only three "regular chaplains" from the Roman Catholic

11. For example, "Chaplains," *Church Intelligencer* 2 (October 4, 1861): 79; *Central Presbyterian* 34 (September 26, 1861): 36. The subject was a matter of vigorous and often heated debate in the *Richland Dispatch* in November 1861—with some arguing that the modest salary effectively "weeded out" unworthy fortune-seekers, leaving the army with only the best and most devoted Christian pastors, and others retorting that the best educated and most qualified chaplains were the ones most impeded from serving by this measure. The latter argument eventually proved more persuasive, and chaplains' wages were raised to (a still meagre) eighty dollars per month in April 1862.

12. Norton, *Rebel Religion*, suggests that not more than fifty Confederate chaplains served for the entire four years (pp. 97, 115–34).

Church: Father Darius Hubert, Father James Sheeran, and Father Giles Smulders; all three were associated with Louisiana regiments.[13] The fact that Lee does not mention Father Hippolyte Gache reflects Gache's detachment from the Tenth Regiment in the fall of 1862, after which he served in hospitals and other Catholic foundations in and around Lynchburg. While several sources state that Gache remained a military chaplain throughout the war, apparently on the basis of a regimental engagement list included with his very brief military record (but which has no notations as to his presence or absence), the last battle at which he was with the Tenth was in fact Cedar Run (August 9, 1862).[14] Lee also fails to mention Father Matthew O'Keefe from Norfolk, Virginia, who was named "brigade chaplain" first to Blanchard's short-lived brigade and then to that of William ("Little Billy") Mahone, previously of the Sixth Virginia. While Father O'Keefe was a noted Southern partisan and sometime visitor to the imprisoned Jefferson Davis after the war, his brigade chaplaincy was essentially honorific and involved no field duty.

One of the particular complications attendant on creating a roster of Louisiana chaplains in Lee's army relates to confusions and duplications in nomenclature that have stymied researchers for years. For example, a Protestant pastor named John Timberlake is sometimes counted among Louisiana Confederate chaplains, but his "Second Louisiana" was not the Southern regiment in Northern Virginia but a Union company raised by Benjamin Butler in New Orleans. Even within the Confederacy, terminology can be vexing: the Methodist pastor Charles F. Evans, sometimes listed as chaplain to the "Ninth Louisiana" and therefore attached to the ANV "Tigers," was actually with the Ninth Louisiana Cavalry Regiment

13. Lee's letter appears in the Conyngham manuscript. The former general added that other Catholic clergy "visited" the men, "of whom the Bishop of Richmond [Father John McGill] was conspicuous." See *Soldiers of the Cross*, pp. 27–28.

14. Father Cornelius Buckley, in editing the Gache letters, makes his situation clear, though still referring to him as chaplain of the Tenth, despite his short tenure and despite the fact that Father Gache stops signing himself as "Chaplain, C.S.A." after November 1862. Others, including Dom Aidan Henry Germain, *Catholic Military and Naval Chaplains: 1776–1917* (1929; rpt. Westminster, MD: Willow Bend Books, 2002), place Gache falsely "at all the major engagements of the war."

(Ogden's), a mounted infantry unit whose sphere of operations was Mississippi and Louisiana.[15]

Of particular pertinence to this volume is the fact that there were two different "First Louisiana" infantry regiments in the Confederacy, both raised almost entirely in New Orleans—one of which spent the war in the Army of Northern Virginia ("Nelligan's"), while the other spent the war entirely in the western theater ("Strawbridge's").[16] For those assembling records, this has been a considerable source of confusion: the western "First" was formally the First Louisiana Infantry Regulars, and some documents add "Regulars" for clarification; others have the abbreviation "Reg." which has understandably been mistaken by some simply to mean "Regiment." Virtually all of the chaplain rosters compiled to date (including Romero's "Louisiana Clergy" and Brinsfield et al., *Faith in the Fight*) fail to make this distinction, thus creating the impression that certain chaplains served in the ANV when in fact they did not.[17]

Such is the case of Father Anthony Carius, a New Orleans Catholic priest who is sometimes said to have been chaplain to the "First Louisiana Regiment, together with the immortal Darius Hubert." But Carius was never in the east; he was a chaplain to the First Louisiana Regulars in the Army of Tennessee, where his reputation was somewhat mixed, at least among the non-Catholic troops.[18] Likewise, an Episcopalian, Ballard S.

15. Other errors arise when soldiers who became chaplains during the war are incorrectly identified *as chaplains* with their unit of enlistment. Thus Marcus Boatner Chapman, a young Louisiana Methodist who served as a private with the Washington Artillery, was later "promoted to chaplain," but not with that unit (despite being listed in that capacity on several rosters); his chaplaincy, which commenced in 1864, was with the Twenty-Sixth Mississippi.

16. "Nelligan's" included also an original company from Caddo Parish in northern Louisiana (Caddo Rifles). Later in the war, two other Louisiana companies—Red River Rebels, from Rapides Parish, and Shreveport Grays, from Shreveport—also served with the eastern First.

17. An otherwise admirably detailed roster appears in the 1964 UCLA doctoral dissertation of Frank Hieronymus, "For Now and Forever: The Chaplains of the Confederate States Army" (appendixes A and B), available as an authorized facsimile (Ann Arbor: UMI, 2000). Though Hieronymus checked service records for accuracy, he too fails to distinguish between the two "First Louisiana" regiments.

18. See Philip Daingerfield Stephenson, *Civil War Memoir of Philip Daingerfield Stephenson, D.D.*, ed. Nathaniel Cheairs Hughes Jr. (Baton Rouge: Louisiana State University Press,

Dunn, who served a scant one-month sinecure as chaplain of the "First Louisiana," and then simply walked away without resigning, was with the Regulars.

A more noteworthy example is the elusive Father Abram Ryan, the "poet priest" of the Confederacy, whose role as a chaplain to Southern troops became the stuff of many legends after the war. Ryan was sometimes said to have been present and offering succor to Catholic soldiers at Fredericksburg and Gettysburg, and was even reported to have been, following Chancellorsville, "at the bedside of Stonewall Jackson." When a life-size statue of Ryan was erected and dedicated in Mobile, Alabama, in 1913, his memorialist hedged: "While we know but little of his life and work as an army chaplain, it seems to be a well-established fact that he did serve throughout the war as a chaplain in one of the regiments in General Lee's army."[19] Ryan's most recent biographers, Don Beagle and Bryan Giemza, noting that evidence is limited, nonetheless grant the plausibility of Ryan having been connected briefly with the Army of Northern Virginia, partly on the basis of records suggesting a connection to the "First Louisiana" regiment. But it is clear that, inasmuch as Father Ryan had any pastoral contact with Louisiana troops, it was with "Strawbridge's" infantry, the western "First." All of his assumed appearances in Lee's army are not "well-established facts" at all, but fictions that Ryan himself made no effort, unfortunately, to correct during his own lifetime.[20]

1998), p. 20. Referring to the "debauched" Irish soldiers in his company who not only drank to excess but engaged in "deeds of secrecy and violence . . . to satisfy immediate lusts, such as marrying green country girls and deserting them when the army moved away," Stephenson complains that "a wicked little priest, Father Carius, would come to them periodically, erect his tent, and absolve them all, they confessing with the greatest outward reverence. Then afterwards he would gamble and drink with them."

19. "Monument to Father Ryan in Mobile," *Confederate Veteran* 21 (1913): 489–90.

20. See Donald Robert Beagle and Bryan Albin Giemza, *Poet of the Lost Cause: A Life of Father Ryan* (Knoxville: University of Tennessee Press, 2008). This correction of the claims that Ryan may have visited the Army of Northern Virginia is now accepted by the authors; their revised account solves many of the riddles of Ryan's whereabouts during the war. See Beagle's "Integrating Digital and Archival Sources in Historical Research: Recovering Lost

The twofold effect of a detailed examination of these records is to amend the impression of a large contingent of clergy, both Catholic and Protestant, ministering among Louisiana troops in the east, and to highlight the lack of Catholic pastoral care overall in the entire Army of Northern Virginia. As such it sets in perspective the enormous spiritual burden carried by the three "regular chaplains" named by Robert E. Lee—Fathers Smulders, Sheeran, and Hubert.

A Roster of Chaplains to Louisiana Infantry in the Army of Northern Virginia, with Some Associated Clergy

CATHOLIC REGIMENTAL CHAPLAINS

Father Louis-Hippolyte Gache, S.J. (Tenth Louisiana Infantry)
One of the French-born Jesuits who came to Louisiana in the 1840s, Father Gache (1817–1907) worked alongside Darius Hubert at Grand Coteau and Baton Rouge. He served with the Tenth Louisiana Infantry Regiment until the fall of 1862, after which he ministered in hospitals in the Lynchburg area. In late February 1865 he was sent with a group of nuns to the Stuart Hospital in Richmond. He was there (not in the "trenches of Petersburg," as some sources claim) when the capital city fell. After the war he went north, where he served in various Catholic universities and churches in Maryland; Washington, DC; Pennsylvania; and New York. He died in Montreal.

Father Egidius ("Giles") Smulders, C.Ss.R. (Eighth Louisiana Infantry)
Born in Holland, Smulders (1815–1900) came to America in 1845, serving parishes in Maryland, Michigan, New York, and Missouri before joining the Redemptorist community in New Orleans, where he was when the war broke out. Though not a Southern partisan, he was sent as chaplain

Knowledge about a Catholic Poet of the Civil War," *Catholic Library World* (March 2011): 201–9; also my "Contrasting Legacies of Confederate Priests Abram Ryan and Darius Hubert," pp. 1–22.

to the Eighth Louisiana Infantry Regiment. He kept no diary and was reticent about his service following the war; one relies on the extensive diary of Father Sheeran, as well as service records, to place him in various campaigns and in hospital service. He was from January 1 through October 31, 1862, absent from his command on "detached service," and then again from November 1863 through February 1865, in North Carolina. In late 1864 Father Smulders initiated a quixotic plan to recruit foreign-born Catholic (especially Irish and German) prisoners of war held in the Salisbury Prison in Rowan County, North Carolina, to take up arms for the Confederate cause; he later admitted that "few availed themselves of the opportunity." Smulders returned briefly to New Orleans after surrender, but his tenure in the South ended soon afterward with his transfer to St. Louis and points north.

Father James Sheeran, C.Ss.R. (Fourteenth Louisiana Infantry)
James Sheeran (1819–1881) was born in Ireland, immigrated to America (possibly via Canada) in his youth, then married and fathered three children. When his wife died, he felt drawn to the priesthood. After he made what were deemed suitable arrangements for his children, Father Giles Smulders, his Redemptorist confessor and effectively his spiritual father, mediated his somewhat rocky transition from secular to religious life. Serving as priest at St. Alphonsus Church in New Orleans when the war commenced, he was assigned chaplain to the Fourteenth Louisiana Infantry Regiment on October 2, 1861. Throughout the war, the garrulous and opinionated Sheeran was "a fixture in the Tigers camps, becoming a particular favorite of the heavily Irish-Catholic Sixth Louisiana."[21] When his Fourteenth Regiment was swapped with the Ninth following the Maryland campaign, he served in the same [Second Louisiana] Brigade as Darius Hubert. Taken as a prisoner of war for crossing Federal lines late in 1864, he was released early in 1865 and returned to Richmond, where he remained in hospital until surrender. After the war he returned briefly to New Orleans but then, like Father Smulders, left the South for good.

21. Mingus, *The Louisiana Tigers in the Gettysburg Campaign*, p. 13.

He eventually had a falling out with his order and died a secular priest in Morristown, New Jersey.

Father Darius Hubert, S.J. (First Louisiana Infantry)

Born in Toulon, France, Darius Hubert (1823–1893) spent his entire adult life in the American South, apart from fleeting ventures into Maryland and Pennsylvania with his regiment during the Civil War. He was the only commissioned Catholic Confederate chaplain in Lee's army to return home permanently to the city of his enlistment. He thus maintained a continuous ministry with survivors of the conflict whose experiences he had shared and whose ongoing suffering he would also share. His personal regard for the Confederate generals under whom he served was expressed frequently and eloquently at veterans' reunions and occasions of public memorial and in the consecration of monuments to fallen soldiers.

PROMINENT CATHOLIC CLERGY LOOSELY AFFILIATED WITH THE ARMY OF NORTHERN VIRGINIA

Father Oscar Aloysius Sears (Lynchburg)

Father Sears was a convert from Methodism and one-time Jesuit novice. Serving at St. Francis Xavier Church in Lynchburg at the outset of the war, he ministered to the wounded in local hospitals while retaining his normal pastoral duties. He worked alongside Father Gache, though their relationship was perfunctory and sometimes tense, and he knew Father Hubert, with whom he seems to have formed a close friendship. After the war Father Sears was sent back to his first parish, St. Joseph Church, Martinsburg, to rebuild and restore a church that had been desecrated by Federal troops. He died in 1867, at thirty-seven years of age.

Bishop John McGill (Richmond)

Bishop McGill was American born, of Irish parents. A strong partisan of the South, he had a reputation not only for pastoral but intellectual leadership in the Catholic Church. The library in his Richmond residence was impressive in scope and range, and his knowledge of church history, canon law, theology, and Scripture was virtually unrivaled among his ecclesiastical peers. Among his many publications of both dogmatic and pastoral nature may be found a "Catholic Devotional for Confederate Soldiers" intended to serve as an aid to the "essential practices of Christian life"—and to counteract the many Protestant tracts flowing into the army. He established a hospital at Richmond for wounded soldiers and made provision for their care. Robert E. Lee mentioned him as "conspicuous" among the Catholic clergy who, though not commissioned as chaplains, provided active spiritual support for Confederate troops. He also visited Catholic soldiers in Libby Prison. Bishop McGill died in 1872.

Father Matthew O'Keefe (Norfolk)

The Irish-born Father O'Keefe made the acquaintance of General Albert Blanchard while the general was on the peninsula early in the war. When Blanchard was promoted to brigadier general, he asked that O'Keefe be named his "brigade chaplain." This title, which carried over to William ("Little Billy") Mahone's Brigade when Blanchard was relieved of field command, was honorific, involving more prayer than presence. There is no evidence that O'Keefe ever followed troops or served on the field, though he clearly wished it otherwise. He revered the Confederate leaders and after the war visited the imprisoned Jefferson Davis.

Father John Teeling (Richmond)

Another native of Ireland and vicar general of the Richmond diocese, Father Teeling is sometimes said to have been chaplain to "Wheat's Tigers," the First Special Battalion, Louisiana Infantry. His name is used in a letter of introduction by Captain R. Going Atkins of the "Tigers" to the Irish Bishop of Kerry, Reverend D. Moriarty, asking that he "dissuade the peasantry of your diocese from emigrating to the northern shores of America "to imbue their hands with the blood of their kindred."[22] However,

22. "A Louisiana Tiger and Mosby Ranger in Ireland," irishamericancivilwar.com/2012/06/09/a-louisiana-tiger-and-mosby-ranger-in-ireland/.

no formal attachment to that regiment exists (or to the First Virginia, to which he is also sometimes said to have been attached), and Teeling seems rather to have been a kind of chaplain-at-large in the early stages of the war in the vicinity of Richmond with troops who lacked formal Catholic ministry. Service records list him simply as "Chaplain, C.S.A.," until March 1862, when he was relieved of duty. In November of that year he was reassigned to chaplaincy in the Richmond hospitals, where he may have worked with Darius Hubert in the late stages of the war. He left his pastorate at St. Patrick's in Richmond in January 1865 for unspecified reasons, and his whereabouts after surrender are unknown; Catholic sources do not list him in active ministry elsewhere in the United States after that time.

PROTESTANT REGIMENTAL CLERGY

Patrick Gibson Robert, Second Louisiana

Robert was an Episcopalian, appointed on July 1, 1861. He left the Second Louisiana for a Christmas furlough on December 24 and was then "relieved from duty" on September 12, 1862, after which he transferred to the Thirty-Fourth Virginia, serving with that regiment until the end of the war.

Robert Hardie Jr., Second Louisiana

Hardie, though a Caddo Parish Louisianan, first enlisted as a private in company B of the Fifteenth Virginia, where he served in the summer of 1861. A Methodist and an aspiring preacher, he applied for and received an appointment as chaplain to the Tenth Georgia Infantry. When he requested yet another transfer the following year, this time to the Second Louisiana, at the suggestion of Colonel Jesse Williams, his Georgian commanding officer Willis C. Holt was disparaging: "Approved, as he was of no benefit to this Regiment." Hardie was evidently the "young preacher" befriended and mentored by Darius Hubert, possibly even before his assignment to the Second, since one of the companies in the First Infantry was raised in his home parish of Caddo, Louisiana, and proximity would have encouraged him to visit his acquaintances there. One gets the impression of an earnest and lovable hothead, for whom mentoring was likely necessary. Captured and exchanged multiple times, he was eventually reassigned to the Virginia reserves at Danville. Late in the war he conceived the idea of raising a company of black soldiers in Halifax County, Virginia, a notion supported by General Zebulon York but that never came to fruition. The final entry in his service records call him a "gallant and worthy officer." After surrender his denomination sent him as a "missionary" to Houma, Louisiana, where local blacks had claimed the church in the name of a newly formed African Methodist Episcopal congregation; he was able eventually to recover the building, but the zealous pastor found the spiritual indifference of white residents more daunting that anything he had faced in the war.

Robert H. Reed, Fifth Louisiana

Though formally (but only fleetingly) attached to the Fifth Louisiana, Robert Reed may not have been a Louisianan at all. A Presbyterian pastor by this name is referred to as "magnificent preacher" in the extant correspondence of two ANV soldiers, both of whom heard him preach to a very large crowd in July 1861.[23] Neither soldier was a member of the Fifth Louisiana; neither was in fact from Louisiana. The chaplain in question would seem to have been Rev. Robert H. Reed of Spartanburg, South Carolina, a friend and protégé of the New Orleans Presbyterian and Southern firebrand Benjamin Morgan Palmer. Reed had, like Palmer, a reputation as a very fine pulpit orator. Palmer may have encouraged his friend to offer his services to the Confederacy. His term of service was only three months; appointed in June 1861, he resigned in September of the same year.

Livias H. Baldwin, Fifth Louisiana

Baldwin's denomination is unknown. His chaplaincy followed that of Reverend Reed, commencing in the summer or early fall of 1862. Captured at Sharpsburg, apparently after going behind enemy lines under a flag of

23. Romero, "Louisiana Clergy," p. 286.

truce, he wrote to General McLellan to request permission to visit family in Newark, New Jersey. The request was denied. He was paroled at Fort McHenry, Maryland, and exchanged at Aikens Landing in November 1862, after which he detached from the Fifth and went home on a Christmas furlough. He spent the remainder of the war as a western chaplain, first in Monroe, Louisiana, and then in Galveston, Texas. While in Galveston he launched a successful appeal to the women of Houston to provide Bibles and tracts for the soldiers under his care and participated in a revival mission "leading to eighty conversions."[24]

William M. Strickler, Fifth Louisiana

A physician and assistant surgeon for the Fifth Louisiana, Strickler served also as acting chaplain following the departure of Baldwin.[25] He was wounded and captured at Gettysburg but eventually returned to service with his Louisiana regiment through the end of the war.

Caleb Dowe, Ninth Louisiana

Rev. Caleb Dowe, an Episcopalian (rector of St. James, Rapides Parish), was formally commissioned as a regimental chaplain to the Ninth in late August 1861 but lasted only a few months, resigning before the year was out.

Florence McCarthy, Ninth Louisiana

A Virginia Baptist, graduate of Richmond College, Rev. Florence McCarthy was initially attached to the Seventh Virginia Infantry, but then transferred to the Ninth Louisiana in September 1863. An ardent partisan of the Southern cause, McCarthy was frequently quoted in the *Religious*

24. Deborah M. Liles and Angela Boswell, eds., *Women in Civil War Texas: Diversity and Dissidence in the Trans-Mississippi* (Denton: University of North Texas Press, 2016), p. 86.

25. Mingus, *The Louisiana Tigers in the Gettysburg Campaign*, p. 13 and note. And see the chaplain list compiled from the recollections of J. William Jones (*Christ in the Camp*) in the second appendix, "Religion in the Southern Army" by S. M. Cherry, in *The Civil War from a Southern Point of View* (Nashville: M.E. Church, 1890), p. 299. Chaplains to Louisiana troops are here listed as Father Sheeran, Robert Hardie, Father Hubert, William Strickler, Father Smulders, and Florence McCarthy.

Herald, in one instance defending Louisiana soldiers against their sometimes raucous reputation: "I have been in many places in the army . . . but nowhere have I seen a more admirable set of people. Their military discipline is the very best, their manners are dignified and friendly, their minds are shrewd and observant, and their hearts are warm and constant. I have never witnessed greater respect for religion and its ministers, greater anxiety to enjoy religious privileges, or more general concern on the subject of personal holiness." It is possible that this rosy assessment did not hold up to closer scrutiny with the particular unit in question; he resigned as chaplain of the Ninth after only two months.

George W. Stickney, Fourteenth Louisiana

Rev. Stickney was Episcopalian rector of St. Matthews Church in Houma, Louisiana, before the war. His service records show a complicated tenure, including an early court of inquiry concerning unspecified "matters" that resulted in his being ordered to "report to duty with his [Fourteenth Louisiana] regiment, [but] with permission to apply for transfer." He transferred in 1862 as chaplain to the "Army of Mobile," where he refashioned himself as army intelligence officer; his constant stream of requisitions for everything from stationery purchases to office cleaning and sweeping drew impatient comment and queries from senior officers. In July 1863 he was sent to Columbus, Georgia, as post chaplain. His duties there were reportedly "very inefficiently performed," his visits to the hospitals "few and far between," with the result that deceased soldiers were often "buried without any of the customary religious rites." The local surgeon general in two rather damning notes recommended his immediate removal so that local clergy could take over the role.

It would have been almost impossible for Father James Sheeran to share duty with any Protestant pastor, but Reverend Stickney would surely have confirmed all of his prejudices. Sheeran does not mention him in his very lengthy war diary. Stickney relocated to New Orleans following surrender; occasional mentions of his war service in local papers (for example, *Times-Picayune*, August 19, 1866, p. 4) are flatteringly inaccurate.

Selected Bibliography

This listing does not include nineteenth-century newspapers and journals consulted and quoted in the footnotes.

Adams, Michael C. C. *Living Hell: The Dark Side of the Civil War.* Baltimore: Johns Hopkins University Press, 2014.

Alexander, Edward Porter. *Fighting for the Confederacy: The Personal Recollections of General Edward Porter Alexander.* Ed. Gary W. Gallagher. Chapel Hill: University of North Carolina Press, 1989.

Anonymous [English combatant]. *Battle-Fields of the South: From Bull Run to Fredericksburgh, With Sketches of Confederate Commanders, and Gossip of the Camps.* 1863. Rpt. New York: Time Life Education, 1984.

Anonymous member of the society. *The Life of Cornelia Connelly, 1809–1879: Foundress of the Society of the Holy Child Jesus.* New York: Longmans, Green and Co., 1922.

Anonymous priest of the diocese [Father Joseph Magri]. *The Catholic Church in the City and Diocese of Richmond.* Richmond, VA: Whittet & Shepperson, 1906.

Archbishop Blanc Administrative Records, 1858–1860. Office of Archives and Records, Archdiocese of New Orleans.

Baker, Vaughan B., and Jean T. Kreamer. *Louisiana Tapestry: The Ethnic Weave of St. Landry Parish.* Lafayette: University of Southwestern Louisiana, 1982.

Bartlett, Napier. *A Soldier's Story of the War, Including the Marches and Battles of the Washington Artillery and of Other Louisiana Troops.* New Orleans: Clark & Hofeline, 1874.

Baudier, Roger. *The Catholic Church in Louisiana.* 1939. Rpt. New Orleans: Louisiana Library Association, 1972.

Beagle, Donald Robert, and Bryan Albin Giemza. *Poet of the Lost Cause: A Life of Father Ryan.* Knoxville: University of Tennessee Press, 2008.

Beckett, Edward F., S.J. "Listening to Our History: Inculturation and Jesuit Slaveholding." *Studies in the Spirituality of Jesuits* 28.5 (1996): 1–45.

Bennett, James B. *Religion and the Rise of Jim Crow in New Orleans.* Princeton, NJ: Princeton University Press, 2005.

Bennett, William W. *A Narrative of the Great Revival Which Prevailed in the Southern Armies During the Late Civil War Between the States of the Federal Union.* Philadelphia: Claxton, Remsen, and Haffelfinger, 1877.

Bergeron, Arthur W., Jr. *Confederate Mobile.* Baton Rouge: Louisiana State University Press, 1991.

———. *Guide to Louisiana Confederate Military Units, 1861–1865.* Baton Rouge: Louisiana State University Press, 1989.

Berler, Anne Karen. "'Unconquerable Defiance': Richmond Newspapers and Confederate Defeat, 1864–1865." MA thesis, Virginia Commonwealth University, 2000.

Betts, Alexander D. *Diary of a Confederate Chaplain.* Ed. W. A. Betts. Big Byte Books, 2014.

Biever, Albert H., S.J. *The Jesuits in New Orleans and the Mississippi Valley: Jubilee Memorial.* New Orleans: Society of Jesus in Louisiana, 1924.

Billington, Ray Allen. *The Protestant Crusade 1800–1860: A Study of the Origins of American Nativism.* 1938. Rpt. New York: Quadrangle Books, 1964.

Blied, Benjamin. *Catholics and the Civil War.* Milwaukee: Benjamin Blied, 1945.

Blight, David W. *Race and Reunion: The Civil War in American Memory.* Cambridge, MA: Harvard University Press, 2001.

Bonekemper, Edward H. III. *The Myth of the Lost Cause: Why the South Fought the Civil War and Why the North Won.* Washington, DC: Regnery, 2015.

Boswell, E.M. "Rebel Religion." *Civil War Times Illustrated* 11.8 (October 1972): 26–33.

Bouve, Pauline Carrington. *American Heroes and Heroines.* Boston: Lothrop, Lee & Shepard, 1905. Pp. 234–45.

Brand, Kathryn. "The Jesuits' Slaves." *Georgetown Voice* (February 8, 2007).

Brinsfield, John Wesley, Jr., ed. *The Spirit Divided: Memoirs of Civil War Chaplains. The Confederacy.* Macon, GA: Mercer University Press, 2005.

———, Benedict Maryniak, William C. Davis, and James I. Robertson Jr. *Faith in the Fight: Civil War Chaplains.* Mechanicsburg, PA: Stackpole, 2003.

Buckley, Cornelius M., S.J., *Stephen Larigaudelle Dubuisson, S.J. (1786–1864) and the Reform of the American Jesuits.* Lanham, MD: University Press of America, 2013.

Bush, Robert. *Grace King: A Southern Destiny.* Baton Rouge: Louisiana State University Press, 1983.

Calcutt, Rebecca Barbour. *Richmond's Wartime Hospitals.* Gretna, LA: Pelican Publishing, 2005.

Carey, Patrick W. *People, Priests, and Prelates: Ecclesiastical Democracy and the Tensions of Trusteeism.* Notre Dame, IN: University of Notre Dame Press, 1987.

Carriere, Marius M., Jr. "Anti-Catholicism, Nativism, and Louisiana Politics in the 1850s." *Louisiana History* 35.4 (Autumn 1994): 455–74.

———. *The Know Nothings in Louisiana.* Jackson: University Press of Mississippi, 2018.

Casler, John O. *Four Years in the Stonewall Brigade.* 1893. Rpt. Columbia: University of South Carolina Press, 2005.

Clancy, Thomas H. "The Antebellum Jesuits of the New Orleans Province, 1837–1861." *Louisiana History* 34.3 (Summer 1993): 327–43.

Coco, Gregory A. *A Strange and Blighted Land: Gettysburg: The Aftermath of a Battle.* Gettysburg, PA: Thomas Publications, 1995.

———. *Wasted Valor: The Confederate Dead at Gettysburg.* Gettysburg, PA: Thomas Publications, 1990.

Colby, Tanner. *Some of My Best Friends Are Black: The Strange Story of Integration in America.* New York: Viking Penguin, 2012. Pp. 225–87.

Coleman, William Head. *Historical Sketch Book and Guide to New Orleans and Environs, With Map.* New York: Will H. Coleman, 1885.

Conyngham, David Power, "The Soldiers of the Cross: Heroism of the Cross, or Nuns and Priests on the Battlefield." Unpublished MS, around 1872. University of Notre Dame Archives.

———. *Soldiers of the Cross, the Authoritative Text: The Heroism of Catholic Chaplains and Sisters in the American Civil War.* Ed. David J. Endres and William B. Kurtz. Notre Dame, IN: University of Notre Dame Press, 2019.

Cox, R. David. *The Religious Life of Robert E. Lee.* Grand Rapids, MI: Eerdmans, 2017.

Crook, Malcolm. *Toulon in War and Revolution: From the Ancien Régime to the Restoration.* Manchester, UK: Manchester University Press, 1991.

Curran, R. Emmett, ed. *American Jesuit Spirituality: The Maryland Tradition, 1634–1900.* Mahwah, NJ: Paulist Press, 1988.

———. "Splendid Poverty: Jesuit Slave-Holding in Maryland 1805–1838." *Catholics in the Old South: Essays in Church and Culture.* Ed. Randall M. Miller and Jon L. Waklyn. Macon, GA: Mercer University Press, 1983.

Cutrer, Thomas W., and T. Michael Parrish, eds. *Brothers in Gray: The Civil War Letters of the Pierson Family.* Baton Rouge: Louisiana State University Press, 1997.

Dabney, Robert Lewis. "Chaplains in the Army of Northern Virginia: A List Compiled in 1864 and 1865." Ed. W. Harrison Daniel. *Virginia Magazine of History and Biography* 71 (1963): 327–40.

Dame, William Meade. *From the Rapidan to Richmond and the Spottsylvania Campaign: A Sketch in Personal Narrative of the Scenes a Soldier Saw.* Baltimore: Green-Lucas, 1920.

Daniels, Morna. "French Newspapers and Ephemera from the 1848 Revolution." *British Library Journal* (1998): 219–33.

Davis, Jefferson. *Papers of Jefferson Davis.* Ed. Lynda Lasswell Crist. Vols. 13–14. Baton Rouge: Louisiana State University Press, 2012, 2015.

Dawson, Joseph G., III. *Army Generals and Reconstruction: Louisiana, 1862–1877.* Baton Rouge: Louisiana State University Press, 1982; 1994.

Dedication of the Tomb of the Association of the Army of Northern Virginia, Louisiana Division, and Unveiling of Statue of Stonewall Jackson at Metairie Cemetery, May 10th, 1881. New Orleans: M. F. Dunn and Bro., 1881.

Deeben, John P. "Faith on the Firing Line: Army Chaplains in the Civil War." *National Archives Prologue* 48.1 (Spring 2016): 1–15.

Didier, Eugene L. "Some Southern War-Songs and Their Authors." *Blue and Gray: The Patriotic American Magazine* 2 (1893): 464–68.

Dimitry, John. *Confederate Military History of Louisiana.* First pub. as vol. 10 of *Confederate Military History.* Ed. Clement A. Evans. 1899. Rpt. Pensacola, FL: eBooksOnDisk .com, 2005.

Dooley, John. *John Dooley's Civil War: An Irish American's Journey in the First Virginia Infantry Regiment.* Ed. Robert Emmett Curran. Knoxville: University of Tennessee Press, 2012.

Dollar, Kent T. *Soldiers of the Cross: Confederate Soldier Christians and the Impact of War on Their Faith.* Macon, GA: Mercer University Press, 2005.

Doyle, Elizabeth Joan. "Civilian Life in Occupied New Orleans, 1862–1865." PhD diss., Louisiana State University, 1955. digitalcommons.lsu.edu/gradschool_disstheses/228.

Duncan, Christopher M. "Benjamin Morgan Palmer: Southern Presbyterian Divine." PhD diss., Auburn University, 2008.

East, Charles. *Baton Rouge: A Civil War Album.* Baton Rouge, LA: Charles East, 1977.

Eastman, William R. "The Army Chaplain of 1863." *Personal Recollections of the War of the Rebellion Delivered before the Military Order of the Loyal Legion of the United States, New York Commandery.* 4th ser. Ed. A. Noel Blakeman. New York: G. P. Putnam's Sons, 1912. Pp. 338–50.

Fabun, Sean. "Catholic Chaplains in the Civil War." *Catholic Historical Review* 99.4 (2013): pp. 675–702.

Falligant, Louis A. *A Monograph of the Yellow Fever of 1876: In Savannah, Georgia.* Savannah, GA: Morning News Print, 1888.

"Father John Abbadie: A Sketch." *Woodstock Letters* 24.1 (1895): 16–36.

Faust, Drew Gilpin. *This Republic of Suffering: Death and the American Civil War.* New York: Alfred A. Knopf, 2008.

Ficklen, John Rose. *History of Reconstruction in Louisiana (Through 1868).* Baltimore: Johns Hopkins Press, 1910.

Foster, Gaines. *Ghosts of the Confederacy: Defeat, the Lost Cause, and the Emergence of the New South, 1865–1913.* New York: Oxford University Press, 1987.

Gache, Louis-Hippolyte, S.J. *Frenchman, Chaplain, Rebel: The Civil War Letters of Pere Louis-Hippolyte Gache, S.J., Tenth Louisiana Infantry.* Ed. and trans. Cornelius M. Buckley, S.J. Tuscaloosa: University of Alabama Press, 1981; 2007.

———. "Our College at Baton Rouge, Louisiana." *Woodstock Letters* 27.1 (1898): 1–5.

Gannon, Barbara A. *Americans Remember Their Civil War.* Santa Barbara, CA: Praeger, 2017.

Garidel, Henri. *Exile in Richmond: The Confederate Journal of Henri Garidel.* Ed. Michael Bedout Chesson and Leslie Jean Roberts. Charlottesville: University Press of Virginia, 2001.

Garraghan, Gilbert J., S.J. *The Jesuits of the Middle United States.* 3 vols. New York: American Press, 1938.

Gassler, Francis Leon. *History of St. Joseph's Church, Baton Rouge, La., from 1789 to Date.* Marrero, LA: Hope Haven Press, 1943.

Gehman, Mary. *The Free People of Color of New Orleans: An Introduction.* New Orleans: Margaret Media, 1994.

Genovese, Eugene D. *A Consuming Fire: The Fall of the Confederacy in the Mind of the White Christian South.* Athens: University of Georgia Press, 1998.

"Georgetown University Search for Slave Descendants." *New York Times,* April 17, 2016.

Germain, Dom Aidan Henry. *Catholic Military and Naval Chaplains 1776–1917.* 1929. Rpt. Westminster, MD: Willow Bend Books, 2002.

Gleeson, David T. *Green and the Gray: The Irish in the Confederate States of America.* Chapel Hill: University of North Carolina Press, 2013.

Gwynne, Samuel C. *Rebel Yell: The Violence, Passion, and Redemption of Stonewall Jackson.* New York: Scribner, 2014.

Harmon, Troy D. "The Great Revival of 1863: The Effects Upon Lee's Army of Northern Virginia." *The American Civil War in 1863.* Gettysburg, PA: National Parks Service, 2001. Pp. 105–30.

Hearn, Lafcadio. *The New Orleans of Lafcadio Hearn: Illustrated Sketches from the "Daily City Item."* Ed. Delia Labarre. Baton Rouge: Louisiana State University Press, 2007.

Hennesy, James. *American Catholics: A History of the Roman Catholic Community in the United States.* Oxford, UK: Oxford University Press, 1982.

Hettle, Wallace. *The Confederate Home Front: A History in Documents.* Baton Rouge: Louisiana State University Press, 2017.

Hieronymus, Frank L. "For Now and Forever: The Chaplains of the Confederate States Army." PhD diss., University of California at Los Angeles, 1964. Facsimile, Ann Arbor: UMI, 2000.

Hollandsworth, James G., Jr. *An Absolute Massacre: The New Orleans Race Riot of July 30, 1866*. Baton Rouge: Louisiana State University Press, 2001.

Hughes, Nathaniel Cheairs, Jr. *The Pride of the Confederate Artillery: The Washington Artillery in the Army of Tennessee*. Baton Rouge: Louisiana State University Press, 1997.

Hymns for the Camp. 2nd ed. Raleigh, NC: Strouther and Marcom, 1862.

Imboden, John W. "The Confederate Retreat from Gettysburg." *Battles and Leaders of the Civil War*. 1887. Vol. 3: p. 424.

Janney, Caroline E. *Remembering the Civil War: Reunion and the Limits of Reconciliation*. Chapel Hill: University of North Carolina Press, 2016.

Jeffrey, Katherine Bentley. "The Contrasting Legacies of Confederate Priests Abram Ryan and Darius Hubert, S.J. *U.S. Catholic Historian* 37.1 (Winter 2019): 1–22.

———. *Two Civil Wars: The Curious Shared Journal of a Baton Rouge Schoolgirl and a Union Sailor on the USS Essex*. Baton Rouge: Louisiana State University Press, 2016.

Johnson, Michael P., and James L. Roark. *Black Masters: A Free Family of Color in the Old South*. New York: W. W. Norton, 1984.

Jones, J. William. *Christ in the Camp: Or, Religion in Lee's Army*. Richmond, VA: B. F. Johnson and Co., 1887.

———. *The Davis Memorial Volume; or, Our Dead President, Jefferson Davis, and the World's Tribute to his Memory*. Richmond, VA: B. F. Johnson and Co., 1890.

Jones, Michael Dan. *The Fighting First Louisiana Infantry Regiment in the Army of Northern Virginia*. St. Charles, LA: CreateSpace Independent Publishing, 2016.

Jones, Terry L. *Lee's Tigers: The Louisiana Infantry in the Army of Northern Virginia*. Baton Rouge: Louisiana State University Press, 1987.

———. *Lee's Tigers Revisited: The Louisiana Infantry in the Army of Northern Virginia*. Baton Rouge: Louisiana State University Press, 2017.

Kein, Sybil, ed. *Creole: The History and Legacy of Louisiana's Free People of Color*. Baton Rouge: Louisiana State University Press, 2000.

Kenny, Michael, S.J. *Catholic Culture in Alabama: Centenary Story of Spring Hill College, 1830–1930*. New York: America Press, 1931.

King, Grace. *Memories of a Southern Woman of Letters*. New York: Macmillan, 1932.

———. *New Orleans: The Place and the People*. New York: Macmillan, 1895.

Koger, Larry. *Black Slaveowners: Free Black Slave Masters in South Carolina, 1790–1860*. Columbia: University of South Carolina Press, 1985.

Kraszewski, Gracjan. "Dogma and Dixie: Roman Catholics and the Southern Confederacy during the American Civil War." PhD diss., Mississippi State University, 2016.

Lankford, Nelson D. *Richmond Burning: The Last Days of the Confederate Capital*. New York: Viking, 2002.

Leigh, Philip. *Southern Reconstruction*. Yardley, PA: Westholme, 2017.

Lonn, Ella. *Reconstruction in Louisiana After 1868.* New York: G. P. Putnam's Sons, 1918.

Markham, Thomas Railey. "Portrait of a Southern Preacher: Excerpts from Writings of Thomas Railey Markham (1828–1894). Unpublished MS. Ed. Frances D. Swann. 1978. Private collection of Markham Dossett, Waco, TX.

Mathisen, Robert R. *The Routledge Sourcebook of Religion and the American Civil War: A History in Documents.* New York: Routledge, 2013.

McCabe, Joseph. *A Candid History of the Jesuits.* London: Eveleigh Nash, 1913.

M'Caleb, Thomas, ed. *The Louisiana Book: Selections from the Literature of the State.* 1894. Rpt. New Orleans: Cornerstone, 2012.

McCall, Gary W. "God of Our Fathers: Catholic Chaplains in the Confederate Armies." MA thesis, University of New Orleans, 2010.

McGreevy, John T. *American Jesuits and the World: How an Embattled Religious Order Made Catholicism Global.* Princeton, NJ: Princeton University Press, 2016.

McKim, Randolph. *Leaves from the Diary of a Young Confederate: A Soldier's Recollections.* 1910. New annotated ed. Ed. Lucy Booker Roper. Southaven, MS: Booker House Publishing, 2012.

Miller, Benjamin L. *In God's Presence: Chaplains, Missionaries, and Religious Space During the American Civil War.* Lawrence: University Press of Kansas, 2019.

Miller, Randall M., and Jon L. Wakelyn, eds. *Catholics in the Old South: Essays on Church and Culture.* Macon, GA: Mercer University Press, 1983.

Miller, Robert J. *Both Prayed to the Same God: Religion and Faith in the American Civil War.* Lanham, MD: Lexington Books, 2007.

———. "Religion and Faith—the Forgotten Factor of the Civil War." *Civil War Book Review* 21.2 (Spring 2019): 1–5.

Millet, Nathaniel. "The Memory of Slavery at Saint Louis University." *American Nineteenth Century History* 16.3 (2015): 329–50.

Mingus, Scott L., Sr. *The Louisiana Tigers in the Gettysburg Campaign, June–July 1863.* Baton Rouge: Louisiana State University Press, 2009.

"Minister's Diary Volume 1, 1837–1855." English trans. St. Charles College Collection, New Orleans Province Archive, Jesuit Archives & Research Center, St. Louis, MO.

Morgan, Sarah. *The Civil War Diary of a Southern Woman.* Ed. Charles East. New York: Simon and Schuster, 1992.

Murphy, Edward F. *Angel of the Delta.* Garden City, NY: Hanover House, 1958.

Murphy, Thomas, S.J. *Jesuit Slaveholding in Maryland: 1717–1838.* New York: Routledge, 2001.

Neyrey, Jerome H., S.J. "St. Charles Borromeo and his 'Daughters.'" *Acadiana Catholic* (October 2016): 20–31; (November 2016): 24–25.

———, and Thomas Clancy, S.J. *Southern Jesuit Biographies.* Lafayette, LA: Acadian House, 2015.

Noll, Mark. *The Civil War as Theological Crisis.* Chapel Hill: University of North Carolina Press, 2006.

Norton, Herman. *Rebel Religion: The Story of the Confederate Chaplains.* St. Louis, MO: Bethany Press, 1961.

Nystrom, Justin A. *New Orleans after the Civil War: Race, Politics, and a New Birth of Freedom.* Baltimore: Johns Hopkins University Press, 2010.

Ochs, Stephen J. *A Black Patriot and a White Priest: André Cailloux and Claude Paschal Maistre in Civil War New Orleans.* Baton Rouge: Louisiana State University Press, 2000.

O'Connell, David. *Furl That Banner: The Life of Abram J. Ryan, Poet-Priest of the South.* Macon, GA: Mercer University Press, 2006.

Pasquier, Michael. "Catholic Southerners, Catholic Soldiers: White Creoles, the Civil War, and the Lost Cause in New Orleans." MA thesis, Florida State University, 2003.

———. *Fathers on the Frontier: French Missionaries and the Roman Catholic Priesthood in the United States, 1789–1870.* New York: Oxford University Press, 2010.

Pastor, Lori Renee. "Black Catholicism: Religion and Slavery in Antebellum Louisiana." MA thesis, Louisiana State University, 2005.

Patterson, Gerard A. *Debris of Battle: The Wounded of Gettysburg.* Mechanicsburg, PA: Stackpole Books, 1997.

Paz, Denis G. *Priesthoods and Apostasies of Pierce Connelly: A Study of Victorian Conversion and Anti-Catholicism.* Lewiston, NY: Edwin Mellen, 1986.

Perrin, William Henry. *Southwest Louisiana Biographical and Historical.* New Orleans: Gulf Publishing, 1891.

Pfeffer, Miki. "'Mr. Chairman and FELLOW AMERICAN CITIZENS': African American Agency at the World's Industrial and Cotton Centennial Exposition in New Orleans, 1884–1885." *Louisiana History* 51.4 (Autumn 2010): 442–62.

Phifer, Thomas H. Civil War Letters. Excerpts. www.countygenweb.com/desotoparishla/phifer.html.

Phillips, Jason. *Diehard Rebels: The Confederate Culture of Invincibility.* Athens: University of Georgia Press, 2007.

Pitrat, John Claudius. *Americans Warned of Jesuitism, or, the Jesuits Unveiled.* New York: J. S. Redfield, 1851.

Pitts, Charles F. *Chaplains in Gray: The Confederate Chaplains' Story.* 1957. Rpt. Penn Laird, VA: Sprinkle Publications, 2003.

Platt, R. Eric. *Sacrifice and Survival: Identity, Mission, and Jesuit Higher Education in the American South.* Tuscaloosa: University of Alabama Press, 2014.

Poll, Michael R. *In His Own (w)Rite.* New Orleans: Cornerstone Books, 2011.

Potter, Gary. "Catholicism and the Old South." Catholicism.org, May 16, 2005.

Power, J. Tracy. *Lee's Miserables: Life in the Army of Northern Virginia from the Wilderness to Appomattox*. Chapel Hill: University of North Carolina Press, 2002.

Quallen, Matthew. "Beyond the 272 Sold in 1838, Plotting the National Diaspora of Jesuit-Owned Slaves." *The Hoya*, April 30, 2016.

———. "Jesuit Slavery: From Washington to St. Louis." Paper presented at Jesuits and Race Research Symposium, St. Louis University, November 11, 2015.

Quarstein, John V. *The CSS Virginia: Sink Before Surrender*. Charleston, SC: History Press, 2012.

Rable, George C. *God's Almost Chosen People: A Religious History of the American Civil War*. Chapel Hill: University of North Carolina Press, 2010.

Reed, Emily Hazen. *Life of A. P. Dostie; or The Conflict in New Orleans*. New York: Wm. P. Tomlinson, 1868.

Reilly, Robert F. "Medical and Surgical Care during the American Civil War." *Proceedings of Baylor University Medical Center* 29.2 (2016): 138–42.

Reynolds, Donald E. "The New Orleans Riot of 1866, Reconsidered." *Louisiana History* 5.1 (Winter 1964): 5–27.

Ricci, Joseph A. "Of Faith and Flags." *Memorial Hall Foundation Newsletter*, December 2012, pp. 1–5.

Robinson-Durso, Pamela. "Chaplains in the Confederate Army." *Journal of Church and State* 33.4 (Autumn 1991): 747–63.

Romero, Sidney J. "Louisiana Clergy and the Confederate Army." *Louisiana History* 2.3 (Summer 1961): 277–300.

Rosenburg, R. B. *Living Monuments: Confederate Soldiers' Homes in the New South*. Chapel Hill: University of North Carolina Press, 1993.

Rumberg, H. Rondel. *Roster of Confederate Chaplains*. Owasso, OK: Truth in History, 2018.

Russell, William Howard. *My Diary North and South*. Ed. Eugene H. Berwanger. Baton Rouge: Louisiana State University Press, 1988.

Schroth, Raymond A., S.J. *The American Jesuits: A History*. New York: New York University Press, 2007.

Schweninger, Loren. "Antebellum Free Persons of Color in Postbellum Louisiana." *Louisiana History* 30.4 (Autumn 1989): 345–64.

———. *Black Property Owners in the South, 1790–1915*. Champaign: University of Illinois Press, 1997.

Sheeran, Rev. James B., C.Ss.R. *The Civil War Diary of Father James Sheeran, Confederate Chaplain and Redemptorist*. Ed. Patrick J. Hayes. Washington, DC: Catholic University of America Press, 2016.

———. *Confederate Chaplain: A War Journal*. Ed. Joseph T. Durkin, S.J. Milwaukee: Bruce Publishing, 1960.

Solomon, Clara. *The Civil War Diary of Clara Solomon: Growing Up in New Orleans 1861–1862.* Ed. Elliott Ashkenazi. Baton Rouge: Louisiana State University Press, 1995.

Southwood, Marion. *Beauty and Booty: The Watchword of New Orleans.* New York: M. Doolady, 1867.

Stern, Andrew H. M. *Southern Crucifix, Southern Cross: Catholic-Protestant Relations in the Old South.* Tuscaloosa: University of Alabama Press, 2012.

Stone, DeWitt Boyd, Jr., ed. *Wandering to Glory: Confederate Veterans Remember Evans's Brigade.* Columbia: University of South Carolina Press, 2002.

Storer, Horatio R. "The Medals, Jetons, and Tokens Illustrative of the Science of Medicine," *American Journal of Numismatics and Bulletin of the American Numismatic and Archaeological Society* 26.1 (1891): 5–9.

Strode, Hudson. *Jefferson Davis, Tragic Hero: The Last Twenty-Five Years, 1864–1889.* New York: Harcourt, Brace & World, 1964.

Strousse, Flora. *Margaret Haughery: Bread Woman of New Orleans.* New York: P. J. Kenedy & Sons, 1961.

Swann, Frances Sleeper Dossett, ed. "The Markham Letters: Story of a Nineteenth-Century Family." Unpublished MS, 1987. Private collection of Markham Dossett, Waco, TX.

Taylor, Richard. *Destruction and Reconstruction: Personal Experiences of the Late War.* New York: D. Appleton & Co., 1879.

Tissot, Peter, S.J. "A Year with the Army of the Potomac: Diary of the Reverend Father Tissot, S.J., Military Chaplain." *Fordham Monthly* (1900): 12–17; 55–62; 128–34; 209–11; 272–76; 342–43; 393–98; 465–72; 529–37; 644–51.

Twichell, Joseph. *The Civil War Letters of Joseph Hopkins Twichell: A Chaplain's Story.* Ed. Peter Messent and Steve Courtney. Athens: University of Georgia Press, 2006.

Unger, Irwin, ed. *Essays on the Civil War and Reconstruction.* New York: Holt, Rinehart and Winston, 1970.

Von Hoensbroech, Paul. *Fourteen Years a Jesuit: A Record of Personal Experience and a Criticism.* Trans. Alice Zimmern. London: Cassell, 1911.

Walker, Jeanie Mort. *Life of Capt. Joseph Fry, the Cuban Martyr.* Hartford, CT: J. B. Burr, 1875.

Walsh, Patrick. "The Irish in South Carolina, Georgia, Alabama, Louisiana, and Tennessee." *Journal of the American Irish Historical Society* 3 (1900): 95–109.

Warner, Charles Dudley. "Impressions of the South." *Harper's New Monthly Magazine,* September 1885, pp. 546–51.

———. *Studies in the South and West.* New York: Harper and Brothers, 1889.

The War of the Rebellion: A Compilation of the Official Records of the Union and Confederate Armies. 70 vols. in 128 parts. Washington, DC: Government Printing Office, 1880–1901. Available online in Cornell University Library's "Making of America" collection.

Washington, Booker T. "The Free Negro in Slavery Days." *The Outlook*, September 18, 1909, pp. 107–14.

Watson, Thomas D. "Staging the 'Crowning Achievement of the Age': Major Edward A. Burke, New Orleans, and the Cotton Centennial Exposition." *Louisiana History* 25.3 (Summer 1984): 229–57; 25.4 (Autumn 1984): 341–66.

Watson, William. *Life in the Confederate Army: Being the Observations and Experiences of an Alien in the South During the American Civil War.* London: Chapman and Hall, 1887.

Welch, Spencer Glasgow. *A Confederate Surgeon's Letters to His Wife.* Washington, DC: Neale Publishing, 1911.

Welsh, William E. "More Loss than Success: Nicholls' Brigade in the Gettysburg Campaign." *Gettysburg Magazine* 54 (2016): 2–20.

Wetta, Frank J. *The Louisiana Scalawags: Politics, Race, and Terrorism During the Civil War and Reconstruction.* Baton Rouge: Louisiana State University Press, 2013.

Wiatt, Thomas T. *Rev. William E. Wiatt: The Life and Times of a Confederate Chaplain and Related Family Stories.* Morrisville, NC: Lulu Publishing, 2018.

Widmer, Mary Lou. *Margaret, Friend of Orphans.* Gretna, LA: Pelican Publishing, 1996.

Wiley, Bell I. "'Holy Joes' of the Sixties: A Study of Civil War Chaplains," *Huntington Library Quarterly* 16 (1953): 287–304.

———. *The Life of Johnny Reb: The Common Soldier of the Confederacy.* 1943. Updated ed. Baton Rouge: Louisiana State University Press, 2008.

Wilson, Charles Reagan. *Baptized in Blood: The Religion of the Lost Cause, 1865–1920.* Athens: University of Georgia Press, 1980; 2009.

Woodward, C. Vann. *The Strange Career of Jim Crow.* 1955. 3rd rev. ed., New York: Oxford University Press, 2002.

Woodworth, Steven E. *While God Is Marching On: The Religious World of Civil War Soldiers.* Lawrence: University Press of Kansas, 2001.

Zanca, Kenneth. *American Catholics and Slavery, 1789–1866: An Anthology of Primary Documents.* Lanham, MD: University Press of America, 1994.

———. "'The Catholics of the South': An Editorial by Abbé Napoleon Joseph Perché, Editor of *Le Propagateur Catholique*, January 26, 1861." *Louisiana History* 58.4 (Autumn 2017): 404–16.

Zwinge, Joseph, S.J. "The Jesuit Farms in Maryland: Facts and Anecdotes: The Negro Slaves." *Woodstock Letters* 41 (1912): 195–222, 275–91.

Index

Notes: Page numbers in italics refer to illustrations; those followed by "n" indicate endnotes.